THE THEORY AND
PRACTICE OF
HOMOSEXUALITY

THE THEORY AND PRACTICE OF HOMOSEXUALITY

John Hart
Department of Applied Social Studies
Sheffield City Polytechnic
Diane Richardson
Department of Sociological Studies
University of Sheffield

With contributions from

Kenneth Plummer

Charles Dodd

Glenys Parry and Ray Lightbown

Rose Robertson

Jeffrey Weeks

ROUTLEDGE & KEGAN PAUL
London, Boston and Henley

First published in 1981
by Routledge & Kegan Paul Ltd
39 Store Street,
London WC1E 7DD,
9 Park Street,
Boston, Mass. 02108, USA
and Broadway House,
Newtown Road,
Henley-on-Thames,
Oxon RG9 1EN
Printed in Great Britain by
St Edmundsbury Press
Bury St Edmunds, Suffolk

British Library Cataloguing in Publication Data

Hart, John

The theory and practice of homosexuality.
1. Homosexuality
I. Title II. Richardson, Diane
306.7'6   HQ76

ISBN 0-7100-0838-4

CONTENTS

ACKNOWLEDGMENTS

In additon to our contributors, we also want to thank Stuart Cameron, Jeanette Leaman, Jane Mycock, Sylvia Parkin and Ann Watkinson. Thanks also to Richard Pinder for compiling the index. Many other friends remain unnamed, but they will know who they are, having had to put up with our total obsession with talking about sexuality during the writing of this book. Finally we want to thank each other, about whom, after a long period of overexposure, we remain enthusiastic.

CONTRIBUTORS

Charles Dodd is Senior Probation Officer (Training) in the Inner London Probation and After Care Service.

Ray Lightbown is a clinical psychologist.

Glenys Parry is a clinical psychologist at the University of Sheffield.

Kenneth Plummer is Lecturer in Sociology at the University of Essex.

Rose Robertson is the founder of Parents Enquiry.

Jeffrey Weeks is Lecturer in Sociology at the University of Kent.

INTRODUCTION

In the past a book on this subject would have been likely to
have defined homosexuality in terms of sexual acts, and to have
seen such acts as evidence of underlying psychopathology. In
addition there has existed a good deal of confusion of homosexuality with transvestism, transsexuality and gender-role
orientation. In this environment homosexuals were seen as either
phobic to the opposite sex, or as wanting to take on characteristics of the opposite sex.

More recent sociological contributions to the literature have
broadened perspectives by distinguishing between homosexual
acts, homosexual lifestyles and homosexual identities. In addition, the rise of the gay and the women's movements has provided an alternative way of seeing homosexuality as the personal
choice of a particular identity and way of life.

As practitioners in this field we are aware that there exists a
lack of synthesis of these differing perspectives which may be
particularly relevant when trying adequately to help a person in
distress who identifies himself or herself as homosexual. As
academics, we do not feel that the available models provide an
adequate conceptual framework to account for the development
and maintenance of a homosexual identity. As individuals enjoying gay lifestyles and identities it is personally important to us
to try to extend the available knowledge about homosexuality to
both fellow academics, practitioners and other gay women and
men.

In Part One of the book we consider in some detail the major
theoretical models relating to homosexuality. We also consider
the treatment implications of such theories, as there continues
to be a good deal of interest in the possibilities of 'cure' or
treatment. As homosexuality is so frequently conceptualized as
being pathological in a moral or clinical sense, it is perhaps not
surprising that homosexuals themselves have introjected such
concepts, and that demand for treatment continues. Interestingly, all treatment strategies would seem to have a low success
rate. In Part One we present a model of homosexuality which
attempts to account for some of the reasons for such low
efficacy, by concentrating on the interacting variables which
are important in both the development and maintenance of a
homosexual identity. Part One is a particularly important section, therefore, given the way that theoretical models inform
practice and, in addition, influence both how homosexuals are
seen in society and how they see themselves.

In Part Two we aim to extend the existing conceptual frameworks related to homosexuality by offering an alternative model which seeks to explain the process of the development and maintenance of a homosexual identity.

Although our view is that homosexuality per se is no more of a problem than heterosexuality, we recognize in Part Three that there are a number of problems experienced by homosexual women and men, as a result of the particular social experiences they have encountered in society and the social meanings they have imparted to these.

We have also emphasized in the book the element of choice, rather than genetic or environmental determinism, in developing a homosexual identity. Such an identity may be assessed by the individual as being preferable to a heterosexual identity, although not necessarily for reasons merely of sexual attraction. Indeed, there may be nonsexual reasons of equal, or more, importance for the individual; for instance, being able to socialize in an atmosphere of reduced gender-role demands and expectations.

On the other hand it may be objected that either of these choices of identity is, in fact, a restriction of choice, given the possibility of bisexuality. We would argue, however, that whilst sexual acts with either sex are clearly possible for many people a bisexual identity or lifestyle is difficult to maintain for reasons which we discuss in Part Two.

Seeing homosexuality as a chosen sexual identity places questions about the evaluation of homosexuality firmly in the moral arena. Such moral questioning relates not just to homosexuality but to the wider discussion of what sex, freed of the trammels of reproductive biology, is for, in the 1980s. We would hope that this book will be an important contribution to that debate. We would argue that it is not so much private sexual acts with which society is concerned, but rather the public emergence of homosexual identities and lifestyles.

Throughout the book we attempt to separate the usage of the term homosexual from that of gay, taking the latter to mean a positive assertion of a certain identity and lifestyle, which challenges both traditional sexual and social relationships between the sexes. There will, however, be occasions in the book when it is not possible clearly to make this distinction.

We do, of course, recognize the importance of two people of the same sex falling and being in love, although in the rest of the book this may not appear to be our central concern.

Part one

THEORY AND PRACTICE

1 THEORETICAL PERSPECTIVES ON HOMOSEXUALITY

Diane Richardson

INTRODUCTION

In this chapter I shall examine some of the explanations that have been offered to account for a homosexual sexual orientation. In no way is it suggested that this will constitute an exhaustive review of the literature; rather the aim will be to provide an evaluation of the more important theories. Important both in terms of their implications for practice, which will be discussed in the following chapter, and in the way they have informed society about homosexuality.

Before going on to discuss each particular theoretical perspective in turn, however, a few general points can be made about the methodological and theoretical inadequacies of much of the research into homosexuality. For instance: the overwhelming male bias, the problem of unrepresentative samples (homosexual subjects often having been drawn from psychiatric or criminal sources, or more recently as volunteers from homophile organizations), a lack of adequate control groups, and the prevalence of an unidimensional view of the homosexual person. These are all features which, irrespective of theoretical stance, continuously emerge from the research literature.

Similarly it can be argued that the majority of studies in defining homosexuality have focused upon sexual acts, and have failed to acknowledge the need to distinguish between homosexual acts, homosexual identities and homosexual lifestyles. As a result, the little attention paid to the latter two areas has meant that the individual and social meanings of homosexual behaviour and identities have largely been ignored. This has contributed to a homogeneous view of both homosexual men and women as predominantly sexual creatures.

There is also frequent confusion in the literature between gender identity, gender-role orientation and sexual orientation, although they have no necessary association with each other.

One other common feature which emerges is the view that sexual orientation is a relatively enduring characteristic, largely determined early in life. Suggestions as to exactly when, why and how this occurs vary greatly of course, ranging from theories which see Oedipal conflicts in the child's early years as of prime importance to those which emphasize prenatal hormonal influences during the third or fourth month of foetal development.

I would point out that in setting out to examine etiological explanations of homosexuality I do not wish to imply or endorse the view implicit in many theories that a heterosexual sexual orientation is somehow a 'natural' development requiring no explanation; nor for that matter that it is necessarily valid to attempt to explain homosexuality in terms of particular etiological factors which are seen as causing the homosexual 'condition'.

MODELS OF HOMOSEXUALITY

At a superficial and highly oversimplified level, a basic dichotomy can be recognized between those models of homosexuality which have placed their emphasis upon biological factors and those which have stressed social influences on the development of sexual orientation. Such a dichotomy is of course a false and meaningless one, it being never a case of biology on the one side and environmental influences on the other, but always a case of a complex interactive process between the two.

Bearing this in mind, let us begin by examining those theories which have stressed the role of biological factors.

Genetic theories: chromosomal sex
In 1940 Lang, influenced by Goldschmidt's (1931) experiments with gypsy-moths, put forward the hypothesis that homosexual men, and by indirect reference homosexual women also, may be regarded as sex integrades. That is to say, female homosexuals were considered to be genetically male, and male homosexuals genetically female, albeit having 'lost all morphological sex characteristics except their chromosome formula' (Lang, 1940). Indirect evidence that this was so, Lang argued, would be the finding of altered sex ratios of siblings in families with a homosexual sibling; according to the integrade theory there being an expected over-representation of males in the case of families with a homosexual male member, and an over-representation of females in the case of families with a homosexual female member.

Direct evidence for Lang's theory was not actually available at that time, as techniques enabling the determination of genetic sex were not developed until the early 1950s. Without direct proof one way or another of the genetic sex of male and female homosexuals, therefore, indirect evidence derived from sex ratio studies acquired particular significance.

Certainly, in reporting a higher male to female sex ratio of siblings in families with a male homosexual sibling, Lang (1940) interpreted this as evidence in support of his original hypothesis. Darke (1948), however, found no statistically significant differences between the sex ratio of siblings of a group of male homosexuals and the normal ratio. Nor did Morrow et al. (1965), in a study of sibling sex ratios of male college students who were not homosexual, find any significant difference to the figures reported by Lang (1940) and Kallman (1952a) for homo-

sexual subjects. In commenting upon this, Morrow points out
that the excessive brother to sister ratios reported earlier may
merely be the product of a statistical artifact, a result of sampling all male populations.

Methodological considerations apart, a higher male to female
sibling sex ratio is in any case open to other theoretical interpretations besides that suggested by Lang (1940). For instance,
we might interpret such findings as merely indicating that male
homosexuals are more likely to come from families in which there
are fewer girls.

One other source of evidence pertaining to Lang's basic
premise, worth mentioning for its wider theoretical ramifications,
is that derived from studies of the offspring of male homosexuals; for if, as Lang suggested, male homosexuals although
phenotypically male are actually genetically female then any offspring they have must be female. Having acknowledged this,
Lang, on examination of the offspring fathered by the married
male homosexuals in his sample, reported that of the total of
238 children born 123 were boys and 115 girls. Lang attempted
to get round the problem this posed for the integrade theory
by evoking the concept of the 'genuine homosexual', implying
that married homosexuals are less likely to be 'genuine' homosexuals. However, nowhere does he explain exactly what is
meant by this term, except indirectly by contrast to 'homosexuality induced predominantly by environmental factors, such
as education in boarding schools or other instances of life in a
restricted society of the same sex' (Lang, 1940).

This assumed dichotomy between so called 'situational' homosexuality and 'genuine', 'true' or 'obligative' homosexuality, is
one which crops up time and time again in the literature. Indeed
its perpetuation has to a large extent been due to the use to
which it has been put in accounting for otherwise contradictory
findings. It is hoped that during the course of this and following chapters, the dichotomy will be demonstrated to be a false
one.

With the advent of techniques whereby nuclear sex could be
determined, it became clear that male and female homosexuals
showed no divergence from that expected for 'normal' male and
female controls: i.e. they exhibited a male and female nuclear
sex pattern respectively (e.g. Pare, 1956; Raboch and Nedoma,
1958). This would seem to be strong evidence against Lang's
theory; however, as Pritchard (1962) pointed out, there was a
complicating factor here in that one could not merely assume
that nuclear sex and genetic sex were synonymous. This was
made clear when in the late 1950s techniques for ascertaining
actual sex chromosome constitution were developed. Of particular
relevance here were individuals with either Klinefelter's or
Turner's Syndrome. Prior to such tests being available, nuclear
sexing of Klinefelter cases indicated the possession of two X
chromosomes, and, in the case of Turner's syndrome, only one
X chromosome. This led to the assumption that such individuals

were in fact cases of intersex, individuals with Klinefelter's syndrome having a male phenotype and female genotype, and Turner's syndrome cases having a female phenotype and a male genotype. On the basis of Lang's theory, therefore, both ought to be homosexual. But this did not appear to be the case (e.g. Raboch and Nedoma, 1958).

Tests of nuclear sex, however, whilst indicating the number of X chromosomes present, give no indication of the presence or absence of the Y chromosome. When it became possible to examine the actual chromosome constitution it appeared that in Klinefelter's syndrome the genetic sex was not XX, as had been thought, but XXY, and similarly in Turner's not XY but XO. Studies of cases of Klinefelter's or Turner's syndrome are therefore of no relevance in assessing Lang's original hypothesis.

Such evidence indicated that one could not merely assume that nuclear sex and genetic sex were synonymous. By implication, therefore, one might question the use of studies of the nuclear sex of homosexuals as evidence against Lang's theory. However, although the presence or absence of the Y chromosome remained unknown, it was unlikely to be absent, as this would have resulted in a XO genotype characteristic of Turner's syndrome, which results in a female phenotype. It could therefore be deduced from studies of the nuclear sex of male homosexuals that none of the subjects had two X chromosomes, implying that, contrary to the predictions of Lang's theory, they could not be genetically female. Further evidence against the theory came from a chromosomal analysis of a small sample of male homosexuals, which also indicated a male rather than a female chromosomal pattern (Pritchard, 1962).

It should be noted that Slater (1962) did not rule out the possibility of chromosomal anomalies being implicated in the etiology of homosexuality, in particular those which might be associated with late maternal age. But the demonstration of an association between late maternal age and male homosexuality could just as easily be interpreted in terms of family dynamics. Moreover, whilst Slater (1962) reports that male homosexuals are more likely to be born to mothers of late maternal age, others have not found this (e.g. Evans, 1972). In summary, therefore, there would seem to be no evidence, on the basis of techniques so far carried out, to suggest that chromosomal error is a significant factor in the etiology of homosexuality.

Finally, mention must be made of studies of the so called 'intersexes' - that is cases of true and pseudo-hermaphroditism - which have implied that it is the child's social environment, rather than chromosomal sex, which is of crucial importance in psychosexual development. For instance, Hampson and Hampson (1961) studied a group of over 110 hermaphroditic individuals who had been assigned to, and reared in, a sex contrary to one or more of the following: chromosomal sex, gonadal sex, hormonal sex, internal sex organs and external genital appearance. In the majority of cases, psychosexual development was consistent

with sex of assignment and rearing, irrespective of chromosomal
sex or, for that matter, gonadal sex, hormonal sex and the
internal and external sex organs.

Genetic theories: statistical genetics
Having discussed theories citing chromosomal error as a possible explanation of homosexuality, it is now appropriate to
consider the implication of genetic factors at a somewhat finer
level of analysis, that is at the genic, rather than the chromosomal, level.

As in other areas where there is interest in the relative
importance of genetic and environmental influences, twin studies
have played a major role. Kallman's (1952a, b) study is of
particular interest here, given its importance in the literature.

Kallman compared a group of predominantly or exclusively
homosexual men with their twin brothers in order to examine
the degree of concordance for homosexuality. In the case of the
twenty six dizygotic (non-identical) twin pairs studied, concordance for 'overt homosexual behaviour' varied from 11.5 per
cent to 42.3 per cent according to whether they were rated
5-6 on the Kinsey scale, or the total range was used. (The
rating scale devised by Kinsey et al., 1948, represents a
continuous gradation of sexual behaviour from exclusively
heterosexual (0) to exclusively homosexual (6).) These figures
are only slightly higher than those reported by Kinsey et al.
(1948) for the male population as a whole, and thus it may be
argued that for non-identical twins there is only a slightly
increased likelihood of homosexuality in the twin brothers of
predominantly or exclusively male homosexuals. In contrast,
the concordance figures reported for the thirty-seven monozygotic (identical) twin pairs studied were particularly striking:
Kallman reporting complete concordance for homosexuality as
rated on the Kinsey scale. Kallman also added that all of the
twin pairs denied any mutual sexual activity, and that most
claimed to have developed their sexual preferences independently,
often living far apart from each other.

This finding, then, of 100 per cent concordance in identical
twins compared to the much lower figure reported for non-
identical twins prompted Kallman (1952a) to suggest that this
  throws considerable doubt upon the validity of purely
  psychodynamic theories of predominantly or exclusively
  homosexual behaviour patterns in adulthood, and correspond-
  ingly strengthens the hypothesis of a genetically determined
  disarrangement in the balance between male and female
  maturational (hormonal) tendencies.
Various important criticisms have been made of Kallman's
study. First, one cannot assume that monozygotic twins are
necessarily genetically identical, and indeed Klintworth (1962)
suggests genetic differences as one possible explanation for the
findings of discordance of homosexuality in monozygotic twin
pairs reported by other researchers (see below).

Second, Kallman's identical twins were not reared apart from one another, and therefore the 100 per cent concordance rate might also be explained by specific environmental factors related to twinship.

Third, a methodological criticism that can be levelled not only at this particular study but at a great many in this area is the unrepresentative nature of the sample of twin pairs used. Interestingly, Kallman himself later reported that the 100 per cent concordance rate observed in the sample of identical twins studied was a statistical artifact (Kallman, 1960).

Fourth, other studies of both male and female identical twin pairs, including one by Kallman (1953) himself, have reported discordance for homosexuality (e.g. Rainer et al., 1960; Kolb et al., 1961; Klintworth 1962; Parker, 1964), or at least only partial concordance (Lange, 1931; Heston and Shields, 1968). Admittedly these studies have employed small samples, often derived from psychiatric sources, where in some instances an alternative 'diagnosis' to homosexuality such as transsexualism (e.g. Klintworth, 1962) or transvestism (e.g. Parker, 1964) would seem to be required. This is an example of how gender identity, gender-role orientation and sexual orientation have often been confused.

Interpretations of such studies have varied from those which emphasize the role of family dynamics in the etiology of homosexuality (e.g. Rainer et al., 1960; Parker, 1964), to those which claim that discordance for homosexuality in identical twins does not invalidate the concept that 'overt homosexuality is a gene controlled variant in the integrative process of psychosexual maturation' (Klintworth, 1962). Others have implied that an etiology based on the interaction of genetic and environmental factors is required to explain these findings (e.g. Heston and Shields, 1968).

Hormonal explanations of homosexuality
Theories which have stressed the role of endocrinological factors in the development of homosexuality have tended to focus upon either postnatal or prenatal influences. These will therefore be discussed separately.

Postnatal hormonal influences   The belief that homosexuality is due to some kind of hormonal imbalance is one which has a long history. Interest in hormonal explanations of homosexuality, however, took on a new significance with the identification of the 'sex' (gonadal) hormones.

For example, in the study by Glass et al. (1940) of the level of androgen and oestrogen excreted in the urine, it is reported that in contrast to a control group of 'normal' males the homosexual group had significantly lower ratios of androgen to oestrogen. Glass accounted for this difference in terms of higher oestrogen values in the homosexual sample, the difference between the androgen values in the two groups being described as 'less striking'. They conclude that it would seem that 'the constitutional homosexual has a different sex hormone chemistry than the normal male' (Glass et al., 1940).

This particular study was severely criticized on both statistical and methodological grounds by Kinsey (1941), who claimed the conclusions reached by Glass were invalid, and that little significance could be attached to their results. In addition, the rather crude bioassay techniques which were available at that time render such studies, in retrospect, of little empirical significance; most studies basing their conclusions about the level of androgen and oestrogen functionally active in the body on measurements of various derivatives and metabolic end products excreted in the urine. As Perloff (1963) points out, the interpretation of measurements like these is fraught with difficulties. For instance, metabolic end products of the sex hormones may derive from both androgens and oestrogens, and therefore cannot be taken as necessarily indicative of either one. The picture is further confused by the possibility of inter conversion of androgens and oestrogens within the body, and the recognition that, in any case, urinary excretion of androgen and oestrogen represents only a small percentage of that which is produced by the body.

The lack of any substantative evidence to support the view that male homosexuality was the result of an altered androgen/oestrogen ratio did not prevent the development of treatment procedures based upon such theoretical assumptions. Two main forms of treatment, based on opposing approaches, were employed with male homosexuals: the administration of androgens (e.g. Glass and Johnson, 1944), and a reduction of androgen levels either by surgical or chemical castration (for a review see Heim and Hursch, 1979). In the case of female homosexuals there would seem to be virtually nothing written about the use of hormonal treatment as a 'cure' for lesbianism. The use of such treatment procedures, and their resultant effects, will be discussed in more detail in the following chapter. We should note here, however, the general finding that the use of sex hormones in the treatment of homosexuality produces no change in sexual orientation, although there may be some change in libido.

Further difficulties for a hormonal explanation of homosexuality were posed by evidence from clinical studies of individuals suffering from various endocrinological disorders resulting in altered levels of androgen and/or oestrogen, which failed to find an increased incidence of homosexuality (for a review see Meyer-Bahlburg, 1977, 1979).

In the absence, therefore, of studies which demonstrated marked and consistent differences between homosexual and heterosexual males on measures of androgen and oestrogen and the 'disappointing' results of the use of these hormones in the treatment of homosexuality, there existed a growing dissatisfaction with theories which sought to explain homosexuality in terms of hormonal influences, and after the 1940s and early

1950s such theories tended to receive little serious attention
in the literature.

The 1970s, however, have seen a revival of interest in
endocrinological explanations of homosexuality. One of the reasons suggested for this has been the development of more
precise and sensitive techniques for assaying the gonadal hormones, in comparison with the relatively crude methods of
measurement previously available (Margolese and Janiger, 1973).

This development cannot, however, be understood purely
in terms of technological advances, but must be seen in the
wider context of a swing towards psychobiological explanations
within psychology (Archer, 1978). A backlash perhaps against
the dominant role that behaviourism, with its appeal to environmental influences as crucial in development, has occupied in
the social sciences in general over the last half century or more.
This is coupled with the more longstanding relationship psychology has had with the life sciences, whereby it is assumed that
the workings of the mind can be ultimately reduced to the
physiological mechanisms of the brain.

This resurge of interest in endocrinological explanations of
homosexuality was marked by the publication of a study by
Margolese (1970), which reported lower androsterone and
etiocholanolone ratios for a group of male homosexuals compared
with a control group of male heterosexuals. Androsterone and
etiocholanolone are metabolites of the 'male' sex hormone
testosterone, which are excreted in the urine.

This preliminary study by Margolese is open to criticism on
several grounds. For instance: small sample size, the results
being derived from an analysis of the androsterone/etiocho-
lanolone ratios of only ten heterosexual and ten homosexual
males; no control for factors other than 'ill-health' which might
have influenced the androsterone/etiocholanolone ratios (e.g.
sexual activity, stress, various drugs); and a lack of discussion
of the 'representative' nature of the homosexual sample and how
it was obtained.

A study by Evans (1972, 1973) of forty-four homosexual and
111 heterosexual men also reported a lowered androsterone/
etiocholanolone ratio for the homosexual group, in support of
the initial findings reported by Margolese (1970). The study of
Evans can however be criticized on similar grounds to those
already mentioned above, with the exception of small sample
size. Also, whilst in the study by Margolese (1970) there was no
discussion of how the homosexual group was obtained, Evans
reports that in his study a highly selected group of homosexual
volunteers was used.

A particularly serious criticism of Evans, however, which
renders his study of questionable significance, concerns the
selection of his control group for which 'no direct information
was obtained as to their sexual orientation and it was merely
assumed that they were all heterosexual' (Evans, 1973).

This was not the case in the study by Margolese and Janiger

(1973) which analysed the androsterone/etiocholanolone ratios of twenty-four heterosexual males (Kinsey 0-1), twenty-three homosexual males (Kinsey 5-6) and nine males falling into the 'intermediate' range (Kinsey 2-3-4). Whilst, as in the case of Evans (1972), the homosexual males comprised a highly selected group, all subjects were rated on the Kinsey sexual inventory. Consideration was also given to various factors which might differentially influence the androsterone/etiocholanolone ratios of the homosexual and heterosexual groups. In this respect Margolese and Janiger reported no significant differences between the two groups in sexual activity or use of drugs (all subjects denied the use of drugs), and on the basis of a physical and psychiatric examination they classified both groups as 'healthy'. In addition they acknowledged the suggestion that differences in the androsterone/etiocholanolone ratios of homosexuals may be accounted for by psychological stress factors associated with being homosexual in a stigmatizing society; given that it has been shown that psychological stress may result in the suppression of testosterone with a simultaneous rise in 17-hydroxy corticosteroids.

This study is also subject to further criticism on statistical grounds given the actual data presented. For instance, the claim by Margolese and Janiger that there were no demonstrable differences in sexual activity between the control and homosexual groups can be questioned on the basis of the statistical analysis used. In addition, the conclusion that this study confirms that by Margolese (1970), in finding significant differences in androsterone/etiocholanolone ratios of healthy male homosexuals compared to healthy male heterosexuals, cannot be assessed without information about the mean values of the androsterone/etiocholanolone ratios of both groups (reported as 1.6 for the control group, and as 1.2 and 0.7 for the Kinsey groups 5 and 6 respectively) and in addition the standard deviations, which Margolese and Janiger do not provide.

In the light of such criticisms and the lack of any data on the androsterone/etiocholanolone ratios of female heterosexual and homosexual groups, we must be very careful in interpreting Margolese and Janiger's claim that this study lends support to the original hypothesis proposed by Margolese (1970) that

the metabolic condition which results in a relatively high androsterone value is the *cause* of sexual preference for females by either sex; whereas a relatively low androsterone value is associated with sexual preference for males by either sex (my emphasis).

In summary, therefore, the criticisms which have already been made of studies that have reported significant differences in the androsterone/etiocholanolone ratios between heterosexual and homosexual males, the failure by certain researchers to find such a difference (Tourney and Hatfield, 1973), the lack of standards for male/female androsterone/etiocholanolone ratios and the sensitivity of androsterone and etiocholanolone to a

variety of influences require us to consider with caution claims
that a relatively consistent hormonal difference between homosexual and heterosexual males has been demonstrated.

Recent interest in endocrinological factors in homosexuality
has not been confined to investigations into androsterone and
etiocholanolone. In a widely quoted study, Loraine et al. (1970,
1971) examined urinary levels of testosterone, oestrone, preg-
nanediol and luteinizing hormone in three male and four female
homosexuals, and compared these with figures obtained for
heterosexual controls. The reported findings were: lowered
urinary testosterone levels in male homosexuals, and, in the
case of homosexual women, lowered levels of oestrone with
raised urinary testosterone and luteinizing hormone values. The
authors conclude that, on the basis of both their own and
Margolese's (1970) findings, endocrine factors are implicated in
the etiology of homosexuality (Loraine et al., 1971).

The work by Loraine stimulated an investigation by Kolodny
et al. (1971, 1972), extensively quoted in the literature, of the
plasma testosterone levels of male homosexuals. In this study a
group of thirty male homosexual students, rated for degree of
homosexuality on the Kinsey scale, were compared with a control
group of fifty heterosexual male students of similar age.
Significantly lowered plasma testosterone levels were recorded
in homosexuals rated 5 and 6 on the Kinsey scale, with decreased
sperm count and increased plasma gonadotropins (luteinizing
hormone and follicle stimulating hormone) compared to the control group. Kolodny also reported an almost linear negative
correlation between Kinsey rating and testosterone level. Subsequent research, however, has been contradictory (see below).

In their discussion of these findings, Kolodny et al. (1971)
take great care not to suggest that 'endocrine dysfunction is a
major factor in the pathogenesis of male homosexuality', and
point out that lowered plasma testosterone levels may be a
secondary result, rather than a primary cause, of a homosexual
orientation.

Both of these studies can be criticized in terms of their
selection of adequate control groups. For example, the heterosexual controls in the study by Loraine et al.(1970,1971) were
chiefly staff members of the Clinical Endocrinological Unit, none
of whom admitted to homosexual inclination or activity; nor, one
could argue, would they be likely to.

In the study by Kolodny et al. (1971), although the
homosexual group were classified according to the Kinsey scale
no such data is presented for the control group, who are therefore presumably assumed to all be at the Kinsey 0-1 end of the
scale. This is a somewhat unlikely assumption given Kinsey's
findings (Kinsey et al., 1948).

In addition to criticisms of the selection of control groups, the
validity of conclusions about homosexuality based on data from
only three male (one of whom was bisexual) and four female
homosexual subjects must be questioned, particularly when such

conclusions are reached as a result of comparison with mean
values derived from a much larger control group sample.

Kolodny's observations are also open to criticism, given the
atypical nature of the homosexual group and the lack of control
for factors which may affect plasma testosterone levels (e.g.
stress, sexual activity). The fact that a high number of drug
'abusers' are reported in the homosexual group confounds the
results, given that many psychotropic drugs have been found to
depress testosterone levels.

In addition we should note that other studies have not found
significant differences between homosexual and heterosexual
males on measures of plasma or serum testosterone, nor differences between homosexuals with different Kinsey ratings
(e.g. Doerr et al., 1973; Barlow et al., 1974). Certain studies
have even reported elevated levels of plasma testosterone in the
homosexual group (e.g. Brodie et al., 1974).

Possible explanations for the variation between studies may
include differences in assay methodology and in sample selection,
lack of control for factors which may influence testosterone levels
(e.g. age, health, drug use, physical activity, sexual activity,
stress), inadequate control groups and the lack of repeated
sampling of testosterone given the high intra-variability of
hormonal levels.

Indeed, in a comprehensive review of the literature, Meyer-
Bahlburg (1977) concludes that

in view of the inconsistency of the results on testosterone
and the methodological shortcomings in many studies, it is
premature to theorize on general mechanisms underlying
endocrine deviations in adult homosexuals derived from
individual studies. The data available make it seem highly
unlikely that deviations in testosterone levels and production
in adulthood can be held responsible for the development of
male homosexuals in general.

There is a similar lack of uniformity in the results of studies
of gonadotropin (luteinizing hormone and follicle stimulating
hormone) levels in male homosexuals (again for a review see
Meyer-Bahlburg, 1977). An example of this is the finding by
Doerr et al. (1973, 1976) of elevated plasma oestradiol concentra-
tions in a group of male homosexuals. These results have not been
replicated, and earlier studies of urinary oestrogen measures
are unsupportive (e.g. Evans, 1972).

In keeping with the predominant male bias which exists in the
literature in general, studies of endocrinological factors in the
etiology of female homosexuality are extremely rare.

In the study already discussed by Loraine et al. (1970, 1971),
lowered levels of oestrone and raised urinary testosterone and
luteinizing hormone values were reported in four homosexual
women. Apart from the statistical and methodological criticisms
that have already been made of this particular study, it must
also be pointed out that three of the four homosexual women
had a history of menstrual irregularities which may have con-

founded the results.

Following Loraine's reports, Griffiths et al. (1974) examined urinary oestrogen and testosterone levels in a group of thirty-six homosexual women drawn from a lesbian organization. Oestrogen levels were reported to be within normal limits for females when stage of menstrual cycle, the menopause and the use of oral contraceptives were controlled for. The authors also report that ten of the subjects had raised urinary testosterone levels. It should be noted however that such observations were based not on comparisons with a control group but with published values of urinary testosterone levels.

In the study by Gartrell et al. (1977), a group of twenty-one homosexual women were compared with a control group of nineteen heterosexual women, matched for age, on measures of plasma testosterone. Testosterone levels were reported to be on average 38 per cent higher in homosexual than in heterosexual subjects.

We must be very cautious in interpreting the results from these very few studies in the light both of methodological criticisms, and the lack of replication of such studies.

Prenatal hormonal influences   There has been a definite distinction in the literature between postnatal and prenatal hormonal influences, particularly in terms of their postulated mode of action. Levels of circulating gonadal hormones in the adult have generally been considered to have a primarily activational role, affecting both the form and intensity of behavioural responses; whereas in the case of prenatal gonadal hormones it has been suggested that they exert a primarily directional influence, in terms of their organizing effect on behaviour (Young, 1961; Diamond, 1965; Leschner, 1978). I will first of all consider the role of the prenatal sex hormones in foetal development.

Quite early in embryonic development the gonads begin to differentiate; male gonads or testes when a pair of XY chromosomes are present, and female gonads, or ovaries, when a pair of XX chromosomes are present. Once differentiated these gonads begin to secrete sex (gonadal) hormones, supplemented by much smaller amounts produced by the foetal adrenal glands.

The main effect of these prenatal hormones is their organizing influence on the differentiation of the reproductive tract and external genitalia (see Fig.1.1). However, it has also been suggested that prenatal androgens play an important organizational role in psychosexual differentiation. Such a model postulates that during the early stages of neonatal or foetal development certain cells in the hypothalamic region of the brain are especially sensitive to androgen. The presence or absence of androgen at this point in embryological development is said to affect the developing central nervous system in two major respects: in the control of gonadotropin secretion by the pituitary under control of the hypothalamus, and in the acquisition and manifestation of gender-role behaviour. It is in this latter area that much interest has been generated in the application of such a model to an understanding of psychosexual differentiation in humans, and, more specifically, to the understanding of homosexuality (e.g. Dörner and Hinz, 1968; Goy, 1968; Feldman and McCulloch, 1971).

Stated briefly, it has been suggested that in the presence of androgen at a critical point in embryological development, hypothalamic centres in the brain become biased in a 'male direction', predisposing the individual to the acquisition and manifestation of certain patterns of behaviour characteristic of males, whether that individual be a genetic male or female (Pathway A in Fig.1.1). In the case of absence of, or foetal insensitivity to androgen, psychosexual differentiation is said to be biased in a 'female direction'. That is to say, the individual is said to be predisposed to acquire and manifest certain patterns of behaviour characteristic of the female, once again irrespective of whether that individual is genetically male or female (Pathway B in Fig.1.1). Note that it is the presence or absence of androgen that is seen to be at issue here, and not the presence or absence of oestrogen.

Theoreticians who have emphasized the organizational influence of foetal androgen in psychosexual development have usually also acknowledged the role of cognitional and learned factors. Such influences are, however, essentially seen in additive terms, as acting upon individuals who at birth are already predisposed to develop in a certain direction. It is in the degree of inflexibility this predisposition is assumed to confer on psychosexual development that traces of biological determinism are apparent (e.g. Diamond, 1965; Hutt, 1972).

As was mentioned earlier, such a model of psychosexual development has led to the suggestion that the presence (in the case of women) or absence (in the case of men) of prenatal androgen may produce a neuroendocrine predisposition for homosexuality. This suggestion is based primarily on animal studies, in particular research carried out with rodents. The castration of male rats neonatally, followed by priming with oestrogen and progesterone in adulthood, results in the manifestation of sexual behaviour characteristic of a normal receptive female placed with a normal male which attempts to mount her. This occurs to a far greater extent than with a normal male, or even a male rat which has been castrated after the neonatal period and has then been primed with oestrogen and progesterone in adulthood (Grady, Pheonix and Young, 1965). Pharmacological castration with the use of antiandrogens such as cyproterone acetate also produces similar effects on sexual behaviour if such substances are injected into male rats during the neonatal period (Neumann, 1966). Similarly, androgen treatment of newborn female rats followed by androgen administration in adulthood results in an increased frequency of sexual behaviour characteristic of the normal male rat (Young, Goy and Pheonix, 1964; Dörner, 1968).

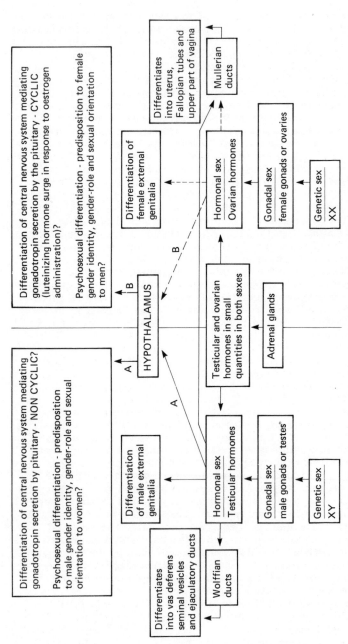

Figure 1.1   Sexual differentiation of the foetus

Of particular relevance here is the research by Dörner (e.g. Dörner, 1968; Dörner and Hinz, 1968), given that on the basis of his studies on rats suggestions have been made about the etiology of homosexuality in humans. Dörner and Hinz (1968) castrated male rats neonatally, and then primed them with androgen in adulthood. Dörner reports that they showed a higher incidence of lordosis (receptive female sexual behaviour) than of mounting and intromission, characteristic of normal males. This is described by Dörner as 'male homosexual behaviour'. He has also reported 'homosexual behaviour' in female rats (e.g. Dörner, 1968). In this case, neonatal female rats were treated with androgen, and then again in adulthood. These rats were reported to show significantly more mounting than lordosis responses. In attempting to explain these findings Dörner (1968) suggests that 'the direction of the sex instinct is completely determined - independently of the genetic sex - by the androgen level during the critical hypothalamic differentiation period'.

On the basis of such studies with male and female rats, Dörner went on to suggest that homosexuality in humans can be understood in similar terms (e.g. Dörner and Hinz, 1968).

There are, of course, many difficulties involved in making inferences about human behaviour from research carried out with animals, especially non-primates. This is particularly apparent in this case where Dörner defines homosexuality in rats in terms of the relative performance of specific acts; in the female rat by an increased readiness to show mounting and intromission behaviour and a decreased readiness to display lordosis, whereas in the male rat homosexuality is defined by the converse.

To go on to equate such so-called homosexuality in the rat with homosexuality in humans is, to say the least, theoretically naive. What are the human homologues of lordosis or mounting behaviour patterns supposed to be? Is a male homosexual displaying lordosis if he acts as the 'passive' partner in anal intercourse, and if so what if on the following occasion he acts as the 'active' partner, does that make him less of a homosexual? In any event, many homosexual men do not engage in anal intercourse.

Similar problems arise in the consideration of mounting and intromission patterns in female rats and their relevance to female homosexuality in humans, particularly as the majority of homosexual women do not adopt strictly defined sexual roles as 'insertor or insertee'. Homosexuality in humans then cannot be defined in terms of specific acts, nor necessarily by the performance of sexual acts with the same sex.

Given these serious criticisms it is disturbing to note Dörner's work being frequently quoted in the media as offering new insights into the causation of homosexuality. The implications of this are all too clear. For instance in the 'Horizon' programme -The fight to be male- (first shown on BBC2, 21st May 1979), the comment was made that Dörner 'expects to prove that low testosterone in the womb leads to homosexuality, *if he does the next step might be to inject more testosterone and so prevent it'* (my emphasis).

So far we have discussed the application of animal research to the understanding of homosexuality in humans. What then of the literature on the influence of the prenatal gonadal hormones in human subjects? Such studies as there are have been largely derived from investigations of individuals with various rare endocrinological disorders which to some extent replicate naturally the kind of experimental conditions already described.

With respect to the possible etiological significance of prenatal androgen in female homosexuals, studies of females with congenital adrenal hyperplasia are of particular relevance. Also known as adrenogenital syndrome, this is a hereditary condition in which defective hydrocortisone synthesis leads to an overproduction of androgen from the adrenal cortex. These genetic females are therefore exposed to heightened levels of androgen whilst in the uterus, and, if they are not treated with cortisone, postnatally also.

Ehrhardt, Epstein and Money (1968) interviewed a group of such girls and their mothers and reported that 'their tomboyism did not include implications of homosexuality or future lesbianism'. It should be pointed out that the possible effect of high levels of foetal androgens on the developing central nervous system of these girls was not contaminated by raised postnatal androgen levels, as they had received cortisone treatment from a very early age. Nor therefore were the results confounded by these girls having a masculinized body appearance, which may be significant in the development of their sexual identifications, and in particular in their view of themselves as sexually attractive to the same/opposite sex.

This may have been a relevant consideration in the study by Ehrhardt, Evers and Money (1968), in which a group of women with congenital adrenal hyperplasia were interviewed. These women had not begun treatment until quite late in life, and had therefore been exposed to high levels of androgen for many years which had resulted in varying degrees of masculinization of the body. The majority of these women were heterosexual, and although some were bisexual none were exclusively homosexual.

A more recent study by Ehrhardt and Baker (1976), of a group of thirteen young women with congenital adrenal hyperplasia who had received treatment from an early age, again reported that whilst some women were bisexual none were exclusively homosexual and the majority were heterosexual.

Although there were no matched control groups in these studies, the preponderance of a heterosexual rather than a homosexual orientation in girls with congenital adrenal hyperplasia does imply that any possible influence of prenatal androgen on sexual orientation cannot be an all-or-none effect, nor a universal one.

In human male homosexuality the suggestion is that a defici-
ency in prenatal androgen should lead to a homosexual orientation. However, because of the small number of males with
endocrinological disorders resulting in foetal androgen defici-
ency, very little data is available to assess this. One study by
Money and Ogunro (1974), of a group of males with partial
insensitivity to androgen, reported that sexual orientation
tended to be in accordance with their sex of rearing. Individuals
were, in all but one case, heterosexual.

Apart from clinical investigations, the other source of evidence pertaining to the possibility of prenatal hormonal influences in human homosexuality is studies which have looked for
evidence of prenatal hormonal abnormalities in homosexuals
themselves.

Anatomical indications, such as abnormal development of the
external genitalia, are rarely found in homosexual men or women.
But it has been pointed out that if differentiation of sexual
orientation occurred at a later stage of foetal development than
differentiation of the reproductive tract and external genitalia,
or if they involved different biochemical mechanisms, then it is
possible that one may be affected independently of the other.

The reported high incidence of tomboyism in the childhood
of homosexual women, and effeminacy in the childhood of
homosexual men, has also been seen as indicative of prenatal
hormonal influences. This is in the context of a number of studies which have reported an increased incidence of tomboyism
in girls with congenital adrenal hyperplasia (e.g. Ehrhardt,
Epstein and Money, 1968; Money and Ehrhardt, 1972). Irrespective of any other criticisms which might be brought to bear, we
must keep in mind that direct observational studies were not
carried out, and that it may be that both girls with congenital
adrenal hyperplasia and their parents are more likely to categorize certain behaviour as an expression of tomboyishness
than would a control group of girls and their parents. In any
case, the association of tomboyism in girls, effeminacy in boys
and later homosexuality can in itself be seriously questioned, in
that virtually all such reports are based on retrospective
accounts by adult homosexuals, who are likely to have recon-
structed their past history in accordance with their present
identity as homosexual.

Finally, the other area of investigation into prenatal hormonal
effects in homosexuals is related to the hypothesis that foetal
androgens have a permanent influence on gonadotropin secretion by the pituitary, under control of the hypothalamus. More
specifically, it is suggested , on the basis of animal studies,
that the presence of prenatal androgen results in a surge in
luteinizing hormone in adulthood in response to increased levels
of oestrogen (see Fig.1.1). Dörner has extended this to
investigations of human homosexuality. He reports (Dörner,
1976; Dörner et al., 1975) that 'intact' homosexual men did

show such a positive feedback effect, whereas 'intact' hetero-sexual men did not. However, as Meyer-Bahlburg (1977) points out, this was not a uniform response in all homosexual men, nor have these results been replicated by other workers.

There would appear to be virtually no studies of the neuroendocrine regulation of luteinizing hormone in female homosexuals, although some preliminary data on transsexual women has been published (Dörner, 1976; Seyler et al., 1978).

In summary, therefore, there would seem to be serious problems involved in the application of a model of homosexuality which emphasizes the role of the prenatal gonadal hormones, based as it is primarily on research carried out on rodents, to an understanding of homosexuality in humans.

Additional problems arise when we distinguish between gender identity, gender-role and sexual orientation. What does the foetal androgen theory have to say about homosexuals who exhibit 'appropriate' gender-role behaviour, with the exception of sexual object choice? Are we to assume that somewhere in the hypothalamus there are different potentiating mechanisms for gender identity, gender-role orientation and sexual orientation, which may be differentially affected by foetal androgens depending, say, on the timing of their action? Alternatively, are we to assume a potentiating influence on all three in the presence of foetal androgen, any discordance being accountable by the 'confluence of circumstances' acting upon this assumed biological predisposition postnatally?

The action of the sex hormones is not yet fully understood, as regards either their possible effects on neural structures, or how this might be translated into behaviour. In any case, the difficulty of disassociating cause and effect in the relation-ship between hormones and behaviour cannot be too strongly underlined.

This kind of explicit recognition of the problems involved in applying such a model of explanation to human homosexuality must be made if naive overgeneralizations are to be avoided.

The explanations of homosexuality which have so far been discussed have tended to pay little or no attention to environ-mental influences, even where the likelihood of a multifactorial etiology is acknowledged. We will therefore now consider those models which have emphasized the importance of such influences, in particular familial factors, in the development of sexual orientation.

Let us first consider what can be loosely categorized as social learning theory approaches to homosexuality, where such pro-cesses as observational learning, modelling and identification, as well as specific learning experiences, are variously stressed.

EARLY SOCIAL LEARNING EXPERIENCES

In common with psychoanalytic explanations, 'social learning theories' have underlined the importance of early experience in psychosexual development. There are, nevertheless, funda- mental differences between the two approaches. Psychoanalysts have tended to focus almost exclusively on family relationships, whilst social learning theorists have, in addition, recognized the importance of wider social influences outside the family, e.g. peer group relationships, the effect of the media and relationships with adults other than parents.

Certainly, a child's parents are one of the most important influences on learning experiences, not least in the way that the child comes to learn the consequences of his/her actions through direct teaching and reinforcement. However, social learning theory would suggest that it is not parental expectations and reinforcements per se which are of prime importance in psycho- sexual development, but the process of identification with, and imitation of, the same-sex parent by the child.

Whilst both psychoanalytic and social learning theorists have emphasized that identification and imitation of the same-sex parent in the early years of life is crucial in gender identity and gender-role development, they hold very different theore- tical assumptions about the way in which this does or does not occur. Psychoanalytic writers view identification as resulting from the resolution of the Oedipus complex, whereas identific- ation in social learning theory terms is said to arise from a perceived similarity between the child and the role model, in this case the same-sex parent. This is within the context of a strong emotional tie to the parental role model.

It should also be noted that the cognitive developmental approach argues that the child's identification with the same-sex parent is not a prerequisite but a result of the child's knowledge of male and female gender-roles. In this way it is suggested that children will have a tendency to imitate their same-sex parent regardless of the actual reward, power or affectional relation- ship they have, although it is recognized that these may be influential variables in the process. Rather it is argued that the tendency to imitate the same-sex parent develops after, and as a result of, gender identity development in the child. Gender identity refers to the cognitive realization that one belongs to a stable category of individuals called either boys or girls. It is this cognitive realization which, it is claimed, then acts as an organizing influence on the gender-role behaviour of the child, rather than the other way around (Kohlberg, 1966).

The concept of identification with the same-sex parent would in any case seem to be far too simplistic a model to explain gender identity and gender-role development. Mothers, for instance, may play a significant role in the psychosexual development of their sons, and similarly fathers in the psycho- sexual development of their daughters (Kagan, 1964). In addi-

tion, gender-role development is likely to be influenced by
many factors besides role modelling figures within the family,
and the assimilation by the child of the values ascribed to such
roles by her or his parents. Nor should we ignore the effect
of siblings and peers, and the values, knowledge and beliefs
assimilated by the child about male and female roles from the
wider social context in which s/he lives and grows up.

At this point we must acknowledge that within the literature
on the effects of early social learning experiences on psychosexual development, the emphasis has tended to be on the
development of gender-role orientation rather than on sexual
orientation per se. Such research however has been of indirect
significance in attempts to understand the development of
homosexuality, where links have been made between 'inappro-
priate' or 'atypical' gender-role behaviour in childhood and a
homosexual orientation as an adult (e.g. Green, 1974a, b;
Rekers, 1977). In this way preadolescent boys who are said to
exhibit 'atypical gender-role behaviour' have been described as
'prehomosexual' and recommended for treatment (see Chapter 2,
pp.58-61). Implicit in such an analysis, of course, is the
assumption that homosexuality is a negative outcome of development.

Green (1974a,b) has emphasized the importance of both
parental and peer group influences. He suggests that these
boys often have problems of identification with their father, who
presents a negative role model. In addition, Green implies that
in such cases father and son are often alienated from one
another; and that parents of so-called 'behaviourally feminine
boys' usually show no consistent pattern of discouragement,
but respond in either a neutral or positive manner to such
behaviour. Green also suggests that these boys are likely to
be labelled as sissys. This may lead to ostracism from male
peers, which may in turn influence adult sexuality.

In mentioning peer group influences it should be pointed out
that various writers have suggested that unisexual peer groups
may be of some significance in the development of a homosexual
sexual orientation. Feldman and McCulloch (1971), for instance,
suggest that one's first sexual experiences may be crucial for
the development of sexual orientation if they occur at a
'critical stage of development'. They suggest that the child is
'at risk' if during this period s/he inhabits a single-sex
environment, where it is likely that sexual partners will be of
the same sex.

It is also important to note that whilst Green suggests that
the 'behaviourally feminine boy' may become homosexual, transsexual or a transvestite, nowhere does he explain why the
individual comes to adopt one rather than another of these three
different identities. A further problem exists in the evaluation
of such 'preventative' research, in that, if it transpires that
after treatment these so-called 'prehomosexual' boys do not
later become homosexual, it cannot simply be assumed that one's

original assumptions about the role of early experience in
homosexuality were valid, without contrasting these boys with
a similar group who have not received treatment. No such follow-
up data is available (see Rekers, 1977).

It is also interesting to note that the focus of interest has
been upon so-called 'prehomosexual' boys rather than girls, and
that female childhood cross-gender behaviour has been rarely
studied, although a few case histories have been reported
(Green, 1974a). This is in keeping with the male bias within
the literature on homosexuality, and can be seen partly as a
reflection of the little interest taken in female sexuality in
general. In addition, and related to this latter point, tomboyism
in girls is seen as being somewhat more acceptable than
sissiness in boys. Indeed, tomboyism is often seen as a transitional phase of female sexual development which many girls go
through. Similarly, whereas the term sissy carries implications
about sexual orientation and may be applied to older boys and
men, the label tomboy does not, and is normally used in
reference to young girls only.

An alternative approach has been to look for 'atypical gender-
role behaviour' in the childhood of adult homosexuals. Saghir
and Robins (1973), for instance, report that two thirds of their
sample of homosexual males described themselves as having been
'girl-like' in childhood, compared to only 3 per cent of the
heterosexual control group. Similarly it has been claimed that
female homosexuals are more likely than heterosexual women
to have been 'tomboys' as children (e.g. Wilbur, 1965; Thompson
et al., 1973).

The retrospective nature of studies which report 'atypical'
gender-role behaviour in childhood for homosexual women and
men presents problems of interpretation, however, given that
a person is likely to interpret past experiences in accordance
with present identity. In this way past experiences may acquire
a different meaning and significance retrospectively. In any
case, the fact that some homosexuals remember demonstrating
cross-gender behaviour when they were children is not of itself
satisfactory evidence of a direct causal link between atypical
gender-role orientation and later homosexual orientation.

Studies which have attempted to explain homosexuality in
terms of early learning experiences have often incorporated
certain deterministic assumptions about development, often
ignoring the way in which children are active in their own
socialization. Indeed, the focus has tended to be upon how
parents influence their children. We must recognize that the
relationship between parent and child is a two-way process, in
which both parties influence each other. This renders
generalizations about the effects of certain types of experiences
on all children highly questionable, given that different children
may respond to similar events in quite different ways. Money
(1961), however, suggests that whilst specific learning
experiences may vary between individuals, there is a universal

'critical period' for the imprinting of sexual orientation. The
notion of critical periods, with the suggestion that there is something special about the process of learning during this time
which overrides later learning experiences, has since been
criticized (e.g. Clarke and Clarke, 1976). This notwithstanding,
the notion of permanancy of sexual orientation is still highly
influential, and is in part the reason why so little notice has
been taken of later socialization experiences and their influence
on sexual orientation.

Having discussed early learning influences at a rather
generalized level, let us now consider specific learning experiences which have been cited as having possible etiological
significance in the development of homosexuality.

Heterophobia
The concept of homosexuality as a phobia or fear of heterosexuality is one which has been postulated by both psychoanalysts and learning theorists, although from very different
theoretical standpoints.

We should initially recognize two main types of response
which have been described in the literature. First, fear of some
aspect, or aspects, of a heterosexual sexual encounter (e.g.
fear or disgust of the genitalia of the opposite sex, or alternatively fear of disease or injury), and, second, fears concerning the individual's performance within heterosocial and sexual
encounters.

Possible explanations which have been offered to account for
the origins of such fearful responses range from early aversive
heterosexual experiences to feelings of sexual inadequacy in
relation to the opposite sex. It has even been speculated that
the rise of the women's movement may facilitate male homosexuality
by increasing performance anxiety in heterosexual sexual situations (Cooper, 1974).

The usefulness of the concept of heterophobia can be seriously questioned on a number of counts. Bieber et al. (1962) report
that 70 per cent of male homosexuals were described by their
psychiatrists as being aversive to the female genitals, in comparison with 34 per cent of the control group. Manosevitz (1970),
however, in a study using nonclinical samples of male homosexuals, finds no significant differences between the homosexual
and control groups in fear of female genitals, nor in fear of
disease or injury to their own genitalia. Similarly Bell and
Weinberg (1978), in their large-scale study of both male and
female homosexuality, report that the idea of having a heterosexual sexual encounter was repulsive to only 1 per cent of
both the black and white male homosexual groups, and to only
2 per cent and 1 per cent of the black and white female homosexual groups respectively. Indeed, a significant majority of
both male and female homosexuals reported that they had
experienced heterosexual sexual arousal (72 per cent of the
white homosexual males, 84 per cent of the black homosexual

males, 79 per cent of the white homosexual females and 80 per cent of the black homosexual females). More specifically, 23 per cent of the white homosexual males, 27 per cent of the black homosexual males, 38 per cent of the white homosexual females and 23 per cent of the black homosexual females reported that they had heterosexual masturbatory fantasies, and an even larger proportion stated that they had heterosexual sex dreams.

This underlines the fact that many homosexual women and men experience feelings of sexual desire and attraction to the opposite sex, and enjoy heterosexual sexual encounters. On the other hand, some homosexual women and men, rather than being aversive, may be merely indifferent to sexual relationships with the opposite sex.

This challenges the concept of homosexuality as a phobic response to the opposite sex. Where aversive feelings towards the opposite sex are reported by homosexual women and men this may in any case be a consequence rather than a cause of homosexual feelings. Certainly, it is difficult to explain within this model why men and women who experience heterophobia do not necessarily identify as homosexual, or similarly why homosexual men and women who experience positive sexual and social relationships with the opposite sex do not necessarily question their identity as homosexual.

In addition, such a view of homosexuality does not highlight the important distinction to be made between homosexual acts and identities, and by focusing on sexual encounters it fails to acknowledge the many nonsexual reasons that are significant for each individual in the development and maintenance of a homosexual identity.

We must also note that the explanation of homosexuality in terms of heterophobia, or negative response to hetero-sexuality, fails to recognize that for many homosexual men and women it is a positive preference for same sex relationships, and not an aversion to cross-sex relationships, which motivates their choice of homosexual relationships. This is in part a reflection of the fact that heterosexuality and homosexuality tend to be viewed as polar opposites, with heterosexuality being seen as the natural and positive pole of development.

Seduction theories
The view of seduction in childhood as influencing the develop-ment of a homosexual orientation in adulthood has taken a variety of forms. Within psychoanalysis, for instance, the emphasis has been upon imagined rather than actual seduction, with particular reference to the child's relationship with the parents; the use of the term 'seductive' being interpreted in terms of the dynamics of the Oedipus complex. On the other hand, actual seduction in childhood (both heterosexual and homosexual) has also been suggested as a significant influence. In the case of heterosexual seduction it has been postulated that such an experience may lead to feelings of aversion to the opposite sex. This is essen-

tially one form of the phobic model of homosexuality previously discussed.

Alternatively, seduction by someone of the same sex has tended to be viewed in terms of the theory of contagion. More specifically, McGuire et al. (1965) have suggested that the nature of the first sexual experience followed by orgasm is crucial in the establishment of sexual orientation. They argue that it is not the seduction experience per se which is significant, but the learning which takes place after the initial seduction scene the first sexual experience being important in providing a fantasy for subsequent masturbation. In this way McGuire suggests that if initial sexual experiences are homosexual then homosexual stimuli, given their association with masturbatory experiences, will become a cue for sexual response. Heterosexual stimuli, on the other hand, are extinguished through lack of such reinforcement. It has been suggested that this may be more likely to occur if the individual has also had early aversive heterosexual experiences, or alternatively if seduction occurs at a particular stage of development. Feldman and McCulloch (1971) suggest that the state at which secondary sexual characteristics begin to develop is the most obvious candidate for this critical stage.

The question that arises is why the individual should choose to masturbate to fantasies of the initial seduction scene rather than to fantasies about other situations, real or imagined, which may include heterosexual encounters. McGuire (1965) suggests that the first actual experience has stronger stimulus value.

Explanations of homosexuality which emphasize the role of early sexual experiences attract little serious attention in the more recent literature. In terms of the general mythology which surrounds homosexuality, however, derivations of such a perspective are still prevalent, and indeed have been influential in recent decisions concerning the employment of homosexuals who work with children (see Chapter 7, pp.145-8).

Concerns about homosexual men and women being 'potential seducers' of children are of course compounded by the frequent confusion of homosexuality and paedophilia.

PSYCHOANALYTIC MODELS OF HOMOSEXUALITY

Central to psychoanalytic thinking on psychosexual development is the concept of the Oedipus complex. This stage of development is where the child is said to experience feelings of sexual desire towards one parent in conjunction with feelings of rivalry towards the other. Prior to this, during the pre-Oedipal phase, the infant is viewed as being primarily attached to the mother. But by the age of four or five the child, in the case of a boy, is said to unconsciously desire his mother and experience aggressive feelings towards his father, whom he views as his rival for his mother's attentions. This is alongside feelings of affection and admiration for the father, and resentment and hatred towards the mother.

At this point Freud's ideas (e.g. Freud, 1905) about the importance of the genital differences between the sexes must be considered. Freud suggests that a boy initially attributes the possession of a penis to everyone, including females. As the boy becomes increasingly aware of genital differences, however, he is said to interpret such differences as indicating that girls have lost their penises, and in turn becomes fearful that he may lose his also.

In terms of the Oedipus complex, the boy's feelings of jealousy and resentment towards his father result in fears in the child that he will be castrated by his father as punishment for such thoughts. The resolution of the Oedipus complex for a boy, therefore, is through what Freud terms the 'castration complex', whereby the child identifies with his rival, the father, thereby gratifying to some extent his sexual desire for the mother whilst at the same time resolving his fear of castration by the father.

In the case of girls, Freud (e.g. Freud, 1920; 1931) argues that they too initially believe that everyone, including boys, have genitals like them. According to classic psychoanalytic theory, the realization that this is not so is associated with the interpretation that the penis has been lost. This discovery and resultant 'penis envy', is seen as bringing about the Oedipus complex in girls. A girl, then, is said to initially experience sexual desire for the mother, the first love object of both boys and girls. When the girl realizes that she does not possess a penis she is said to interpret this as a loss rather than a lack; as punishment for the incestuous desires she holds for the mother. Blaming her mother for what she perceives as her apparent castration, the girl transfers her feelings of love to the father, who in a sense can satisfy her wish for a penis. In this way the girl experiences feelings of hostility towards the mother, now viewed as a rival for the father's attentions, both for not having provided her with a penis and for her apparent castration. This is alongside feelings of affection and admiration for the mother as well as resentment and hostility to the father. Finally, the girl identifies with her rival, the mother, thereby gratifying her incestuous desires for the father and satisfying to some degree her 'penis envy', whilst at the same time resolving her feelings of aggression towards the mother.

Through the Oedipus complex, then, girls are seen as coming to identify with their mothers and boys with their fathers, and, having so identified, as acquiring behaviour and knowledge considered appropriate to their sex. Without entering into a detailed critique of such a model we should note here criticism of the notion of 'penis envy', which has formed the cornerstone in psychoanalytic thinking of an understanding of the psychosexual development of women. Indeed, the question of why a girl who has never possessed a penis, and therefore does not know its value from her own experience, comes to regard it as so precious, is an important one.

Having described the Oedipus complex in both boys and girls, we are now in a position to discuss psychoanalytic theories of homosexuality. The concept of bisexuality is of significance here, in that Freud (1905) puts forward the hypothesis that there is an innate and unconscious sexual predisposition to both opposite and same sex partners in each individual. The expression of such predispositions in adulthood was said to depend upon experiences of the individual in early childhood, particularly during the Oedipus complex. Those who are homosexual are seen as being at an arrested stage of psychosexual development. Such a perspective has encouraged the view that homosexuality is an immature form of behaviour.

Having implied that pathological parent-child relationships and 'castration anxiety' during the Oedipus complex have been seen by psychoanalysts as being of prime significance, we must acknowledge that Freud himself does not assume unresolved Oedipal feelings to be the only etiological pathway in the development of homosexuality. He suggests, for instance, that homosexuality may occur when the individual 'narcissistically' takes him or herself as the love object, rather than the mother or father, and searches for a person who resembles this love object. A variety of other mechanisms have been suggested by the neo-Freudians such as Ernest Jones, Harry Stack Sullivan, Karen Horney, etc., some of which are reviewed by Bieber et al. (1962, pp.3-11).

We should note that certain writers have placed particular emphasis on pre-Oedipal, rather than Oedipal, conflicts. Melanie Klein (1932), for instance, regarded the oral phase of psychosexual development as the most important stage in determining a homosexual orientation. In this respect, oral frustrations were seen as leading to a fixation to a particular erogenous zone (the breast) rather than to a particular person. Homosexual acts therefore have been understood by some writers as symbolic expressions of fixations to a particular bodily region. Socarides (1979, p.269), for instance, states that fixation at the pre-Oedipal stage of development results in the most 'serious cases of homosexuality', in which the individual is described as having to compulsively engage in homosexual acts in order to achieve a transient stabilization of self identity.

The overall emphasis within psychoanalytic thinking on homosexuality, however, is on early parent-child relationships, hence the need to critically examine studies which have paid particular attention to the parental background of male and female homosexuals.

Let us first consider female homosexuality. Freud drew attention to a gap in psychoanalytic theory and research relating to female homosexuality as long ago as 1920; since then the situation has changed little. What literature does exist tends to emphasize the significance of the mother-daughter relationship, although this does not exclude consideration of the relationship

with the father. For instance, both Freud (e.g. 1931; 1933) and
Deutsch (e.g. 1932; 1947) imply that the existence of, and
retreat from, the Oedipal relationship with the father is a
significant factor in the genesis of female homosexuality. (For a
historical review of psychoanalytic theories of female homosexuality see Socarides, 1963.)

Where poor relationships with the father are discussed they
are 'frequently regarded as only a consequence of the deep-
seated conflicts between the daughter and her mother' (Bene,
1965a). More specifically, McDougall (1979) has suggested that
in 'prehomosexual' girls the conflicts and desires experienced
in relation to the father are dealt with by identifying with him
rather than with the mother, who once more becomes the love
object, Wilbur (1965, p. 76) describes the typical family constellation of the homosexual female as:

> a father who tends to be passive, unassertive, gentle and
> detached, a mother who is dominant, domineering, guilt-
> inducing, and hostile; and a daughter who is hostile towards
> her mother, who cannot turn to her father because of what
> she perceives as his weakness, and who suffers from severe
> feelings of rejection and longing.

If we consider what has already been said about the Oedipus
complex in girls, a heterosexual orientation is achieved by her
transferring her libidinal attachment from the first love object,
the mother, to the father. However, if her attachment to the
father is too strong it has been suggested that she may later
reject men because of the incest fears which have been transfer-
red to them, with a resultant homosexual orientation (e.g. Romm,
1965). Alternatively, lesbianism has been seen to result from
the girl failing to reject the mother as a love object, instead
becoming fixated on her (e.g. Deutsch, 1932).

The view of female homosexuals as 'mother fixated' has been
important in the way in which homosexual relationships between
women have been seen as re-enactments of the mother-child
relationship (e.g. Socarides, 1963; Storr, 1964). This denial of
the erotic aspects of homosexual relationships between women by
perceiving them as pseudo mother-child relationships is very
interesting to contrast with the equally prevalent view of both
male and female homosexuals as primarily sexual creatures.

The very few studies which have been carried out into the
parental background of female homosexuals do not tend to
reflect this emphasis on disturbed mother-daughter relationships. We should note here, of course, that such studies are
based on recollections by adult homosexuals of their childhood
and not on any direct evidence of parent-child relationships.

Bene (1965a) reports a far greater difference between the
recollected feelings of homosexual and heterosexual control
groups for their fathers than for their mothers. Indeed, no
significant difference was found between female homosexuals
and heterosexual controls in their reported feelings towards
their mothers. This, Bene suggests, indicates that 'female

homosexuality tends to be connected with unsatisfactory relations between the girl and her weak and incompetent father'
(Bene, 1965a).

Similarly, Thompson et al. (1973) report that it is having a
weak and/or hostile father which is of etiological significance
for both male and female homosexuals, with no clear role for the
mother in the etiology of female homosexuality. In contrast to
this, the role of the mother is reported as being etiologically
significant in the development of male homosexuality.

If we now turn to psychoanalytic studies of male homosexuality, we can note that there has been a primacy placed on
the role of the mother. Classically, this admiration and love
of the mother, or 'mother-fixation', has been interpreted in
terms of Oedipal conflicts, whereby the son copes with his
feelings of hostility and aggression towards his mother by
identifying with her rather than with his father. The understanding of such a process of identification has been set in the
context of a weak or absent father in conjunction with a
domineering and dominant mother (e.g. Fenichel, 1946). This
is reflected in the psychoanalytic literature, where the close
attachment to a dominating mother, an unsatisfactory relationship with the father, or both, have been variously stressed.

Of particular notice here are the views of Bieber (e.g. Bieber
et al., 1962; Bieber, 1965). In the widely quoted study by
Bieber et al. (1962), seventy-seven psychoanalysts were given
a questionnaire and asked to rate on items pertaining to family
relationships a highly selected group of male homosexual and
heterosexual patients who were undergoing psychoanalysis.
The basis for this was the psychoanalysts' interpretations of
the retrospective accounts given by the patients of their family
background.

Bieber et al. (1962, p.172) report significant differences
in the assessment of the reported backgrounds of the two
groups, describing the 'typical' parent-child relationships of
male homosexuals in the following way:

> The 'classical' homosexual triangular pattern is one where
> the mother is close binding and intimate and is dominant and
> minimizing toward a husband who is a detached father,
> particularly a hostile-detached one. From our statistical
> analysis, the chances appear to be high that any son exposed
> to this parental combination will become homosexual or deve-
> lop severe homosexual problems.

Indeed, they go so far as to actually say that 'a constructive,
supportive, warmly related father *precludes* the possibility of
a homosexual son' (p.311). Evans (1969) points out, however,
that the data presented by Bieber et al. would suggest that a
moderately good relationship with the father does not in fact
preclude the appearance of homosexuality.

Contrary to classic psychoanalytic theory, Bieber also
suggests that most men are not 'latent homosexuals', but rather
all homosexuals are latent heterosexuals. This challenges

Freud's view of the inherent bisexual nature of man, and instead proposes that homosexuality is not a preference for same-sex relationships, but an inhibition of an inborn sexual responsiveness to the opposite sex. Bieber (1965) suggests that this may take the form of, for example, a fear of and aversion to the female genitalia, or anticipation of sexual rejection, humiliation or hostility from women. The most disturbing fears, however, Bieber claims, are associated with the expectation of being physically attacked by another man during sexual intercourse with a woman. This view that the male homosexual essentially fears and hates other men, whilst loving although avoiding women, is once again at variance with traditional psychoanalytic thinking, in which the female is seen as the centrally feared and hated figure. Such a fear of same-sex partners who are perceived as powerful and threatening is seen by Bieber as having its roots in the Oedipus complex, and as being the key to understanding both male and female homosexuals.

A number of other studies have reported the typical 'triangular system' parental constellation in the background of male homosexuals described by Bieber (e.g. West, 1959; O'Connor, 1964; Evans, 1969; Thompson et al., 1973). Evans (1969) points out, however, that we cannot simply assume that findings which are in general agreement with those of Bieber et al. necessarily uphold the conclusions they reached about the etiological significance of parental relationships in the development of homosexuality.

We must also note that other researchers have reported different patterns of parent-child relationships (e.g. Bene, 1965b; Apperson and McAdoo, 1968). In the study by Bene (1965b), for example, a nonpatient group of male homosexuals were compared with a group of male heterosexuals on measures of family relationships. Whilst the findings indicated some support for the view that male homosexuals remembered having had bad relationships with their fathers, there was no evidence to suggest that male homosexuals were more likely than the heterosexual group to recollect being overprotected by, over indulged by or strongly attached to their mothers. Indeed, Bene reports that compared with the heterosexual group the homosexuals recollected somewhat more hostility and less affection in their relationship to their mothers. More fundamentally, other researchers have seriously questioned whether family relationships have any necessary association at all with later sexual orientation (e.g. Hooker, 1969; Siegelman, 1974).

In this respect Siegelman's study is particularly important. In this study the recollected family backgrounds of a large nonpatient group of exclusive or predominantly exclusive male homosexuals were compared with those of a control group of male heterosexuals. The overall findings were rather similar to those reported by Bene (1965b), in that the homosexual group more often reported a rejecting and distant father. And, in contrast to the prevalent characterization of the mother as close-

binding and intimate, the homosexual group more often described their mothers as more rejecting and less loving than did
the heterosexual group.

What Siegelman claimed as the most striking result of the
study, however, was the complete lack of significant differences
in parental background between the homosexual and heterosexual groups rated as low on neuroticism. Thus it is possible
that the reported differences between homosexuals and heterosexuals on measures of family relationships is related to differences in neuroticism, rather than to anything specific to
homosexuality. This is all the more significant given that this
study was not subject to many of the methodological and sampling inadequacies which tend to characterize studies in this
area. Siegelman (1974) concludes that such findings 'seriously
question the existence of any association between family relationships and homosexuality vs. heterosexuality.'

In evaluating the literature on the parental background of
male and female homosexuals we must be critically aware that
the majority of studies have made generalizations about the
etiology of homosexuality from findings based on emotionally
disturbed or criminal populations (e.g. West, 1959; Bieber et al.,
1962; O'Connor, 1964; Nash and Hayes, 1965). Even where
nonclinical or noncriminal subjects have been used there is still
the problem of the representative nature of the sample, given
that subjects are usually volunteers from homophile organizations, and are thus likely to constitute a highly selected group
(e.g. Evans, 1969; Bene, 1965a,b; Siegelman, 1974).

In addition, many studies have failed to employ control
groups, and where these are used they have usually been poorly
matched. A good example is the lack of control for level of
adjustment, which, as Siegelman (1974) illustrates, may directly
influence results.

Various other methodological criticisms can be made of such
studies. For instance, the findings of Bieber et al. (1962)
represent only psychoanalysts' interpretations of the retrospective accounts of male homosexuals and heterosexuals, and
it is surely no surprise therefore to find that these support
psychoanalytic conceptualizations of the parental background
of male homosexuals. Similarly, other studies have based their
conclusions on the interpretation by psychiatrists or psychoanalysts of case histories (e.g. West, 1959).

Alternatively, investigators have based their findings directly
on retrospective accounts obtained from adult homosexuals
(e.g. Bene, 1965a, b; Evans, 1969; Thompson et al., 1973;
Siegelman, 1974). In the absence of any direct evidence, or
evidence from corroborative studies based on the parents of
homosexuals, we must be careful in the interpretations we make
of such data. This is especially so given the low reliability of
retrospective accounts. Also we should note that a person's
recollection of past events will be significantly influenced by
their present perceptions of themselves.

A related problem in interpreting retrospective accounts of subjects who are in therapy is that the therapeutic process will in itself influence the versions of the past they will give. Thus homosexual patients undergoing psychoanalytic treatment are likely to give accounts of their family background which are influenced by psychoanalytic theories of homosexuality. In such circumstances we must clearly be very careful in using such accounts as validatory evidence of particular theories.

We must also recognize that an association between a certain type of parental background and homosexuality in adulthood does not of itself indicate a cause and effect relationship. Evans (1969), for instance, points out that certain family constellations may not be causative of homosexuality, but rather may be a consequence of the child's effect on the parents. Such influences are often ignored, in contrast to the emphasis placed on how parents affect their children. The acknowledgment that the parent-child relationship is a two-way process underlines the fact that one cannot make generalized statements about the effects of certain familial influences on all children; in this case a weak or hostile father or a close-binding and over-intimate mother.

SOCIAL INTERACTIONIST MODELS

In its almost exclusive concern with causation and treatment, research into homosexuality has largely ignored sociocultural variables. This is a reflection of the predominance of personal pathological models of homosexuality in the literature, in which homosexuality is viewed as a 'condition' of the individual. Moreover in their search for etiological explanations theoreticians have tended to assume that homosexuals constitute a homogeneous group subject to similar motivating and causative influences. This perception of homosexuals as belonging to a uniform category is in part a result of the emphasis there has been on sexual orientation and sexual acts, both in defining and explaining homosexuality. More importantly, the social meanings of such acts for the individual, and the relationship they may or may not have to a homosexual identity, has been largely ignored. In this way, as has already been noted, there has been a lack of distinction between homosexual acts and homosexual identities, it generally being assumed that one follows on commonsensically from the other.

This distinction is clearly recognized within a social interactionist perspective, and the emphasis is placed upon homosexual identities rather than sexual acts. A homosexual identity in this sense, however, is not assumed to be an inborn and permanent characteristic, although it may be construed by the individual in this way. Rather, sexual identity is considered to be socially constructed and maintained through the process of social interaction. Within such an analysis, therefore, it is

important to look at the social context in which homosexual acts
occur and identities develop, and the individual meanings each
person ascribes to these.

Studies of homosexuality within institutionalized settings
(e.g. prison) have paid some attention to situational factors, in
viewing homosexuality as a response to a particular social context rather than the manifestation of an underlying 'condition'
(e.g. Ward and Kassebaum, 1965; Gagnon and Simon, 1974). In
addition, the rise of interest during the 1960s in the 'sociology
of deviance' produced a number of studies which attempted to
understand the individual homosexual woman or man by reference to the homosexual subculture in which s/he interacts
(e.g. Hooker, 1965; Schofield, 1965; Humphreys, 1970; Bell
and Weinberg, 1978).

We should at this juncture note two important points. First,
that sociological studies of lesbianism are rare (e.g. Simon,
1967; Warren, 1976). Second, that whilst the sociological literature has underlined the diversity which exists amongst male
and female homosexuals in terms of social class, race, marital
status, etc. it has not in the main questioned the association
between sexual activity and sexual identity. Thus, whilst they
have placed homosexual acts and relationships within a social
context, such studies have not directly addressed themselves
to the construction and maintenance of a homosexual identity.
This important question is discussed in more detail in Part Two
of the book, and in particular Chapter 3.

Having discussed the importance of placing homosexuality in
a social context, some mention must be made of theories which
have attempted to view homosexuality within a historical and
political setting (e.g. Plummer, 1975; Weeks, 1977; Ettorre,
1980). In acknowledging the development of theories of homosexuality which have explicitly recognized their political implications, however, it must be pointed out that all models of homosexuality are in a sense political theories. Certainly any theoretical model of homosexuality does not stand apart from the
society from which it has sprung, but both moulds and is
moulded by it. In this way, scientific opinion on the subject of
homosexuality has influenced how society at large views homosexual women and men, and thus has played an important role in
matters of social acceptance and reform. For example, genetic
explanations of homosexuality were used by early reformers such
as Krafft-Ebing and Havelock Ellis to gain sympathy for homosexuals who at that time were viewed as criminals and/or sinners.
The assumption that homosexuals were 'suffering' from some
inherent biological abnormality carried with it the suggestion
that they therefore ought not to be blamed for a condition over
which they had no control, and for which there could be no
cure. Deterministic assumptions about the permanency of the
homosexual 'condition' were also embedded in the reasoning
within the Wolfenden report, which recommended the 1967 law
reforms on male homosexuality in England and Wales.

The perception of homosexuality as a choice; a positive preference for relationships with the same sex rather than an aversion, or dislike, of relationships with the opposite sex, also raises important questions about social acceptance. It is one thing to accept someone as 'born like it' and quite another to accept homosexuality as a choice between relationships and lifestyles - the possibility of which is therefore, assumedly, open to us all.

We should also be aware that models of homosexuality will influence the meaning homosexuals themselves will ascribe to same-sex relationships and acts, and more importantly, their identification as homosexual. The possible influence such models may have on the self image of homosexual women and men is all the more significant given the negativistic assumptions implicit, or in some case explicit, in the majority of explanations. It is just such assumptions which have been challenged by homosexuals who, in coming out as openly gay, have asserted and affirmed the view of homosexuality as a positive preference. Once again, we can find examples in the literature of how this has been defused by interpreting being open about one's homosexuality as psychopathological (e.g. Munro and McCulloch, 1969), or as a defence mechanism (e.g. Romm, 1965).

The explicit recognition of the close relationship between the politics and science of homosexuality becomes all the more important at a time when there is an increasing demand for social change in the area of social and legal discrimination of homosexuals. Under such conditions, scientific theories and models of homosexuality themselves assume increased social and political significance: hence the need not only to be aware of what these theories are, but also to recognize the methodological and theoretical inadequacies of much of the research in this area.

2 THEORETICAL EXPLANATIONS IN PRACTICE

John Hart

WHY, IN PRACTICE, WE HAVE TO TAKE ACCOUNT OF THEORY

> until more is known about the origins of heterosexuality
> it is difficult to believe that meaningful insights will be
> reached regarding the origins of homosexuality.
> (Masters and Johnson, 1979, p.411)

To begin discussing theories about the causation of homosexuality is to risk the appearance of accepting the assumption that
the etiology of homosexuality is in some qualitative way different
from that of heterosexuality. This is something we do not
believe, for reasons which will be clarified in our discussion of
interactionist and political theories of homosexuality. The dangers involved in searching for 'answers' were brought home to
me when the literature search turned up a psychiatrist's comment (Neustatter, 1954) that applied without reservation to my
own situation: 'Some homosexuals are said to be unable to
whistle and to have a strong preference for the colour green -
a favourite colour in children.'

Why has so much time, energy and moral fervour been devoted
to investigating, treating and trying to change this minority
sexual orientation? Whatever the true figures may be about the
incidence of homosexual acts, these will be unlikely ever to
overtake solitary masturbation as the major sexual act and
fantasy preoccupation of women and men. Certainly masturbation has been the subject of some medical and moral concern in
the past, but in private it was never illegal as was, and sometimes is, a sexual act between men. Heterosexual conduct is
possibly reduced more by acts of solitary masturbation than by
homosexual acts, but the threat to heterosexual relationships
and identities has been seen as coming from sexual behaviour
between people (men more often than women) of the same sex.
If we are considering whether a person's sexual conduct is
dangerous, to others or to society, then clearly it is likely
numerically to be heterosexuality which is the 'cause' of the
greatest amount of trauma. As neither masturbation nor heterosexuality, as generalized conditions, attract the same amount of
interest in theorizing about causation, prevention and cure as
does homosexuality, we should acknowledge that it must be
providing society with a powerful symbol, beyond any logical
concern about its contribution to sexual behaviour or other
human conduct; indeed it may be that we should conclude that

the concern to theorize, treat and generally obsess about homosexuality in our society is a displacement of much wider concerns about the way people relate to each other. All the theories discussed here, therefore, should be seen as political theories, although I shall leave until the end a discussion of political theories about homosexuality which are openly identified as such. We have to study the reasons why people have been so obsessively determined to explain and thereby control homosexuality. We will note the kinds of explanations that have been advanced at certain times by 'experts', and the reception that these theories have experienced from society at large and from homosexuals themselves.

THE EFFECT OF THEORIES ABOUT HOMOSEXUALITY ON HOMOSEXUALS

We need to consider the responses of groups of people who may have different perspectives on the 'evidence' presented. First we have homosexual people themselves. Of course, we should recognize that sexual orientation has many different personal meanings, and homosexuality may be a very tenuous common denominator between people. The views that 'they' have therefore of theories about their lifestyle or sexual behaviour will differ widely in relation to their own political and moral beliefs, and their social and cultural situation.

The fact that until comparatively recently all homosexual men were sexual outlaws, and stigma was attached to women whose acts were not technically the concern of the criminal law, meant that as a group homosexual people had some investment in remaining socially invisible (or rather blurred), and there was little hope of group solidarity in public advocacy of their orientation. What homosexual women and men do have in common, and what separates them from heterosexuals, is the experience of having to ask and answer the question, 'WHY AM I HOMOSEXUAL?' The answers to this question are wide ranging, personal and yet also part of a repertoire provided by (heterosexual) society. Only recently have gay people attempted to redefine this question-and-answer process for themselves, rather than accept being labelled as sick or maladjusted. In looking now at some of the past and current answers to the question, I should like to consider the effects of theorizing by somewhat artificially dividing homosexual people into two groups. I shall consider those women and men who have directly experienced some professional interest in their sexual orientation, and the larger group whose sexuality has never become a concern of anyone outside a close group of friends. If their families are included one is less sure their situation is free from professional influence, as their parents or spouses may consult the GP, the vicar, friends, popular magazines or academic literature, and carry over the theories received there to their interactions with the homosexual person. We do not know the ways that the homosexual woman or man who does not directly come into contact with professionals concerned with the phenomenon views her or his own sexuality. Much of the past theorizing about homosexuality has been based on very special groups of people, usually men in trouble with the law or having personal problems. The issue is further complicated by the 'hidden' state of the majority of homosexual people. There are formidable methodological problems in surveying sexuality, and this of course also applies to homosexuality.

'The Spada Report' (1979) claims 'an unequaled overview of the entire gay scene in America today'. What the report does in fact provide are the fascinating responses of over 1,000 men who responded to Spada's questionnaire. We learn that 'Most of the respondents stated either that there was "no reason" that they were gay or that they were born that way' (p.274). There was also a range of other reasons given for being homosexual which relate to theories discussed in this volume. Another American work which communicates a lot about certain gay women and men without claiming to be representative of all homosexuals is 'The Gay Report' (Jay and Young, 1979); however, these authors deliberately decided not to ask their respondents questions about their view of causation.

The way people whose sexuality has been the subject of professional concern view themselves depends partly on the reason for 'the referral' - being apprehended by the police is of a different order to seeking help for worries about your sexual orientation. Only a very small number of homosexual people do come into direct contact with professional helpers or controllers, because of sexual orientation. In Britain it would certainly be less than the figures quoted in the American study of Jay and Young (1979, p.722). In their group, 20 per cent of the gay men and 8 per cent of the gay women had been to a therapist to be 'cured'. Also, 12 per cent of the men and 18 per cent of the women were currently seeing a therapist 'for any reason'. We should also note, however, that homosexual people may be particularly vulnerable to explanations of felt sexual differences provided by 'experts'. It seems likely that in many 'true case histories', a reconstruction of past events may go on to make them fit more comfortably with those of the expert. An example of this may possibly have occurred in West (1960), when the author presents 'two typical cases' of (male) homosexuality, including one who had sought treatment for his sexual orientation and was 'known to me outside the patient-doctor relationship' (p.81). West states (pp.85-6):

He knew about the psychological theory that male homosexuality arises from mother-fixation, but he did not seriously think that this had much relevance to his own case. However, after a discussion of his behaviour towards his mother and its contrast with his attitude to his father, he developed a violent headache.

My own experience emphasizes the ways in which explanations / theories /labels can be introjected by individuals even when these are strongly prejudicial. A former colleague, who was homosexual and a counsellor, whose training has been psycho-dynamically dominated and who had been in psychoanalytic psychotherapy, viewed his homosexuality as being a 'personality disorder', and would comment on other homosexual men's behaviour with some variation on, 'Well, they are the most unstable section of the community'. Such views are related to a point in time when the social conditions were right for the emergence of a particular theory, explanation, label and the development of a particular self concept. This same colleague described to me his unhappy position as a sexual outlaw prior to the 1967 Sexual Offences Act, his thirteen years in a monas-tery and his emergence as a middle-aged man in the late 1970s in an apparently liberated world where the rules about manag-ing one's sexuality had changed and everyone appeared 'glad to be gay' - at least if they were under twenty-five.

Contact with professionals may provide a sickness identifica-tion of one's sexuality, or a raising of consciousness to a political analysis. The effect of theories about sexual orientation on homosexual men or women are influenced by the interaction between those theories and the self, and, specifically, by the power of the professional encounter.

THE PERSON IN THE STREET

Assumptions are frequently made by those with a professional interest in homosexuality about general societal attitudes, and it is to these that we next turn. Green (1974b, p.309), in justifying his research and therapeutic endeavours related to changing -The behaviourally feminine male child-, asks,
    What if the very feminine boy is prehomosexual? ... Can we
    expect a style of behaviour that is illegal in 80% of the
    United States, labelled until 1974* a mental illness by Ameri-
    can psychiatry, considered a sin by most organized religions,
    and a social threat by so many Americans, be comfortably
    embraced in time for today's prehomosexual boy?
The answer to the question is that it depends upon what society / societies you are concerned about, and what aspects of 'a style of behaviour' you are referring to, and at what point in time. Of course the answers people give do to some extent depend on 'the way you ask 'em!' For example, Levitt and Klassen (1974) reported on a 1970 American National Survey one of the purposes of which was to look at attitudes and perceptions concerned with homosexuality. Of this sample, 77.7 per cent considered that sex between two same-sexed persons was 'always wrong' when they 'have no special affection for each other'. This view was

* It was in fact 1973. (J.H.)

shared by 70.2 per cent when the persons 'love each other'. The possible responses provided a choice from 'always wrong' to 'not wrong at all', which may have lead respondents in a certain negative direction with closed-answer questions. Along- side this observation I would place another reported finding, that masturbation was 'still considered always wrong by 26% of our sample of 3,018'. In this survey there was no opportunity to offer views as to 'causation' within a political or interaction- ist framework.

However, we cannot deny the implication of Green's (1974b) views, that undoubtedly some sort of 'homophobia' does exist in western societies. An interesting discussion of the causes of such attitudes is reviewed by MacDonald (1976). He concludes that among the major sources of negative attitudes is 'the need to preserve the double standard between the sexes, thereby avoiding confusion of the sex-roles'. Green (1974b, p.309) asks about the possibilities of achieving a change in 'laws and public opinion so as to render the adult homosexual's life comparable with that of the heterosexual'. In terms of the perception of homosexuality probably being part of a more general question as to what sexuality divorced from reproduction is for, we can expect a diversity of attitudes in society and a general trend which may be towards repression. We cannot be optimistic that social attitudes towards homosexuality will support equality of opportunity in terms of 'laws and public opinion'. What we can ask about, however, is the effect of generally hostile attitudes on homosexuals themselves.

An interesting aspect of recent studies of homosexual women and men not confined to those who come into contact with pro- fessionals (because of the law or their psychological problems), is the way in which, despite obvious societal pressures, homo- sexuals are able to report on their own positive attitudes to their lifestyles. For example, to Spada's (1979) question, 'Would you rather be straight?', 85 per cent of 541 gay men responding replied 'No' while 72.1 per cent of 1,038 gay men answered 'Yes' to the question, 'Do you consider yourself happy?' (pp.337-8). Jay and Young (1979) asked their respondents, 'If you could take a pill to make you straight, would you do it?': 95 per cent of the lesbians and 77 per cent of the gay men said 'No'. This may illustrate the stability of sexual orientation.

Findings about the possibilities of achieving a satisfactory adjustment come from Weinberg and Williams (1974) on male homosexuals in Europe and the USA and Bell and Weinberg (1978) on gay women and men living in the San Francisco Bay area.

Such findings do not prevent beliefs being held by apparently informed persons that the reverse is true. For example, the Working Paper on the Age of Consent in relation to Sexual Offences (1979, p.20):

Most of us believe that in the vast majority of cases the homosexual way of life is likely to be less satisfactory than

heterosexual relationships and more likely to lead to
unhappiness. This stems to some extent from society's
disapproval of homosexuality and homosexual acts which it
was suggested to us, are considered degrading and objec-
tionable by a great many people.

How is it, then, that 'we all know' that homosexuals are unhappy people, less reliable than heterosexuals (especially when
they are security risks), have stronger sexual drives, unhappy
childhoods, defective genes, are a danger to children (especially their own)? Frank Pearce (1973, p.284), looking at the
situation prior to the 1970s, is still helpful here: 'heterosexuals
have little chance of learning through their own experience how
essentially similar homosexuals are to themselves. Cases such as
child molesting are predominantly the ones presented to the
public.' Pearce sees the mass media as managing the contradictions inherent in a view of normal and abnormal conduct
(pp.299-300):

> The newspapers' treatment of homosexuality is comprehen-
> sible as an attempt to come to terms with the anomalous
> nature of the activity. Homosexual acts call into question
> the 'natural' order which has been so necessary for indus-
> trial capitalism.

He comments on 'how hard the newspapers have to work to
suppress the information that destroys both their conception
of homosexuality and of the normal moral world.'

Essentially, popular views which characterize the 'homosexual
condition' appear to be of two kinds, both of which can be
demonstrated as existing (often co-existing) from survey data
and our own everyday experience. These are (i) deterministic,
'born that way', early parental upbringing experience or victim
of seduction, and (ii) the voluntaristic, seeing homosexuality
as sinful behaviour. Of course, it is common to blame parents
for a range of 'undesirable' conditions in society, from the
macro - 'the cycle of deprivation' - to individual disorders such
as schizophrenia, truancy and lack of respect for authority.
Certainly it is the experience of counsellors working with
parents of homosexual children that they frequently ask 'Where
did we go wrong?'

There exist many apparent reinforcements to such deterministic beliefs, whether in warnings to parents not to smoke in
front of the children or in the presumed effects of growing up
in a lesbian household (see Chapter 8). Behind such concerns
is a view of happy family life which protects its members from
social deviations and dangers, and prepares them to reproduce
another generation in their own image. Threats to such a
socialization process are recognized in the courts and by the
Church (viz. -The wayside pulpit: the family that prays
together stays together-). As Pearce (1973) implies, openly
gay people are a symbolic contradiction to a society which has
been experiencing in this century a range of critical pressures,
both economic and ideological. In this situation we can gener-

alize that on a popular level, the theories of homosexuality which
have filtered through are concerned with parental failure and
shock at the 'abnormality' (possibly seen as connected with biological or genetic factors) of the homosexual son or daughter.
In a 'series about how those closest to us can turn out to be
strangers with terrible secrets' in 'Woman' (21 October 1978),
Brenda Barambas tells of her responses on finding out her son
was homosexual:

> My main feeling was guilt. I went over Peter's upbringing
> time and time again trying to find somewhere I'd made a
> mistake. I thought about him playing with dolls and prams
> when he was little - he used to love that. But then all my
> sons did - and so do a lot of other little boys.

There exists the idea that mothers or fathers, because of a lack
of complete satisfaction with, or criticism of, their own gender
role, or their own 'weakness', have failed to provide an adequate
model for their daughters or sons.

As mentioned in Chapter 1, theories about the causation of
homosexuality have, in this century, been in interaction with
other dynamic processes in society, with the result that hereditary, hormonal, psychoanalytic and social learning theories have
been subject to swings of fashion; we can however generalize
that a version of inadequate parenting, whether because of
hereditary or psychological factors, has been the most consis-
tently held and popularized theory. Along with such beliefs is
also held the view of homosexuality as being contagious. This
presumably is adapted from a social learning theory in which
seduction is seen as the cause of later deviant sexual orientation.
The homosexual is therefore seen also as dangerous, a 'carrier'
of the contagious condition. In this report from the 'Guardian'
(3 April 1976), a judge sentenced a teacher for indecent assault
on his ten- and eleven-year-old pupils:

> One reads again and again in histories of young men invol-
> ved in homosexual activity, that at an early age they were
> subject to some homosexual attack. There is no medical
> evidence I have heard to suggest that that cannot but have
> in some cases, a very serious effect and may well have done
> in this case.

Such generally held beliefs about the causation of homosexuality may well be in for a revival, not so much because of
increasing interest in social learning theories, but as a response
to those gays who are asserting their rights and attempting to
redefine their sexual preference in political rather than personal
pathological terms. We are also benefiting from the (post-Kinsey)
sociologist's ability to distinguish homosexual acts from homosexual lifestyles. Such developments have involved the notion
of choice of sexual orientation, and for those holding beliefs
about the essential correctness of monogamous heterosexual
relationships there is the implication that homosexual behaviour
should be the subject of conversion rather than compassion.
Gay people are not deterministically seen as being less than

totally responsible for their 'inversion', but instead as being
morally autonomous and therefore capable of a conscious decision to abstain from homosexual conduct. Such a view is not
new: for example Bailey (1955, p.39) wrote of the need for
Christians to distinguish between 'the homosexual *condition*
(which is morally neutral) and homosexual *practices*'. Gay
liberation politicians now see the 'homosexual condition' as a
moral question, and this new analysis has not escaped the attention of theologians. The Save Our Children campaign, fronted
by Anita Bryant in America, in its literature referred to
tolerance 'based on the understanding that homosexuals will
keep their deviate activity to themselves, will not flaunt their
lifestyles, will not be allowed to preach their sexual standards
to, or otherwise influence, impressionable young people'
(reported by James Treloar in the 'Sunday News Sunday Magazine', Detroit, Michigan, 5 June 1977). The concept of choice
of lifestyles is recognized by Mary Whitehouse in Britain and
Bryant in America; as the latter has put it, 'I don't hate
homosexuals. I love homosexuals. It's the sin of homosexuality
I hate' (reported in 'Newsweek', 6 June 1977, Richard Steele
with Tony Fuller in Miami). Although Bobys and Laner (1979)
have questioned how easy it is to be seen as an 'ex-homosexual',
the 'born again' Christians on both sides of the Atlantic feature
'ex-homosexuals' who give their 'testimony' at evangelical meetings. Clearly here is the idea of a choice of lifestyle, even if
the choice requires some help from prayers and therapy. For
some, the strain on their previously held liberal attitudes to
homosexuality can be glimpsed in this response from 'The Spada
Report' (1979, p. 275): 'God made me gay, bless Her!'

The emergence of an openly political theory of sexual orientation may well have provided the problem, for both theologians
and the general public, that they may still 'hate the sin', but
can they love the unrepentant sinner?

THE WAY THAT PROFESSIONALS VIEW HOMOSEXUALITY

If we include in this group all those who partly earn their
living by treating, preaching for or against, prosecuting or
researching homosexuality, I think we should, as a preliminary,
consider that they may have some investment in theories which
lead to the abolition, eradication, continuation or expansion of
homosexuality. Within such groups, individuals will have their
own reasons for wishing to promote a certain type of theory.

If we look more closely at the way those professionally
involved in the subject of homosexuality view the phenomenon,
it may seem at first that as theorists they would perceive the
world through one or more particular theoretical perspectives.
However, if we consider the situation specific to the encountering and treatment of homosexuality, we realize that no such
purity is likely to exist.

Let us first consider personal influences on professionals in
their practice. From my own study of social workers and probation officers (Hart, 1979), I tentatively concluded that it may
not be the professional's sexual orientation which 'determines'
her or his responses to sexual conduct, but rather her or his
own moral/political assessment of the conduct as the employee
of welfare organizations. This is likely to include a calculation
about the effects of certain behaviour on their employers. For
example, in my experience it is possible for aversion therapy for
homosexuals to be administered in psychiatric units where a
large number of the staff are currently 'suffering from the same
condition' which they are treating. If the personal response to
the individual patient or client was as important as some of the
counselling literature suggests, then the treatment would in
such situations presumably not take the form of aversion therapy
but of co-counselling, assertion training, encounter or
consciousness-raising groups to help people whose lifestyle was
causing them stress. There are after all so many psychologists,
social workers, nurses, psychiatrists and medics who are in a
position to empathize with the homosexual 'condition'! Of course,
the effects of stigma have ensured that it is not only practitioners who have avoided personal involvement; theorists also
have used their personal contacts to provide material for theories about homosexuality without declaring their own interests
in the subject of their research or theorizing. The study by
Delph (1978), on the other hand, involved the investigator in
'passing for homosexual', and is of interest for the way in which
'the observer' maintains his social distance from the label
'homosexual' in the presentation of himself in his writing. We
must consider the professional's actions within her or his
political experience. Within such a perspective we can understand the emergence in recent years of the 'professional gay'.
This has been made possible by some law reform and by the
apparent increasing tolerance in our society for discussion of
sexual matters. Such free speech has, however, very definite
limits (see Plummer, 1981, on the attempts by paedophile groups
to have a public platform). Our society also has some limited
toleration of 'successful deviants'. The attitudes of professional
gays towards theories are influenced by their advocacy of the
gay lifestyle and developed through a knowledge of gay history;
it is a personal, political and professional commitment beyond ·
objectivity. If such persons are also therapists we might expect
their aims to be, similar to Thomas's (1977, writing of feminist
therapy), those of integration. It is the opposite of the professional response I cited earlier:

Integration is, in fact, the making of multiple connections
and feminism and feminist therapy can be seen as the making
of connections on many levels - connections between feminism
and therapy, between one woman and all women, between
one's personal problems and one's social awareness, between
one's beliefs and what one does, and between what one does

in therapy and how one lives one's life.

One more factor we should note in considering the personal responses of the professionals to theory, concerns the findings of Truax and Carkhuff (1967). These suggest that no matter whether the theorist is psychoanalytic, client-centred, behaviourist or eclectic, the effective therapist is one who can demonstrate accurate empathy, non-possessive warmth and genuineness. The findings relate to therapies which acknowledge the importance of the personal encounter. Such considerations are still important in personal encounters with professionals who see themselves as involved mainly in chemical or behavioural procedures. The Truax and Carkhuff results do require acceptance and non-defensiveness from the effective therapist. This would involve having some personal comfort with one's own and the client's sexuality. It is difficult to see how such conditions for successful therapy could be achieved by professionals who either hold personal pathological models of homosexuality, or who are anxious about their own sexual orientation for personal or professional reasons.

So far we have assumed that theories guide actions. This must be seen in the context of both the society in which people operate as professionals, and specificially within the organizational constraints which may be felt to impinge on professional behaviour. But this is perhaps allocating too much power to the concept of 'theory'. After all, just as the majority of homosexual people do not become the patients, clients or charges of professional helpers or controllers, so the majority of professionals are unlikely to be in the business of pushing back the frontiers of knowledge about homosexuality. As busy social workers, psychiatrists, counsellors, GPs, psychologists and clergy, they are the consumers of ideas about treatment procedures.

It would be easy to characterize the market for many of us involved as helping professionals as requiring a 'digest' of theories and treatments, in a series including perhaps 'Freud's Greatest Hits', 'A Masters and Johnson Sampler' and 'The World of Gagnon and Simon'. What may happen in such a situation is that the original papers and research are never studied. As Rogers (1976, p.176) has warned in relation to attempted explanations of 'sexual deviations':

> Naive extrapolation is, I am afraid, far too common, particularly when subsequent workers latch on to, and quote, previous work without reading it carefully or without enough knowledge in the area to properly assess it. One fears for the psychiatric profession in this respect.

(See Chapter 1, which attempts to review critically some important research on homosexuality.)

The sorts of conditions required to generate theories occur when enthusiastic or ambitious people have the time to devote to the task, in the appropriate political climate and economic situation, where there are either public funds available for research or private-practice patients or clients ready to pay for therapy, or, more recently, a 'way in' to organized gay groups or, especially in the past, to a captive population. A good example of the importance of the latter comes from a Parliamentary Report dealing with the prison medical service, featured in the 'Lancet' (vol. 1, p. 632, 1949), 'Research, partly therapeutic in character, into the psychiatric and endocrinological aspects of homosexuality is being conducted at two selected prisons, and homosexuals will also benefit from research which is in progress into psychopathic personalities.'

This reminds us that the samples of homosexual men and women referred to in the literature frequently have special characteristics beyond their sexual orientation – for example, they are in prison, in analysis or in Southern California.

Faced with knowledge of the elite nature of theory (including specifically political theory) on homosexuality, and the individual client in distress, the professional person may well fall back on some variant of saying 'I accept you.' It is one of the objectives of this present volume to provide some of the things to say after that (see also Richardson and Hart, 1980, on counselling). We must recognize that such a task involves a consideration of the specific treatment implications of theories of homosexuality.

PROFESSIONAL AND PRACTICAL IMPLICATIONS DERIVED FROM THEORIES ABOUT HOMOSEXUALITY

Born that way?
Any theory which stresses prenatal or genetic factors in the etiology of a pathological condition does not always lead to therapeutic optimism – except of course in terms of genetic or biochemical engineering. A 1979 BBC television programme on the work of Dörner has discussed the future possibilities of the prevention of 'potential homosexual' offspring (see Chapter 1, pp.19-22).

A more sophisticated approach to the nature/nurture debate is to consider the way in which inherited factors may render the individual more susceptible to certain environmental influences, and also how, for example, environmental stresses may themselves affect the production of sex hormones. There is little evidence that such sophistication has been present in the way that professionals have viewed homosexuality. There has been far more emphasis on showing that 'the condition' is caused by prenatal or postnatal influences. The possible interaction of such influences has been acknowledged in some of the more recent literature (see e.g. Rogers, 1976).

In the light of the problems of methodology and replicability of those studies which have apparently shown biochemical differences in male homosexuals, it seems unlikely that any basis is provided either for social engineering efforts with those 'at risk', or to change the direction of sexual interest of people who become homosexual. After looking at reported biochemical differences, Barlow, Abel, Blanchard and Mavissakalian (1974) conclude: 'it would certainly seem premature to base treatment or theory on biological differences between homosexuals and heterosexuals.' In reviewing psychoendocrine data on lesbian and transsexual women, Meyer-Bahlburg (1979) concludes: 'I was unable to find any concrete clinical reports on actual attempts at "curing" lesbianism by compensatory administration of estrogens or by antiandrogen treatment.' As we have indicated, however, amongst the general public, and amongst homosexuals themselves, there is some support for theories upon which such treatment is based. Levitt and Klassen (1974) found that 13.6 per cent of respondents said they thought 'more than half' of all homosexuals are 'born that way', with 16.7 per cent responding that this was true for 'all or almost all' homosexuals. However, 43.9 per cent thought it true for 'hardly any or none', and 18 per cent thought it true for 'less than half'. It seems likely, then, that professionals will sometimes be faced with having to make some statement to clients or other interested people about the status of genetic or hormonal theories. Re-education of the public and of individuals holding such deterministic beliefs is not necessarily an easy task, given the appeal of 'scientific' findings which provide explanations of sexual difference in terms of factors apparently outside the control of individuals. As we will later discuss, alternative perspectives which emphasize choice may not be so comfortable either for society or homosexual people. However, the practice implications of an adherence to genetic or hormonal theories may form a basis for liberal 'acceptance' (other theoretical models may lead to similar attitudes). In the present state of knowledge one could not ask for more from practitioners using such a model. We should note here the extreme possibilities of non-acceptance of homosexuality. After reviewing the scientific and ethical status of castration for sex offenders, Heim and Hursch (1979) report that

> there always exists a theoretical gap between the etiology of sex deviations and the various kinds of somatic or nonsomatic treatment. As to castration as a somatic kind of treatment for sex offenders, however, it is justified to say that the gulf just mentioned is the largest among all treatment possibilities available; and it is.... unbridgeable.

Such a conclusion may also apply to stereotaxic surgery, which, however, has been used in Germany for the treatment of 'pedophilic' homosexuality. The age of sexual interest for these male patients in fact ranged from seven- to 22-year-olds (Roeder, Orthner and Müller, 1972). Dieckmann and Hassler (1974) report on such treatments applied to three homosexuals, and feel able to state further that 'sufficient anatomical and experimental knowledge of the hypothalamic control mechanisms of sexual function now exists to justify treating certain forms of disturbed sexual behaviour by selective destruction of specific regions or nuclei of the hypothalamus.'

They consider their results as having the same but superior effects as antiandrogen, and it is to hormonal treatments of homosexual behaviour that we now turn.

Such treatments have been seen as an effective way of controlling the 'libido', usually of sexual offenders, where the aim has been not the redirection of sexual interest but the suppression of sexual urges. We should note here the way in which male homosexuality has been seen as synonymous with a sexual offence. It is therefore understandable that it is law enforcement professionals such as probation officers, prison medical officers and policemen who most likely will have been involved in the operation of a 'hormonal theory in action'. It is interesting to note at this point how homosexuals who have committed criminal offences may get categorized with other sex offenders. For example, a probation officer defines sexual offenders for whom he is advocating a libido suppressing drug as those 'convicted of rape, attempted rape, indecent assault, buggery, etc.' (Shaw, 1978). In America prior to 1973, homosexuals could be seen by professionals as 'sociopaths', and Peters and Roether (1971) describe a group psychotherapy approach to probationed sex offenders: 'The homosexuals who are arrested are more likely... to rationalize most of their behaviour, questioning the social norms which classify them as antisocial and deviant. They rarely examine their feelings of sexual inadequacy'.

The problem with a theoretical orientation which stresses the hormonal determinates of homosexuality and the use of libido suppressing drugs rests specifically on a lack of proven specific effectiveness, and on the serious side-effects, of treatment. There is also the equation of homosexuality with sexual acts in isolation from identities and lifestyles. This is acknowledged by careful commentators and clinicians such as Bancroft (1974; 1979). The professional problem I wish to concentrate on here is the pressure which professionals working in the correctional field may feel when dealing with people who have been in trouble for homosexual conduct perhaps with young people. As a probation officer in my study (Hart, 1979, p.87), put it:

> Dealing with prisons who have psychiatric units with sex offenders may find the probation officer in dilemmas when their idea of treatment is different from the prison medical staff. And the prisoner of course is faced with the dilemma of 'What will get me out of prison quickly and is it worth the risk?' I think this is a vast area which is very much uncharted.

The 'Guardian' (29 March 1980) reported that in London prisons the 'use of implanted female hormones in sex offenders has been abandoned' because of side-effects, the most obvious being the growth of breasts, and because 'they are not 100% effective'.

Such caution does not extend to all practitioners. Shaw (1978) believes the limitations of success with sex offenders on libido-suppressing drugs such as cyproterone acetate has to do with

social factors. Group therapy was therefore instituted to
'internalize the need for regular taking of the drug, to examine
guilt and to help the offender gain insight'. Failure to attend
the meetings or 'to keep any appointment necessary for the
efficacy of the treatment will result in immediate breach proceedings under Section 6 by the C.J.A. (Criminal Justice Act)
in the case of a probationer, or in the case of a parolee, information being made available immediately to the authorities concerned.'

We can then make an interim conclusion that at present drug
treatments are used most often on captive patients, and are
directed at the suppression, rather than the redirection, of
sexual interest. They have severe problems in terms of side-
effects, personal motivation and social implications, in that they
are essentially an avoidance, rather than an encountering, of
sexuality. It is precisely because homosexual people are particularly vulnerable to legal attitudes to their behaviour that a
heavier responsibility is placed on those professionals working
in the correctional services to ensure that anyone facing the
opportunity of drug treatment is given as much freedom of
choice as is possible. Alternative treatments do exist, and one
is described in the Atascadero project in America where im-
prisoned paedophiles were given the opportunity to learn social
skills by interacting with adult gays as role models (Serber and
Keith, 1974). The grey area in which hormonal theories and
treatments are being tested requires specific attention not just
from medical personnel but from organizations like the British
Association of Social Workers.

In the American study previously cited, Levitt and Klassen
(1974) reported on their respondents' 1970 statements concerning 'Homosexuality is a sickness that can be cured' as being
true for 'all or almost all homosexuals', 37.9 per cent; 'more
than half', 24.0 per cent; 'less than half', 16.5 per cent; 'hardly any or none', 12.9 per cent. Let us take these figures at
their face value, and speculate that a large number of Americans
may see homosexuality not just as a sickness but also as curable.
The fact that the American Psychiatric Association did not dis-
agree with them until 1973 is ignored by the authors in their
curious remark, 'This, of course, represents population lag
behind the profession of psychiatry'. One could equally well
read the figures of 16.5 per cent who thought this true of 'less
than half', and 12.9 per cent 'hardly any or none', as examples
of people who were in 1970 ahead of the profession of psychiatry! Socarides, an American psychoanalyst, was still able in
1979 (p.275) to refer to homosexuality in the context of 'the
commitment to the attempted alleviation of this important and
serious disorder'. Professional and public attitudes are in a
state of interaction. It seems likely that reported or expected
'successes' in the treatment of homosexuality will influence
beliefs about 'the condition'. Many professionals, whether they
be medics, counsellors or clergy, encounter homosexuality still

presented as a sickness and are asked for advice about the possibilities of cure. Although in Britain we have not made such general statements as the American Psychiatric Association, if one turns to the standard psychiatric textbooks, for example Stafford-Clark and Smith (1979), we find that homosexuality is no longer necessarily seen as a disease to be cured. However, if the person is presented, by her or himself, by the family or by society as being sick, the concepts frequently in use would imply a medical model which is seeking to treat a condition or illness, rather than a person with her or his own particular behaviour and meanings. We have noted that libido-suppressing drugs are one way of treating 'a sickness' - by the suppression of 'symptoms'. We shall now look at another theoretical model which has also been associated with seeing homosexuals as sick.

The psychoanalytic model in practice

To state that the influence of psychoanalytic theory has been out of all proportion to its scientific status or clinical practice is almost a statement of the obvious. It cannot be denied, however, that for a large number of professionals working in the field, psychoanalytic concepts are a convenient way of viewing a homosexual orientation: the emphasis on the primacy of the family and intense feelings within, the emphasis too on the need to develop insight into behaviour rather than act out, are attractive ideas, especially to harassed social workers or probation officers dealing on the one hand with adolescents 'flaunting' their sexuality, and on the other with a society which expects its agents of social control to act 'as if' a consensus morality existed in our society.

Freudian psychoanalytic writings, in linking anatomical differences with psychological functioning, have also been popularized as giving explanations of gender-role disturbances being caused by, for example, too close a relationship with mothers or small girls wishing for a penis. The importance of possessing or not possessing a penis assumes enormous dimensions for some psychoanalytic writers, for example Khan (1964, p.224) in quoting Freud (1925): 'masturbation... of the clitoris, is a masculine activity and ... the elimination of clitoridal sexuality is a necessary precondition for the development of femininity.' Socarides (1979, p.258) notes that the adult male homosexual 'constantly yearns and searches for masculinity, and by engaging in homosexual acts incorporates the male partner and his penis, thus "strengthening" himself'. Such theoretical perspectives can get translated into explanations of effeminate men or butch women. This confusion of gender-role, gender identity and sexual orientation is common amongst both the public and professionals, and is at least partly rooted in the half-remembered Freudian theory of many practitioners.

Psychoanalytic theory is also influential in the idea that much behaviour can be seen as a defence against repressed wishes, and, in certain cases, specifically against the emergence of

unconscious homosexual wishes - alcoholism, paranoid schizophrenia and even social work itself have all been placed at some
time under this umbrella. The fact that little work has appeared
to refute or verify such statements (see e.g. Klaf, 1961) does
not mean that they are not around in the professional's 'world-
view' of emotional disturbance. A helpful discussion of psychoanalytic viewpoints on the 'symptom' of homosexuality in relation
to psychopathology is given by Limentani (1979), who differen-
tiates between the 'true homosexual' and homosexuality as a
defence against the emergence of a neurosis or psychosis.

There does exist a vague feeling amongst many professionals
that homosexuality 'is something to do with your upbringing',
and this is seen not so much in terms of social learning, but
as something rather deeper in the unconscious aspects of early
relationships. It is a deterministic view of human sexuality in
which very early experiences are seen as all-powerful in determining later gender-role, gender identity and sexual object
choice. Crucial to this is the notion of anxiety being the block
to heterosexual development because of an unresolved Oedipal
situation. Brown (1964, p.206) writes:

> The male homosexual is not as he supposes indifferent to
> women, but is actually afraid of them when it comes to sex.
> It is another illustration of how desperately fearful and
> insecure he is in the possession of his masculinity. This
> original sexual fear of women or rather fear of women as
> sexual creatures, tends to make his relations with them
> artificial and superficial. That is apart from his original
> relationship to his mother which is very strong and highly
> ambivalent. It is probably always worth making the point to
> the patient that he tends to deny the realities of normal
> growth and development; in particular that the vagina is the
> normal complement to the penis, as the woman is to the man.

Bieber et al. (1962, p.303) conclude their important study of
male homosexuals in psychoanalytic therapy in New York City in
the 1950s with the assertion that 'fear of heterosexuality under-
lies homosexuality'.

I think it important to consider now the actual practice of
psychoanalytic therapy, to focus on what has been for many
professionals the basis of their counselling. Scott (1964, p.106)
is helpful in giving some guidelines to the appropriate therapeutic method:

> if it can be shown that the patient has at some time been
> capable of sound personal and heterosexual relations, that
> he has been sufficiently mature to hold a job and to accept
> responsibilities of community life, and if at the same time
> a careful history reveals for each lapse into perverse action
> an adequate precipitating factor, or, more often, constella-
> tion of factors, then we are dealing with a regression. If on
> the other hand the patient has never succeeded in attaining
> healthy personal and love relationships (and) indulges his
> perverse actions without adequate precipitating factors,

then we are probably dealing with an arrest of psychosexual development. While it may be true that ideally, both types should be treated by analysis, experience shows that there is an excellent chance in many cases of the regressive type, that non-analytic methods will suffice.

Scott is, however, careful in his therapeutic claims that therapy can alter the direction of 'intensely homosexual drives'.

If we consider the process of psychoanalytic treatment, it is obviously only available to a small number of people who have the finance, energy and time to devote to what is in fact a reconstruction of their view of their behaviour and feelings, several times a week over several years. The therapeutic encounter is potentially a very powerful one given the motivation that is necessary for the patient to continue in treatment. Wilbur (1965, pp.279-80) writes, on the psychoanalytic treatment of female homosexuality:

Treatment has been carried out successfully on a once-a-week basis, but two to four times a week are preferable and should be considered necessary. Patients should be told that they will need to remain in treatment three to four years or perhaps longer.

The published results of these therapies are disappointing for clinicians who wish to utilize psychoanalytic concepts in treating homosexuality. If the aim is cure then their success in achieving this seems poor given the amount of investment by worker and patient in what might appear to be an ideal environment for change. Bieber et al. (1962, p.301) report that 27 per cent of 106 homosexual men who undertook psychoanalysis, either as exclusively homosexual or bisexual, became exclusively heterosexual. Of the seventy-two who began as exclusively homosexual 19 per cent became heterosexual. Of the thirty who began as bisexual, 50 per cent became heterosexual. In relation to the duration of treatment, only 7 per cent of those who had fewer than 150 hours of analysis became heterosexual, whilst 47 per cent of those who had 350 or more hours became heterosexual. However, Bieber et al. (1962, p.319) assert that 'We are firmly convinced that psychoanalysts may well orient themselves to a heterosexual objective in treating homosexual patients rather than "adjust" even the more recalcitrant patient to a homosexual destiny.' Similar results and conclusions about psychotherapy treatment and follow-up of male and female homosexuals are reported by Mayerson and Lief (1965). However, Socarides (1979, p.263) reports 'that of the 44 overt homosexuals who have undergone psychoanalytic therapy, 20 patients, nearly 50%, developed full heterosexual functioning and were able to develop feelings of love for their heterosexual partners.'

If we now turn to what some psychoanalysts, and others, would see as a dilution of psychoanalytic treatment - psychotherapy - we have to consider not just 'cure', but also 'adjustment'. Some therapists, such as Brown (1964, p.197), are optimistic: 'the majority of patients treated derive very great help from the treatment, and about one in ten can be considered to be cured'. The case illustration Brown gives is useful in highlighting the commitment involved in some individual psychotherapies - eighty-two one-hour interviews over two years - and also the need to be clear about what it is that is being treated. The patient in this case was a teenage boy referred for putting on his scout shorts and defecating in them. During treatment the therapist found that this was a 'favourite game' for dozens of boys in his school. However, he sees the boy aged sixteen as homosexual and reports that by the end of the treatment, when he was eighteen, he was involved with a girlfriend. Brown (p.210) interpreted to the boy that his interest in shorts involved 'the paired knees and the barely hidden flesh as the two breasts; the original source of refreshing drinks whether in imagination or in fact'.

Psychotherapeutic techniques of the dynamic schools place much emphasis, in the explanation of sexual orientation, on childhood relationships within the family, although there may be theoretical disagreements about concepts such as the contribution of hereditary and biological factors, the centrality of bisexuality and consequentially whether it is blocking, avoidance, or arrested development of a heterosexual orientation. Bieber et al. (1962, pp.3-11) provide a useful discussion of the Freudian and neo-Freudian theoretical positions on homosexuality. The line taken by the therapist who holds notions of family pathology would be in helping the client to re-examine her or his early family experiences, especially those where a 'faulty' relationship existed with the mother or father. Through the provision of verbal insight and emotional modelling and experience, the therapist can provide an atmosphere in which the client could see that present assumed difficulties with the opposite sex derived from possibly pre-object relationship trauma or Oedipal problems with her or his mother or father, and sometimes later experiences with peers. Socarides (1979, p.269) discusses the treatment considerations:

> An important criterion is that the patient experiences inner feelings of guilt capable of being used analytically. This strong inner feeling of guilt derives from the unconcious wishes of an aggressive and libidinal nature, experienced under the disguise of homosexuality... Once the patient sees that his guilt arises from internal conflict, and not simply from the mores of a condemning society, he is at last on a path towards the begining of the resolution of his homosexuality.

Socarides (1979, p.273) also emphasizes the importance of the transference relationship in the 'analysability' of homosexual patients. He sees this as both permitting the development of a working alliance between patient and analyst, and also safely enabling regression and 'abreaction' to occur, 'and furthers the patient's understanding of his earliest nuclear conflicts which

were causative of his condition'. In this model, same-sex orientation is assumed to be based on avoidance of or antipathy
towards the opposite sex. This may have certain implications in
relation to the sex and perhaps sexual orientation of the therapist. Such therapeutic reconstruction work is costly in terms of
time and emotional energy even if available on the NHS.

If dynamic psychotherapy is only available to a few, it is
still influential in the work of semi-professionals like social
workers who may be faced with young people who are 'sexually
acting out' in a homosexual direction. A good example of a
treatment approach in an American residential setting is given
by Wasserman (1968, p.264):

> the worker chose to provide casework that was ego-
> supportive, on the theory that this had much to offer an
> adolescent whose previous symptom was homosexual acting-
> out.... He pointed out the unacceptable behaviour (homo-
> sexual acting-out), conveyed the feeling that the adolescent
> could control this, and supported him when he did show
> control.

Wasserman's orientation is a casework derivation of psychoanalytic ego-psychology. His situation in working with this
teenage boy is typical of many problems faced by field and
residential social workers. The problems may be clarified, if
not resolved, if such behaviour is seen in the context of adolescent sexuality in general and the rights of children in care to
sexual expression. The decision to see same-sex behaviour as
more than just a phase should be based on the meaning it holds
for each young person, rather than an apparent automatic
theoretical assumption such as Wasserman's that such behaviour
should be of concern as evidence of a future 'pathological adjustment'.

Behavioural treatment strategies available to the therapist
There exists a wide range of behavioural treatment techniques.
They include aversion therapy, systematic desensitization,
orgasmic reconditioning and positive conditioning of heterosexual
responses (see Bancroft, 1974; 1979; and Fischer and Gochros,
1977). These are all based on the idea that homosexuals should
be negatively reinforced in respect of their homosexual interests
and/or positively reinforced in respect of their heterosexual
interests (with or without the aid of chemicals or electronic
technology). Bancroft (1974, p.214) would favour emphasizing
the latter approach and discusses how treatment should be
geared to the expressed needs of the individual, and may be
focused on four main areas, involving attempts to reduce
heterosexual anxiety and increase heterosexual responsiveness
and satisfactory behaviour, and reduce homosexual interest.

Such an approach would emphasize the educative and
retraining aspects of therapy, rather than seeing homosexuality
as a sickness to be cured. Bancroft would see behaviour therapy
as providing, via limited behavioural goals agreed with the

patient, the opportunity for learning new skills (in this case
related to heterosexual behaviour). Such a stance is widened
in some recent applications of behaviour therapy, to focus on
the choice of the individual in the development of either heterosexual or homosexual orientations. Therapists may therefore
see themselves 'desensitizing individuals to socially elicited guilt
and shame whilst providing them with skills to ensure adjustment
in their chosen sexual orientation' (Higginbotham and Farkas,
1977, p.231). Duehn and Mayadas (1977) discuss assertion
training using video to enable homosexuals to deal with social
and interpersonal problems involved in a gay lifestyle. However,
we should note that treatments are also in use which are a
development of aversive conditioning. For example, in covert
sensitization the patient is relaxed and told to imagine a scene
in which he is attracted to a naked man, pursues him and finds
him

> floating on his back in a cesspool. There's an awful stench –
> from fecal matter and urine. It's smeared all over him....
> Then you puke. It goes all over you and some of it goes into
> the cesspool. He swims toward you.... reaches out for you.
> Now you're really disgusted (Cautela and Wisocki, 1977,
> p.158).

Bancroft (1974) is careful to emphasize that the reported
successful outcome of all kinds of therapy for 'changing'
homosexuals – behavioural, psychoanalytic, psychotherapeutic –
is in the range of 30-40 per cent, and therefore with such a
'success' rate it is important to single out those patients who are
most likely to be in this category. Factors such as motivation,
previous heterosexual interest and sex (again very few women
are featured in the literature) are of importance. As both
psychoanalytic and behavioural approaches stress that 'the
condition' is in some way a response to fear of the opposite (that
is, usually female) sex we are left with the interesting question
as to why such 'timid' persons should resort to homosexual
experiences given that they are characterized in the clinical
literature as illegal, sometimes dangerous, emotionally difficult
and unsatisfying and the subject of much social stigma.

Masters and Johnson (1979, p.271) are more careful than most
writers and clinicians to state their base line in treating homosexuals, whom they conclude are not physiologically different
in their sexual functioning from heterosexuals; the homosexual
'is basically a man or woman by genetic determination and is
homosexually orientated by learned preference'. They take into
account the reasons for the individual wishing to change or
improve a homosexual orientation, and report on their treatment
of homosexual dysfunction: 'there is real potential of a professional breakthrough in the treatment of homosexual dysfunctions'
(p.402), although treatment of homosexual dissatisfaction
(conversion and reversion to heterosexuality) was not so
successful. This was moreover in a selected group with a high
motivation to change. The failures may be related to lack of

support of clients post-treatment, as well as more general problems of accounting for a person's lifestyle and the meanings that sexual orientation holds for her or him. Masters and Johnson show that it is possible to help homosexual people in heterosexual relationships. It requires certain conditions in terms of personal motivation, wishing for and being able to adapt to a change of lifestyle. The rarity of such situations should not either prevent us from studying the careful assessments and techniques of Masters and Johnson, or assuming that the goal of heterosexuality is in any way appropriate for the majority of homosexual women and men, any more than a change of sexual orientation would necessarily be indicated by the problems presented by heterosexual persons.

The majority of homosexual people will not come into contact with such specialized treatments, and the majority who do may not, from the published accounts, change their orientation. We shall now consider a more general approach to social learning as this has potentially wider applicability.

A SOCIAL LEARNING APPROACH

This takes consideration of the development of a homosexual orientation out of the laboratory or clinic, and into the ordinary experience of people in their families, peer groups and all the other socializing influences which impinge on the individual's development. Such an approach does, of course, also imply that we can analyse the development of a heterosexual orientation in a similar way. The implications of a social learning approach have given some clinicians an amount of therapeutic optimism so necessary in treatment, for, as we have seen, the results of attempts to 'cure' homosexuality are depressing or encouraging according to your view of sexuality. To put it plainly, treatment does not seem to work, but what about the prevention of homosexuality? Social learning theory does refocus the discussion on to the environmental contributions to learned sexual behaviour. Consideration of environmental influences, and specifically the learning about sexuality which takes place in the family, led Johnson and Robinson (1957) to state that 'the family physician and the pediatrician... can "vaccinate" large segments of the population against the "virus" of sexual deviation.' This was to be achieved by education of the parents to avoid over-stimulating of the child, or covert or overt seduction of the child sexually. It was based on a belief that such parental behaviour stimulates the child into 'perverse sexual aberrations', including homosexuality, by 'distorting the instinctual sexual development of the child'. This model, although emphasizing the effects of the child's environment, does still appear rooted in psychoanalytic formulations.

In order to consider practical treatment possibilities, we need to move to the literature on the development of gender identity

and gender-role development, for it is here that links are made
both in theory and practice between social learning experiences
and the development of a homosexual orientation. In Chapter 1
the errors involved in directly linking such concepts as adult
homosexual behaviour with childhood behaviour in relation to
masculinity and femininity have already been discussed. The fact
that some homosexuals may remember exhibiting cross-gender
behaviours in childhood is not satisfactory evidence in itself
that a direct causal link exists. The subjects may be recon-
structing their past to fit in with generally held notions of
homosexual behaviour. (For illustration: Levitt and Klassen,
1974, asked their respondents for opinions about the statement
that 'Homosexuals act like the opposite sex'; 22.1 per cent
'strongly agreed' and 46.7 per cent 'somewhat agreed'.) It is
interesting to place studies which are concerned with gender-
role development in a social/historical context. With the increasing influence of women's liberation ideology, it seems likely that
what is 'proper behaviour' for girls and boys will become somewhat less clear. At the same time some homosexual men are
reacting against effeminate stereotyping by becoming 'super
macho'; if they were to be joined by homosexual women choosing
to adopt traditional feminine behaviour, what, one wonders,
will be the type of childhood behaviour referred to as being
'gender-disturbed' for future generations?

The (American) literature (Zuger, 1966; Green and Fuller,
1973; Green, 1974b; Rekers, 1977), assumes that 'If the gender-
disturbed child does not develop to be transsexual or transvestic
in adulthood, the evidence indicates that he will probably develop as an effeminate male homosexual' (Rekers, 1977, p.279). As
has been indicated in Chapter 1, such evidence is by no means
conclusive, and the studies do not always make the necessary
clarifications of homosexuality, transvestism and transsexualism
as separate outcomes, nor of the need to separate gender role
from gender identity and sexual orientation. We should note,
however, that research/treatment programmes are being conducted in America. Green and Fuller (1973) provide a clear
outline of their group therapy approach with 'boys who behave
as girls' and their parents. This group of seven boys was then
aged between four and nine years, and they met for one hour
weekly with a male therapist; part of these sessions involved
the boys being 'reinforced for activities using large muscles or
for bravery, such as climbing high on the monkey bars, plung-
ing head first down a slide, running, or kicking a ball'. Their
parents were also seen and counselled to encourage their sons
in 'appropriate' gender-role behaviour and discourage apparent
cross-sex behaviour or 'role-taking'. The fathers were
encouraged to take an interest in activities with their sons, so
that in the future 'camping' would describe a healthy outdoor
pursuit for them both.

Such specialized treatments may seem somewhat extreme and
to reflect particular parental or cultural anxieties, but the ideas

behind them are, I would suggest, widespread. To give an
example: I was consulted by a probation officer who had to provide a court report for a judge in a matrimonial case. A boy
aged eight had been showing signs of effeminacy - putting his
hand on his hip, pouting, etc. The mother had been very
concerned and related it to her divorced husband's sexual
orientation, in that after they had separated he had been living
with another man. During access visits the boy had stayed
overnight with his father. The mother claimed it was the man's
lover and his friends whom the boy was imitating, and she
wanted the overnight stays to end for fear that the boy would
grow up into a homosexual. The judge asked for a probation
officer's report, specifying that the question of the boy's
future sexual orientation be considered. The probation officer
was sympathetic to the husband's situation and had no wish to
discriminate on the grounds of the man's sexual orientation,
indeed he wanted to find a way of answering the judge's concern satisfactorily. He told me that he found the case had made
him face the questions, 'What about the development of homosexuality - is it influenced by an ambience such as the one in
this case, and how much are effeminate gestures a precursor?'
Similar sorts of concerns can of course be expressed in lesbian
custody cases. A fuller consideration of these problems requires
reference to our interactionist model (Chapter 3), but we can
here examine the limitations of a social learning theory approach
and clarify the practice implications of an interactionist perspective.

We should note first that effeminate mannerisms are not
necessarily indicative of anything we should take seriously. The
'News of the World' (16 December 1979) reported on the 'homo-
sexualist' references in Larry Grayson's 'Generation Game'
television show, and the concern that 'Mr.Grayson's mannerisms
also anger parents because children find him tempting to imitate'.
Certainly this is social learning but the meanings of such
behaviour seem unlikely to have much to do with a preference
for a homosexual identity. Those of us who can still remember
childhood same-sexed sexual acts can also recall that the kids
involved would also vehemently put down 'poofs and queers'
(see our case example of Stuart, pp.79-87). Social learning
reflects the ways in which the culture socializes its young
people into appropriate gender-role behaviour and gender
identity. The implication is that the majority sexual orientation
experience will be heterosexual; the result of parental example,
the media, advertisements, romantic stories in popular magazines
and sex education programmes. There are few openly homosexual
role models available. When they do happen to be available to
the child, as in my case example, the question is how influential
are they? Undoubtedly they do have an influence, but certainly
not in a deterministic way. The little boy in question will probably grow up knowing more about same-sex relationships than
his peers, but whether he will prefer them, given the alter-

natives, will depend on what value he comes to place on heterosexual norms or a bisexual identity. What, however, of the
centrality of same-sex parental identification? This process is
an important one, but, as Mischel (1967) implies, the same-sex
parent is not the exclusive source of identification, and the
perceived power of male and female adults is important in affecting identifications (see also pp.23-5 and 153-6). Sexual orientation cannot be seen as necessarily developing from parental
relationships in isolation. I know of no evidence which links
being a homosexual woman or man with having homosexual
parents. That studies such as Whitam (1977) report that male
homosexuals remember certain factors, for example being
regarded by other boys as a sissy, may be a reconstruction of
events (the men are not all 'effeminate' homosexual adults), and
does not explain the development and maintenance of an identification as homosexual. In the case we are considering, we
should evaluate the boy's behaviour within the context of its
present meaning for him, his parents and other people in his
environment. We should separate concern for his future sexual
identity from his sexual interests, his gender-role orientation
and his gender identity; considering this 'in the round' within
the context of his experience of parental behaviour in general
and the other important influences in his life - friends, relatives,
school, professionals, etc. In such a way we may come to some
idea of the meaning of his behaviour now for himself, and interpret this to the interested parties as part of an interactive
process which may lead to adolescent and post-adolescent
heterosexual, homosexual or bisexual identification(s).

Let us consider another area where social learning explanations of homosexuality are encountered in practice. This is in
the notion of seduction, usually by male homosexuals, of adolescent and pre-adolescent boys. This learning experience is sometimes seen as crucial in determining (or rather blocking) the
future of heterosexual interest. Levitt and Klassen (1974) write:
'Of the four causal notions probed, the most popular propositon
is that "young homosexuals become that way because of older
homosexuals".' Our response to this should be to remember the
young people one has known in single-sex institutions who
engaged in situational homosexuality, but identify now as
heterosexual. Also we should keep in mind the evidence from
other cultures where widespread homosexual activity does not
necessarily lead to homosexual identities or lifestyles. I know
of no homosexual clients or friends who would describe 'unwilling
seduction' as being an accurate account of their first homosexual
experience, and I find, interestingly, that many young homosexual men recall how they avoided sex games with other boys
at school because sex in the showers meant something different
to them than it did to their peers.

INDIVIDUAL MEANINGS

To generalize, we could say that the ways of looking at homosexuality and its treatment so far considered have emphasized
sexual acts and the meanings other people attach to these acts
when performed by same-sexed people. We have said little
about the meanings ascribed to their behaviour by those most
intimately involved. Homosexual actors are regarded as being
in public performance. This is sometimes because of their own
public displays (e.g. 'cottaging'), but also because the wider
society uses its agents of law enforcement and therapy to search
out and confront the homosexual person. It also happens that
homosexual people will become visible by seeking help because
of felt psychological or social stresses. The fact that society
has, as we have seen, been very interested in finding theories
which would explain homosexual behaviour, and that this has
affected the homosexual's view of her or himself should not any
longer deflect us from considering a central view we hold,
namely that 'Only the actor himself can give an authoritative
report on the monitoring of his own behaviour' (Harré and
Secord, 1972, p.8). An alternative perspective on the way in
which the girl or boy, woman or man can come to identify her
or himself as homosexual is included in Chapter 3. Here it will
suffice to say that such a theoretical orientation looks not at
the frequency of sexual acts, but rather at the way individuals
deal with their sexual interests at a particular time by ascribing
meanings to the act which are syntonic with their current image
of themselves. It is therefore possible to meet in counselling
young men who are acting as prostitutes to men, all involved in
similar acts but identifying as homosexual, heterosexual or
bisexual. Later these same people may be involved in homosexual
acts which hold a different meaning for them because of their
social experiences. The essence of counselling is to desensitize
oneself to homosexual behaviour and to guard against voyeur-
istic indulgences; to ask instead how is it that this person, at
this point in time, is ascribing a particular meaning to her or
his behaviour, and how does this relate to lifestyle, both now
and idealized. As we will argue, 'counselling the homosexual'
should not be the objective, rather it should be counselling the
man or woman who is now engaging in same-sexed acts, whose
meaning for him or her will be related to self identity and lifestyle at that time. I hope it will be obvious by now that with
such a view the concepts 'it's immature', 'it's just a stage' or
's/he is a confirmed homosexual', are not very useful in counselling. We have instead to understand the ways in which
individuals interpret sexual acts in the context of their own
society history, current relationships and hopes for the future.
Identities change and so do interpretations of behaviour; we
have no reason to think that with the wider society in the throes
of social change the meaning of sexual behaviour will be
immune from the process. The life experience of heterosexual

people, especially in families, may be felt as being under threat because of economic pressures; also consciousness-raising in sections of the women's movement will have implications for both homosexual and heterosexual experiences and lifestyles. As Bell and Weinberg (1978, p.128) noted:

> It may be that homosexuality is more frequently construed by males as a failure to achieve a 'masculine' sexual adjustment, while lesbians, many of whom have experienced considerable sexual contact with males, more often experience their homosexuality as a freely chosen rejection of heterosexual relationships.

A CHOICE OF SEXUAL IDENTITY?

We have here the emphasis on choice, the political and therapeutic implications of which we will now consider. To do this we move from deterministic push/pull theories of sexual behaviour into the world of individuals being open to placing a range of interpretations on their capacity for sexual arousal. Plummer (1975, p.137) asks, 'why, when so many people are potentially available for homosexual experiences and identification, do so few enter stable homosexual roles?' The answer to this important question is within the experience of all of us, and relates to the societal pressures to encourage heterosexual conduct; indeed readers of the first two chapters of this book may well be experientially in a position to appreciate this, just by reading descriptions of attempts to bring homosexuality under control! Certain people do at specific times, however, choose to ignore or challenge such attempts. The contributions to such a choice may come from genetics, biochemistry, parental experience, peer groups, adult relationships or the general political climate. All these influences will be in an interactive process, and the individual will make sense of them by interpreting them as part of a general sense of self and then adapting to or striving to achieve a particular lifestyle. This is what we should confront as theorists, counsellors, moralists, politicians, law-makers and enforcers. As I have mentioned, 'political gays' have already been taken on by some theologians. I am aware that these theologians are sometimes also politicians, law-makers and enforcers. The result may be attempts to use the law as an alternative to treatment in order to try to control gay lifestyles or behaviour. But some clinicians would see the assertion that a gay identity is a 'sexual preference' or 'political choice' as itself a psychological defence. I would recognize that a political analysis of one's sexual orientation may provide a positive identity for many people; let us therefore look at some lifestyle implications of certain political stances.

Hocquenghem (1978), for example, sees homosexuality not as leading to a gay lifestyle, but rather to a way of undermining present society by emphasizing sexual desire (especially casual

and anal sex), and destroying disciplinary agencies like the
family. Such a view says nothing directly about lesbians. It also
implies a free market where access to sex as a commodity is
equally available. This is not the experience of most of us,
especially in our role as counsellors. It may be that we are
working towards such a situation, but meanwhile there are problems experienced by individuals such as legal restrictions,
feelings of personal inadequacy and lack of job security which
are our political and professional concerns. Undoubtedly we
will encounter people with such a political analysis and I do not
see the resultant lifestyle as necessarily cause for our concern.
Many homosexual people, especially men, do seem to be able to
separate their sexual acts from their need for supportive social
contacts. Casual sex may be OK and possibly politically important, but as Masters and Johnson (1979, p.216) write, on the
problems of 'a "cruising" lifestyle':

> The concept of maintaining high levels of subjective sexual
> involvement by constantly changing partners works well,
> particularly when the man or woman... is relatively young
> and acceptably attractive. But this circle of freedom con-
> stricts when one grows older, or unfortunately, is no longer
> physically or socially attractive enough to acquire new part-
> ners with satisfactory regularity.

We should, as in other situations, be careful to distinguish
the differences in the experiences of homosexual men and women
(see Hart and Richardson, 1980). Balanced against the greater
opportunity for social and sexual relationships available to
homosexual men in our society, we should account for the way
in which identification with the general aims of the women's
movement and the possibility of identifying as a political lesbian
(i.e. to choose to live in close relationships which are free from
masculine domination), enables gay women to enjoy social and
political support which is just not available to gay men in
Britain. A 'men's movement' has to cope with the surrendering
of the traditional masculine role, the fear of which may be
involved in hostility to male homosexuals by heterosexual men;
hence the difficulties for males in identifying politically as gay
men. A committed feminist gay man may well feel isolated in
sexist male homosexual culture, and without much hope of many
men sharing his perspective. We should also note the existence
of sexist attitudes amongst homosexual people themselves,
especially among homosexual men. As we have earlier reviewed,
homosexual people are at risk of introjecting explanations of
their orientation which may appear as 'I couldn't do it with a
man/woman.' It is the problem of false consciousness, and
although there have been some successes in consciousness raising therapeutic exercises, I know of no evidence that most
helping professionals have managed to include this method in
their interventive strategies.

A similar task faces us when the homosexual person has
introjected a sickness model of their identity and behaviour.

What do we say? A tirade against self oppression is unlikely to achieve much. I would suggest that we retain our basic belief in the primacy of the individual's explanation of her or his world. We should have this with our customary 'respect for persons'. We can then offer an alternative perception of their homosexual identity and behaviour. I do not think we should be tentative about this, for there are plenty of alternatives around, with which the individual will clearly be familiar. We will not always succeed. To give a personal example; a young gay man aged eighteen joined a gay group for which I have some responsibility. After a very unhappy adolescence during which he had made two suicide bids, he had 'come out' to his mother who was a psychology graduate. She had been understanding and had helped him to contact other gay people. However, he still found a lot of tension at home, centred on his mother's wish to hide his orientation from his father - 'He's had enough disappointments in his life already.' One day a row broke out between Simon and his mother on whether there should be gay radio programmes; his mother shouted, 'It's nothing to be proud of, you know.' His mother also disapproved of the left wing gay friends he had made, and would almost daily comment on these, claiming, 'They are only after you for your body.' This went on for several months, and Simon experienced a lot of conflicts in attending group meetings on such topics as 'coming out' and 'sexism'; he was an apprentice electrician and was terrified of discovery. He was also very worried about his straight friends knowing he was gay. After I had tried to offer him a political analysis of his situation as a homosexual man, he expressed his conflicts to me as: 'I just don't know who to believe, you, my mother, or my boss at work.' I responded that he should believe the people whose explanations he could most identify with his own life experiences. Shortly afterwards he stopped coming to the group except for social events and began to go frequently to the local gay pub where he had made a number of friends. He had found a 'way in' to meet homosexual people socially and had rejected an openly gay lifestyle. This was obviously right for him at that point in time.

As I have indicated, consciousness raising should be in our repertoire of helping strategies, but of course people will make their own choices. They may not be permanent or enduring; all we can do is attempt to provide an analysis which, unlike those involving deterministic explanations, extends people's sense of choice and thereby control over their own lives.

The above case example brings together considerations of both interactionist and 'political' theory. Clearly my attempts at consciousness raising failed because for Simon his self concept as homosexual was interacting with other core constructs such as 'being a good son to his parents' and 'being one of the lads at work'. For Simon, an openly gay identity would threaten not just his view of himself and his relationship with his parents, but also his view of himself (perhaps realistic) as a good

employee. We can see that for Simon a more openly gay identity
was not possible, as according to his perception of the world
such a commitment would entail considerable losses in other areas
of his life that were central to his self identity. So Simon at that
time chose to identify as homosexual only to himself and within
the limits of the commercial gay scene. During the rest of his
life he would pass for straight. His concept of himself would
prevent him from linking his homosexuality with a political
analysis of the function of gender roles, and the control of
sexuality by the State. For Simon, the gay group gave him some
contacts to enable him to function on the commercial gay scene,
which meant going to the local gay pub and meeting with the
regulars there. He no longer felt isolated, although he still had
to live with the contradictions inherent in the rest of his lifestyle. Consciousness raising efforts with homosexual people
should always take into account the social investments of the
individuals' current lifestyles and the costs involved for them
in change.

SOME COMMENTS ON PRACTICE PROBLEMS OF THE THEORIES UNDER REVIEW

I would first make a general comment: readers may consider
that a larger question than that of efficacy of treatment methods
is raised in this Part. This concerns the question of what is
'good' and 'bad' in sexual conduct. I am sympathetic to such a
concern, and consider that professionals should cease to see
themselves as neutral technicians and instead recognize their
role as moral agents (see also Hart, 1979). Such an orientation
is especially important in dealing with those people who have
little choice as to whether or not to accept 'treatment for their
homosexuality' (see pp.47-58).
    Let us now ask why it is that homosexuals have proved so
resistant in the past to therapies of different sorts. An obvious
problem is that of motivation; treatment was undertaken with
legal or family pressures pushing the individual, rather than a
felt personal need for change. We must account also for the
meanings that a homosexual identity has for each person. Such
meanings may not have been accounted for by the therapist,
in that a homosexual identity is very different from a catalogue
of homosexual acts; the latter being performed by a large percentage of the population, probably with a limited amount of
personal involvement, whilst for many people a homosexual,
heterosexual or bisexual identity is one of the fundamental ways
they have of viewing themselves and their world. Any therapy
which seeks to deal with homosexual behaviour must account for
the person and for the way that the behaviour relates to the
person's lifestyle; and therefore assessment is necessary in
terms of the meanings of homosexual behaviour for the individual,
and the costs and benefits involved in changing a person's

lifestyle. This may partly account for the interesting findings of Bieber et al. (1962, p.277). In their study, equal numbers of heterosexuals and homosexuals were likely to experience improvement in certain non-sexual areas of behaviour, although the homosexuals may not have achieved heterosexuality. Our model (see Chapter 3) allows that sexual identity is subject to change throughout a lifetime, but, like any oppressed group, homosexual women and men would see their identity as being hard fought for and needing some protection; this may well appear in the guise of rigid adherence to a view of homo-sexuality as being permanent. I would agree with Masters and Johnson (1979) in their view that it is possible to achieve 'reversion' or 'conversion' to heterosexuality (or homosexuality, of course), but such a statement remains at an academic level until the meanings of homosexual (and heterosexual) behaviour, and the wish to change or adapt to such behaviour and achieve a certain lifestyle, are accounted for within an interactionist perspective. Of course, within this perspective specific tech-niques of helping may be used which come from behavioural or dynamic psychology.

The experience of Diane Richardson and myself in discussions with professionals concerned with helping (young) people is their concern to be able to offer them the hope of a positive identity when they think they may be homosexual. In this Part, we are attempting to change the direction for practitioners away from a search for 'etiology' towards considering the meanings of behaviour for the individual, and the possibilities of having a historical awareness of the importance of sexual orientation as a symbol, which has previously taken little account of individual meanings or of feelings about sexual conduct. Such a perspec-tive will, of course, be helpful in acknowledging the possible development of a positive homosexual identity. It will also remind both helper and helped of the limitations of individual therapy in compensating for the negative, and enjoying the positive, experiences of people in our society choosing to have social and sexual relationships with the same sex.

Part two

IDENTITIES
AND LIFESTYLES

Our focus in this Part on the diversity of homosexual identities and lifestyles is contrary to the way homosexuals have been seen: as primarily sexual creatures, all subject to similar motivating and causative influences. In considering the meaning of a homosexual identity for each individual, we attempt to account for the relative stability of sexual orientation as a core construct of a person's self identity.

We have also stressed in this Part the importance of considering the differences between men and women in becoming and being homosexual. In addition, we have pointed to the different meanings that being homosexual may hold for each individual according to the particular historical time and cultural milieu in which she or he may live.

Adopting such a perspective, we would stress the importance of having to consider sexual acts within their social and cultural context, and the particular social meanings of such acts for the individual. In this respect, engaging in homosexual behaviour may not necessarily lead to a person's considering her or himself to be homosexual.

Such a view of homosexuality as relating mainly to sexual acts, in isolation from the individual meanings of such behaviour, may affect the way in which homosexual women and men see themselves. This emphasis on sexual behaviour is reinforced for homosexuals by the limitations they encounter in the public expression of their relationships. This may result in a feeling of heightened sexuality in situations where such expression is allowed. In addition it may, for the homosexual person, result in their seeing their sexual orientation primarily in terms of sexual acts.

Apart from describing male homosexual and lesbian identities and lifestyles, this Part also attempts to extend conceptual frameworks about homosexuality by offering an alternative theoretical model.

As this model is concerned with attempting to explain the development and maintenance of a homosexual identity, we must consider the question of why it is that only a small minority so identify. We might, alternatively, pose the question as why it is that so many people are not homosexual, given the possibilities of a generalized sexual responsiveness.

The model which we outline suggests some of the reasons why the incidence of 'exclusive homosexuality' appears to be small. At the same time our model does contain an implication that, with more people living openly gay lives, the destigmatization of homosexuality and the increased opportunities to have homosexual relationships will engender a larger number of people coming to identify as such.

3 THE DEVELOPMENT AND MAINTENANCE OF A HOMOSEXUAL IDENTITY

Diane Richardson and
John Hart

As we have reviewed in the previous Part, there has been a continuous search for the answer to the question, 'Who or what made me homosexual?', both by homosexuals themselves and by those who have been involved in the control, treatment and investigation of homosexuality.

When such a question has been asked, the definition of homosexuality has largely been in terms of sexual acts. Indeed much of the clinical literature has characterized homosexuals as being obsessed with sex. However, as has already been outlined in chapters 1 and 2, we must distinguish homosexual acts from homosexual identities; given that many people engage in same-sex acts without necessarily identifying as homosexual. Alternatively, a person may not have actually engaged in same-sex sexual acts, although they would define themselves as homosexual.

In this chapter we will address ourselves to the complex question of how a person comes to identify as homosexual, and thereafter maintains, or not, such an identity. We must recognize here that the cognitive awareness of oneself as homosexual, heterosexual or bisexual usually occurs during early adolescence, with the onset of the development of formal abstract thought and the capacity for self reflection. After this, redefinition of sexual identity may occur at any stage in the life cycle, regardless of sex or marital status. This is contrary to the common assumption amongst many theoreticians that sexual orientation is fixed at an early stage. An illustration of this process would be the elderly person who has been married, has grandchildren and who at the age of seventy falls in love for the first time with someone of the same sex and comes to identify as homosexual. Their experience of homosexual attraction and the meaning of a homosexual identity for them will obviously be very different from that say of a fourteen-year-old boy, or alternatively that of a 28-year-old woman with a lesbian feminist analysis of her sexuality, or of a middle-aged married woman whose children are leaving home and who falls in love with the girl next door.

How then does each of these individuals come to identify as homosexual (a process which, as we have already stated, has no necessary association with homosexual acts)?

It is commonly acknowledged that many adolescents experience attraction to the same sex, and this usually is regarded as being a transitory stage in psychosexual development. However, it is our contention that many people could and do continue to find persons of the same sex sexually, emotionally and socially desirable, and yet we recognize that it is only a minority who categorize this attraction in terms of a homosexual self identity. For the majority who do not so identify they may adopt a variety of explanations for such experiences which enable them to develop and maintain a heterosexual identity.

Our theoretical orientation therefore is that we should really be asking questions about the development and maintenance of any sexual identity, rather than assuming a natural inevitability about the development of a heterosexual identity. However, for our present purposes we are going to focus on how a person comes to identify as homosexual. In order to clarify the theoretical model we are presenting we will first provide two detailed case examples which emphasize the importance we would attach to considering, for each individual, the meaning of a homosexual identity, and the process whereby such an identity is or is not maintained.

Let us consider Janet, who at twenty-five identifies as homosexual. Janet was brought up in an upper middle-class home, experienced private education at a convent school until eleven, and then a single-sex grammar school, followed by single-sex higher education.

Janet recalls her earliest sexual encounter as playing 'doctors and nurses' with another girl at the age of eight, which involved both of them undressing and touching each other. Whilst neither had an orgasm, Janet experienced this as exciting but prohibited behaviour.

At grammar school, in common with many of her peers, she developed close emotional relationships with other girls, one of which, at the age of fifteen, involved kissing and cuddling with another girl in bed. Janet had already begun to have romantic fantasies about women, although her masturbatory fantasies were about men. However, whilst her friends also went out with boys, Janet did not, because she saw no reason to. Given the common experience they all had of enjoying relationships with girls, the question that presents itself, therefore, is why her peers chose also to have relationships with boys, whereas Janet felt no need.

What we have so far described might not, for someone other than Janet, have resulted in the development of a homosexual identity; this requires us therefore to look more closely at her individual experience of these events.

The fact that Janet went to a single-sex school, had few friends outside of school and was interested in sporting activities which were often single-sex occasions, meant that most of her interactions with persons of her own age were with girls. This, of course, is a common experience for both boys and girls. Indeed, even in co-educational schools same-sex friendships are usually the norm prior to heterosexual dating. Janet experienced such relationships as positive and enjoyable. This is a necessary but in itself not a sufficient factor to explain why she did not feel the need at that point to seek close relationships with boys, as did many of her peers who experienced a similar lack of opportunity to meet the opposite sex. Apart from the comparative opportunities for the development of same-sex and opposite-sex relationships, the knowledge, beliefs and values concerning homosexual and heterosexual relationships that each individual assimilates will be highly significant in the choices about relationships which s/he makes at any given point in time. In Janet's case she not only experienced the kind of heterosexual taboos which most adolescent girls are made aware of, i.e. the possible sexual dangers in male-female relationships, but also the specifically negative and prohibitive attitudes of her parents towards her having a boyfriend at that age. The meaning of such messages about heterosexual relationships for Janet has to be seen in interaction with the positive experiences she had of same-sex relationships, and the fact that these were encouraged by her parents as an alternative to heterosexual relationships, which were seen as potentially harmful.

Janet's view of heterosexual relationships was also influenced by her mother's subservient attitude to her father and her older brother, and her brother's deprecative attitude towards women in general. Prior to adolescence Janet had expressed a desire to be like her brother, whom she saw, as a male, being more favoured. This took the form of wanting to dress in similar clothes to him, and play with his toys. Such an evaluation of the relative privileges of being male and female is, of course, a common experience of many girls in our society.

The possible stigma of not having a boyfriend, which for other girls may have been an important influence in encouraging cross-sex relationships, was at least partially avoided by Janet by reason of the fact that her time in and out of school was devoted mainly to single-sex sports and accompanying social activities. This enabled her to legitimately claim to herself and significant others that she had little time and opportunity to form relationships with boys.

At this point we should note that a keen interest and participation in sporting activities is often seen in women as indicating atypical gender-role orientation. That gender-role orientation is often confused with sexual orientation has meant that such interests are often associated in many people's minds with homosexuality in women. The fact that PE is seen in this way may be, for girls who, like Janet, enjoy sports and positive same-sex relationships, an influence in their ascription of the term homosexual to themselves and to such relationships. Similarly, when physical acts between women can be construed as homosexual behaviour this may provide opportunity for identification as homosexual. At the same time, however, such an identification may limit the public expression of such acts for individuals, because of the meanings they have acquired.

Janet's particular Higher Education College was one with a
long tradition of single-sex education for PE teachers. It was a
stately home in the country, isolated from the social facilities of
the town and nearby city. Social events were organized which
enabled the girls to have a self-sufficient community. Janet
found herself in a hostel with a number of girls who had a high
status in the college and who identified as homosexual. She had
therefore positive role models for identifying as homosexual, and
a social and working environment conducive to same-sex relationships. It was through this socializing process that Janet was
able to continue and develop the kind of relationships she had
been enjoying since adolescence. At this point Janet began to
engage in sexual acts with women, firstly in a one night stand,
and then in a particular relationship with a fellow student who
herself identified as homosexual. This relationship was to last
throughout Janet's time at college.

The identification of Janet's partner as homosexual made it
difficult for Janet to see her own involvement with this woman
as anything other than homosexual. If her partner had not so
identified it might have been possible for a similar relationship
to have gone on without either of the partners describing themselves as homosexual.

In this relationship Janet, then aged nineteen, experienced
orgasm for the first time with another person. As we have noted
in Chapter 1 the first sexual experience to orgasm with another
person has been seen as having possible etiological significance
in the development of homosexuality (pp. 27-8). Whilst, for
reasons later discussed in more detail, we would question the
universal importance of such an incident in its association with
the development of sexual identity, we recognize that for some
people their initial sexual experiences may be interpreted by
them as having significance for their identity as homosexual,
heterosexual or bisexual. In addition, a person's sexual
experiences may affect the meaning such an identification may
hold for them. For instance, in the case of someone who has had
positive sexual experiences with both sexes and who identifies
as homosexual, it would seem unlikely that she or he could
account for homosexuality in terms of a phobia about having
sexual relationships with the opposite sex.

By this time, in common with most of her close friends, Janet
had adopted a homosexual identity. The alternative to such a
self identification for Janet would have entailed risking social
ostracism from relationships she valued highly. This would have
faced her with the problem of having to form a new network of
friends. Prior to this point Janet had found no definite need to
identify her enjoyment of same-sex relationships as homosexual,
but by this time the social expectations, even on middle-class
young women, are that they should be involving themselves in
courtship behaviour. Janet, however, for the reasons so far
outlined, saw no advantages, and indeed certain disadvantages,
in being involved in such heterosexual behaviour. The fact that

this is expected of young persons in our society meant for Janet that she had to answer the question of why she was not engaging in such typical behaviour. The answer that Janet came to was a product of her past experience of close same-sex relationships, her current positive interactions with women friends and an evaluation of the advantages and disadvantages for her in adopting a homosexual identity in that milieu at that particular point in her life.

Janet experienced this not as a change in identity from heterosexual to homosexual, but rather as a conscious recognition of an identity which she had always assumed. The point we would make is that in a society which organized the meanings of sexual encounters in a different way, i.e. sex of partner not indicating lifelong sexual preference, then Janet might not necessarily have come to this identification, nor would she have necessarily explained her past behaviour as being indicative of a homosexual orientation.

Janet's experience of same-sex relationships could be seen as a lack of choice, not merely in terms of men not being socially available, but also her being sexually unattractive to them. This is indeed one explanation that is offered to account for same-sex preference, the notion of 'she can't get a man'. In fact Janet has always experienced herself as attractive to both sexes, and has had this aspect of her self image confirmed by being asked out by both men and women. Indeed, Janet did very occasionally go out with men, and found kissing pleasant but had no wish to engage in any further sexual involvement.

It is interesting at this point to note the economic aspects of Janet's situation. The sense of financial dependence on her family which Janet experienced had been continually met in the form of clothes, holidays, cars, gifts of money. She therefore had no economic reasons to form relationships with men, as might other girls of her age from less privileged backgrounds. One of the costs of these financial rewards for Janet, however, was that she had to be careful to avoid parental disapproval of the relationships she was having. A crisis occurred when someone at college informed Janet's mother that Janet was homosexual. The reaction of Janet's mother to this information was one of disapproval, but she took the view that it was the particular environment, and the people Janet mixed with, which were responsible.

Janet attempted to cope with her mother's disapproval in a number of ways, without denying that she was homosexual. These involved avoiding open discussion of her homosexuality, which enabled Janet's mother to ignore Janet's homosexual identity. At the same time this allowed her to maintain such an identity without the costs which would have been entailed in the loss of parental approval and support.

We have so far concentrated on Janet's experiences whilst undertaking higher education. On leaving college Janet took up a job as a PE teacher and then as a care assistant, before becoming a social worker.

The fact that Janet, because of her educational attainments, was able to pursue such careers with their social and financial rewards, meant that for her the possibility of becoming economically dependent on a man held few attractions. This, of course, has to be seen in association with the financial supports which were still being provided by her parents. That Janet had identified as homosexual says little about how, unlike some of her friends, she maintainec such an identity after leaving college. For them the perceived costs and benefits of a future heterosexual identity outweighed those of a homosexual identity. Why was this not so for Janet?

Janet remained in the same geographical area and continued to be in contact with many of the friends she had known at college. This provided for her, outside of the confines of the rather special experience of single-sex higher education of the kind that Janet had encountered, a reference group and continuity in relationships, which was one factor in encouraging and enabling her to maintain a homosexual identity. This situation could be interpreted by Janet to mean that her homosexuality was not situationally specific to college life, but that it was part of her perception of herself and the relationships she wanted with other people. Alongside this Janet began an influential relationship with a woman who strongly identified as a lesbian feminist. This woman was open about her homosexual identity in her work and social environments. It was more difficult therefore for Janet to see the previous long-term relationship she had had at college as an isolated experience with one particular woman, rather than a feature of the choices she was making in forming relationships in general. The potential of Janet's new relationship would have been difficult for her to fulfil without her developing a gay identity, because her new partner demanded a similar openness in their relationship to the one she already practised in her social and work environment. Once again Janet's partner's self identification as homosexual consolidated Janet's own perception of herself.

Through this relationship Janet met other women and men who defined themselves as gay and had a political analysis of sexuality. In the case of homosexuality, their analysis was that relationships with the same sex were a positive alternative to sexist relationships with people of the opposite sex.

By this time Janet is on many levels heavily invested in maintaining a homosexual identity, and continues to have same-sex relationships. Whilst she does have some social contacts with men, and may go out with them, she is not interested and sees no need for further intimacy. Indeed, if she did many of her current satisfactions in her personal relationships would be in jeopardy. This is partly because, being a minority group, homosexual men and women are generally censorious about behaviour which appears to contradict a homosexual identity, and partly because it may seem that the person is taking on the

values of the society which is stigmatizing them as homosexual.
In Janet's case any change in her self identification as homosexual would involve this threat of social and personal loss. We
would not rule out that in the future she may make a different
evaluation of her sexual identity, depending upon the interaction between the way that society perceives homosexuality and
the way, through personal experiences, Janet sees herself.

We have discussed the development and maintenance of Janet's
homosexual identity, highlighting some of the important interacting factors. In adopting a social interactionist perspective
we recognize that there are many more subtle influences that
may affect such a complex process which we have not acknowledged in our account. This is for reasons of space, and because
of the difficulties inherent in gaining access to an understanding of such influences in any one person's life. What we have
done, therefore, is presented an account of Janet's experiences
in a way which emphasizes the costs and benefits implicit in the
choices that were made by her, not necessarily consciously, in
adopting a particular identity and lifestyle. An important aspect
of this account is that the identification as homosexual for Janet
did not involve her questioning whether she was heterosexual
or homosexual, but merely seemed a 'natural' process. This
taking for granted of one's sexual identity is of course the
experience of those who identify as heterosexual. However, the
need to question one's sexual identity is a feature of some
people's lives, and can be illustrated by the following case
example of Stuart.

Stuart was the youngest child in a working-class family where
all the children had entered higher education. At the age of
twenty-one he identifies as bisexual.

Stuart's first sexual experiences were with girls at the age of
six, when he was involved in playing 'doctors and nurses'. The
next sexual experience he remembers was when, at the age of
nine, a group of older girls began masturbating him. This
particular experience was traumatic for Stuart because his older
brother interrupted this and later told his schoolfriends, who
ostracized and humiliated Stuart. When he was ten Stuart
experienced a number of sexual acts with boys, during which
he achieved orgasm for the first time with another person by
body rubbing. The position he enjoyed most was that of having
a boy on top of him, which he saw then as the 'female position'.
This had worried Stuart at that time because he feared he might
get pregnant. In addition, Stuart also felt that his mother knew
he was engaging in such acts, and he regarded her response
as one of silent hostility. This impression of disapproval was
strengthened when Stuart informed his mother that an older
boy had made sexual advances towards him. His mother's
response was to warn Stuart not to go near the boy again.
Further negative messages about homosexual encounters came
when at thirteen Stuart was stopped from visiting a friend of

his brother's, a choirmaster, who his mother described as homosexual, having had a warning about the man from the vicar. Stuart did not see this relationship as sexual, nor did any sexual acts occur. He regarded the concern about the relationship as being rooted in his mother's perceptions of his friend as undesirable.

Stuart's early sexual experiences with boys were important for him in that he recalls that the other boys involved would make derogatory remarks about 'puffs' and 'queers'. This led Stuart to think to himself, 'but what we are doing is no different from them'.

By the age of ten, therefore, Stuart had experienced both heterosexual and homosexual acts. The way he interpreted and evaluated these was affected by the degree of pleasure he obtained in each instance, the responses of his partners, his knowledge about sexuality, his mother's responses, as well as peer-group influences. We must note here that Stuart's memories of these early homosexual experiences were later selected out by him as being important in the development of his sexual identity from adolescence onwards.

Stuart moved to a new school, and had no further sexual experiences with either sex until the age of sixteen. His masturbation fantasies during this period were exclusively heterosexual, and Stuart recalls no homosexual desires or fantasies. At this point, as we have outlined, Stuart had had a number of sexual experiences with both boys and girls. He had found those with boys to be more enjoyable. The social meanings surrounding these homosexual acts which Stuart encountered, however, were predominantly negative and prohibitive both in the messages he received from society at large, and, more specifically, from his family and peer group. On the other hand, the social meanings surrounding Stuart's heterosexual experiences included both positive and negative elements. We should note here that whilst heterosexuality is viewed as positive and necessary in society, for young adolescents heterosexual acts are usually discouraged.

At about age thirteen Stuart had started to ask girls to go out with him, but without success. His opportunities to form relationships with girls were limited both by partial segregation in school and, outside, by the fact that he wasn't invited to the parties which served for his peers as important occasions for finding a boyfriend or a girlfriend.

Stuart by now was asking himself two questions: 'Am I homosexual?' and, 'What if I am?' The interacting influences which in Stuart's case led him to question his sexual identity included messages that he was different from other boys; his mother saw him as 'sensitive', and he was isolated from his peers in that he did not share many of the traditional interests of the other boys, e.g. football. Such behaviour in a boy in our society is often seen as having implications about sexual orientation, of which Stuart was aware. In addition, the significance of such messages for Stuart has to be seen in interaction with his lack of success in finding a girlfriend.

The interpretation by Stuart of this difference from other boys as being a sexual one was also influenced by his past sexual experiences, and the meanings, previous and current, they held for him. In particular he became concerned, in retrospect, about his homosexual experiences, which took on a new significance in the light of his current questioning of his sexual identity.

Stuart's inability to get a girlfriend was seen by him as being a further indicator that he might not be heterosexual. For many teenagers the assumption can be made, 'I do not have a girlfriend, therefore I am not attractive to the opposite sex, therefore perhaps I'm attracted to the same sex.' This does not necessitate the prior existence of homosexual attraction or homosexual desires in the individual. Indeed, as in Stuart's case, quite the reverse process may occur in that homosexual feelings of attraction may be evoked as a consequence of such an evaluation. For Stuart this took the form of starting to fantasize about men whilst masturbating.

In the context of Stuart's total personality he enjoyed being different, and associated this with homosexuality. The messages that he had encountered and taken in, however, were that homosexuals were dangerous people (the choirmaster), who were the object of ridicule (peer reactions) and who engage in prohibited acts (mother's warnings). One important aspect of such meanings for Stuart was that if his schoolfriends thought he was homosexual they would ridicule and ostracize him. His way of dealing with this was to adopt a 'camp clown' role at school, so that, in Stuart's words, 'they'll think I'm only pretending to be gay'. In terms of Stuart's relationships with girls this made him less of a sexual threat. This had the benefit for Stuart of enabling him to form close relationships with them, although at the same time he saw this as restricting his sexual opportunities with females.

At sixteen Stuart began mixing with a new social group, and was invited to a party where he had intercourse with a thirteen year old girl, whom he saw as a 'slag'. This was a disappointing experience for Stuart. Although the girl had an orgasm he did not, and he had difficulty in penetrating her. Shortly after this Stuart formed a close sexual and emotional relationship with a girl at his school. Stuart remembers that during this relationship his concern decreased about his sexual identity being other than heterosexual, and he was enabled to engage in masturbatory fantasies about men.

This relationship was both a very committed and sexually enjoyable one for Stuart, although he faced considerable disapproval from his mother and the school, and, because the girl was below the age of consent, there was the threat of legal action.

His girlfriend was at this time experiencing a number of personal difficulties at home, and was eventually taken into care

by the local authority. This encouraged her dependency on
Stuart, which he found very satisfying. This bond was
strengthened by the fact that after the girl was taken into care
she was widely seen as a 'prostitute', and Stuart was warned
by a social worker to keep away from her. Interestingly, whilst
Stuart's mother had also expressed disapproval of his relationship with this girl, she was also relieved that he had now got a
girlfriend, as she had been anxious about his sexual orientation.
Within his family this concern was reinforced by comparisons
with his strongly heterosexually orientated older brother.

The negative reactions of Stuart's mother to his relationship
with this girl, the response of social services, the threat of
legal sanctions and the way the girl was seen by most people,
including the teaching staff at their school, finally persuaded
Stuart to give up the relationship, albeit reluctantly.

This decision has to be seen in the context of Stuart having
already begun another relationship with a girl (Mary), who was
much approved of by Stuart's mother in preference to his previous girlfriend. His mother encouraged their going away on
holiday together without Mary's mother's knowledge. Stuart
remembers his first sexual encounter with Mary as being the
most enjoyable he had had up to that point, and after three
weeks he proposed marriage.

The social group Stuart and his girlfriend mixed with saw
bisexuality as 'trendy', and in this environment Stuart felt able
to state he was 'gay' to certain other boys who he felt would
accept this. One of the reasons why Stuart decided to announce
that he was gay was that it amused him to shock people, and he
felt that in the context of such a group he would be seen as
a more interesting person. In terms, however, of his own self
identification and the way he described himself to Mary, Stuart
started to say that he was bisexual.

By this time Stuart was eighteen years old, had left school
and was about to go into higher education some distance away
from his home town. Mary, a year younger than Stuart, was
still at school.

Soon after his arrival at his college of higher education the
subject of homosexuality arose during a discussion with a mature
student (Ray) he had got to know. Stuart saw this as another
opportunity to announce that he was homosexual, in order to
shock Ray. He told him that he had 'homosexual tendencies' but
was getting married shortly. To Stuart's surprise this announcement was greeted by Ray without any disquiet, and instead he
asked, 'Do you know that I am homosexual?'

At that point Ray was concerned that Stuart seemed to be
showing some anxiety, and interpreted this as Stuart having
conflicts about his sexual orientation. He therefore asked Stuart
if he would like the opportunity to discuss this on another
occasion, and with some hesitation Stuart agreed. Stuart was
experiencing a mixture of discomfort that the 'game' he had been
playing had misfired. In this context Ray taking Stuart's

announcement seriously, made Stuart once more have to confront his own feelings about homosexuality.

Before their next meeting Stuart had started to ask himself
the question he had asked before: 'Am I homosexual or heterosexual?' He discussed this with Mary, his girlfriend, who showed
some anxiety about the possibility that Stuart might choose to
identify as homosexual.

On meeting Ray again Stuart expressed this ambivalence in
saying that he did not know whether he was heterosexual or
homosexual. After a detailed discussion Ray said he felt Stuart
should take his homosexual interests seriously, and that
irrespective of his sexual orientation he should not rush into
marriage at such an early age. Stuart responded to this advice
by saying that he would like to explore his homosexual interests
but without sexual involvement. Ray suggested therefore that
they might meet weekly and go to gay discos and clubs, to which
Stuart agreed.

This enabled Stuart's homosexual interests to be expressed
whilst at the same time being safely contained, in that Ray had
agreed to Stuart's prohibition of sexual involvement. Such
limits were important to Stuart in terms of his loyalty to Mary
and his commitment to their forthcoming marriage. Also any
further homosexual involvement might have posed a threat to
Stuart's current sexual identity.

Mary was also in agreement with this weekly arrangement
between Stuart and Ray. She had met Ray and liked him, and
believed that he and Stuart would respect the limits which
Stuart had imposed.

Through this relationship with Ray, Stuart was introduced
to a number of openly gay women and men who had an analysis
of homosexuality as a positive choice they had made in their
lives. Such an analysis Stuart adopted, whilst maintaining a
bisexual identity. Stuart was attracted to the lifestyle he saw
Ray and his friends enjoying, and occasionally mixing in this
milieu provided him with a sense of excitement, and of being
different.

His relationship with Ray continued for about a year, and
although Ray and Mary did meet, Stuart was concerned to keep
them apart from one another as they represented two different
lifestyles for him, and therefore some potential conflict for
Stuart in the way he was leading his life.

Ray had found it increasingly difficult during this time to
continue to accept the limits Stuart had imposed on their
relationship, both in terms of the restrictions on sexual contact
and Stuart's determination to marry within a short time. He
considered that Stuart was not, as he had advised, taking his
homosexual interests seriously. Stuart, however, claimed that
his homosexual interests were being fulfilled by his affection
for Ray, and by the social contacts he had made through Ray
with other gay men and women.

Although Stuart was enjoying his relationship with Ray he did not feel able to take on a homosexual identity or any further involvement in a homosexual lifestyle. Some of the reasons for this were Stuart's own view of homosexuality as involving transient relationships in which the partners were not faithful to one another. Being someone who valued stability and welcomed dependency, Stuart found such a prospect unattractive. On the other hand, however, Stuart saw a positive advantage in the possibility within homosexual relationships of not having to conform to delineated roles.

Specifically in his relationship to Ray the difference in their age, and interests, emphasized for Stuart the likely problems in their relationship becoming more committed, and he compared this unfavourably with what he saw as being available in his relationship with Mary. With her he had the security of someone who was dependent on him and who had a monogamous view of relationships. In addition his prospective marriage to Mary was widely approved of by their parents, and Stuart did find it more socially comfortable to commit himself to a heterosexual relationship.

The rightness of his decision was reinforced for him at the time of his marriage by social acceptance from his relatives and friends. In addition to this, Stuart had been influenced by the early marriage of his older brother, which he saw in very positive terms because a number of rewards had resulted, including getting a nice home and being seen as a 'respectable married couple'. In contrast, Stuart saw his parents' marriage rather less positively, this being influenced by the family having to accommodate his father's alcoholism.

Ray at this point decided not to attend Stuart's wedding, and to end his relationship with Stuart, as by this time he felt frustrated by its lack of development both sexually and socially. Stuart was sad to hear this and felt let down by Ray, but he had to accept that Ray saw him as having made a choice in favour of a heterosexual identity and lifestyle.

After getting married Stuart experienced similar rewards to his brother, and saw his marriage as being significant in obtaining a new flat which was certainly preferable to the bed-sitter he had been living in previously. The flat, however, was many miles away from the friends Stuart and Mary had made, and from the college Stuart was attending. This increased their dependency on each other, which Stuart welcomed.

During the first year of the marriage, which Stuart found very enjoyable, he did not see Ray. He continued to have homosexual interests but these were limited to masturbatory fantasies about men.

Ray and Stuart did, however, come into contact again in the college situation. Stuart told Ray he had been having some disagreements with Mary, since he had felt he would like to be able to have sexual relationships with either sex outside their marriage, whilst Mary was still committed to monogamy.

In addition to wanting other sexual relationships, Stuart also desired the social rewards which he had experienced in the past with Ray and his friends. He perceived Ray's social group as leading glamorous and exciting lifestyles, and felt that he could overcome Mary's resistance to the possibility of his having relationships outside their marriage by involving her in this social milieu, from which she had previously been excluded. Indeed, Stuart envisaged the possibility of Mary herself having homosexual encounters and therefore not being so concerned with his behaviour.

Ray's response to this was welcoming, whilst warning Stuart that he would not tolerate renewing their close relationship without the possibility of sexual contact between them. Stuart's reply was that whilst he desired such a relationship with Ray, the possibility of this occurring was dependent on Mary's agreement. Ray then suggested that Stuart attend a gay party with Mary to test out her response.

This was agreed and the couple attended the party. Mary spent most of the time sitting on the sidelines watching Stuart, who was behaving in a more openly sexually manner with men than he had ever done before as an adult. During the party Stuart constantly sought reassurance from Mary, who became more and more withdrawn. It was to be several weeks before she was able to talk to Stuart about her negative reactions to his behaviour at the party. She said that she had never realised 'that was how homosexuals behaved', and that she had feared that Stuart would sleep with Ray that night, which she had never wanted to happen. Stuart expressed some surprise at her response but took note of her strong reactions.

Prior to the party, Mary had not taken Stuart's declared bisexual identity very seriously; she had seen him as essentially heterosexual, with politically sympathetic views about homosexuality, and as someone who was anyway 'obsessed with sex'.

At this point Stuart had, after a year of rewarding married life, attempted to operationalize his bisexual identity. Mary's response was not merely in terms of the possibility of extramarital sex, but was also about her realization that Stuart's homosexual interests were not confined solely to Ray, and might involve close emotional and sexual relationships with other men.

Stuart also experienced some anxiety in that he could no longer view his homosexual feelings as being contained by his relationship with Ray. In addition, his very positive reaction to the first gay party he had attended meant that he had to confront the meaning of what being attracted to men might mean for him, in terms of both sexual acts and a homosexual identity. He also realized that a homosexual lifestyle could be a real alternative.

This resulted in Stuart experiencing a number of conflicts which related to anxieties he had never fully resolved about the costs, as he saw them, of having a homosexual identity. These included the threat of the loss of the relationship he had with Mary, and the associated social and personal rewards including the possibility of having children. He also saw homosexual relationships as more unstable than heterosexual relationships, involving social stigma and pejorative attitudes towards homosexuality which he had experienced from his family, peers and the wider society.

Stuart chose to focus this conflict on Mary's response to his behaviour, and announced to Ray that because of Mary's strongly expressed views homosexual involvement with him, or with any man, was not possible, at least for the moment.

From asking himself in adolescence 'Am I homosexual?' Stuart has come to see himself as having a bisexual identity. He has been able to continue with this view of himself by enjoying a committed heterosexual relationship with Mary, and by limiting his homosexual experiences to masturbation fantasy and to one particular person. This equilibrium was threatened when Stuart had to confront the acting out of his homosexual interests in a gay milieu and the perception by other men, and to some extent Mary, of him as homosexual.

The way in which Stuart is viewed by people he knows varies from being seen as a married homosexual, and therefore having problems in his marriage, to being seen as heterosexual but with politically sympathetic views about homosexuality which extend to considering the possibility of sexual encounters with men himself. We see exemplified in Stuart's case, therefore, the pervasiveness of the polar assumption that one is either heterosexual or homosexual, and the difficulties for the individual of maintaining a bisexual identity.

For Stuart a homosexual identity would have greater costs and fewer benefits then maintaining a bisexual identity. Such costs include the more stigmatized perception of homosexuality relative to bisexuality, which in some circles is seen very positively as the 'way we should all be really'. Stuart's view is that a homosexual identity, or heterosexual identity for that matter, is a restriction on the possible choices one might wish to have in forming relationships. Stuart sees himself as attractive to women and not to men, which may also play a part in affecting his choice of relationships. A bisexual identity also enables him to experience himself as being different, without the same degree of social rejection that would be involved in a commitment to a homosexual identity.

This has to be seen in the context of Stuart being married to Mary. If he had a similarly committed relationship with Ray and was still identifying as bisexual he would not have been spared the homosexual stigma, and his bisexuality would probably have been viewed with some suspicion and possible hostility by both heterosexuals and homosexuals alike. In that situation, therefore, Stuart might perceive that not to adopt a homosexual identity, and to maintain instead that he was bisexual, would offer few advantages and might involve considerable social and personal loss. In fact Stuart states that had he met Ray before meeting Mary he would have chosen a homosexual identity.

At this point Stuart identifies as a monogamous bisexual. He

still has homosexual interests but regards his relationship
with Mary as the crucial factor in the maintenance of his
sexual identity. Any change therefore in his evaluation of
his relationship with Mary may enable a change to occur in his
lifestyle and identity. If Mary left him Stuart says he would
probably adopt a homosexual identity. Assuming this will
not happen, Stuarts says that in the future he thinks it likely
that he will gradually come to identify as heterosexual if he
has no homosexual contacts. In saying this Stuart is
recognizing that it is likely that a person will identify with
the sexual contacts and lifestyles s/he chooses, which in
Stuart's case are heterosexual, and that in the absence of
homosexual contacts he will find it difficult to maintain a
bisexual identity.

THEORETICAL OVERVIEW

The two case examples we have given illustrate the process
for each individual of developing and maintaining a particular
sexual identity at any given point in time. The essential
uniqueness of this process of identification has had little
recognition in the literature on homosexuality. Indeed, rather
than looking at the meanings homosexual behaviour holds
for each individual, research into homosexuality has been
almost exclusively concerned with etiological considerations.
    Most explanatory models of homosexuality, whilst
emphasizing the universal effect of specific etiological factors,
claim to adopt a multi-factorial approach to causation by pay-
ing lip service to other predisposing factors which may not
have been emphasized within their own particular model. Such
an approach to homosexuality has in the main been seen in
additative rather than interactionist terms. The underlying
assumption has been that each factor can be assessed dis-
cretely, and therefore that the outcome for the individual can
be viewed as the sum total of each of these discrete factors.
    Theoreticians have accounted for differences between
individuals in terms of relative weightings attached to particular factors. This can be illustrated by the Fig 3.1,
where the predisposing factors (A, B, C, etc.) that have
been suggested as having etiological significance include:
pre-Oedipal development, Oedipal conflicts, prenatal hormonal
influences, seduction, peer group experiences and so on (see
chapters 1 and 2). In each theoretical model such factors
will be given a weighting according to: (i) the theoretician's
particular perspective and (ii) the way in which, for each
individual, the relevance of these selected factors is seen.
Some theoreticians may also acknowledge that in a particular case certain factors relevant to their model may not
in fact apply.
    In such models homosexuality is seen as developing from

certain predisposing factors (A, B, C, etc.) which have been
selected as having etiological significance. We would argue,
however, that the etiological significance of any one factor in
the development of a homosexual identity depends upon the way
in which it interacts with other factors, and the meaning such
interactions hold for the individual. In this way no one factor
or summation of factors can be seen as predictive of the
development of a homosexual identity. Indeed, rather than a
summation of factors selected by a particular theoretician as
being specific to the development of homosexuality, it is, we
would suggest, the interaction of a whole range of factors
specific to the particular individual and their significance in
the individual's total life experience which is crucial in the
development of sexual orientation. This interactive process can
be represented by Fig 3.2, where A, B, C, etc. represent an
infinite number of life experiences encountered by the individual.
In using the term 'life experiences' we would include the social
experience of constitutional factors. For example, the experience
of being 5ft 3ins tall and male, or 6ft 1in and female, in our
society.

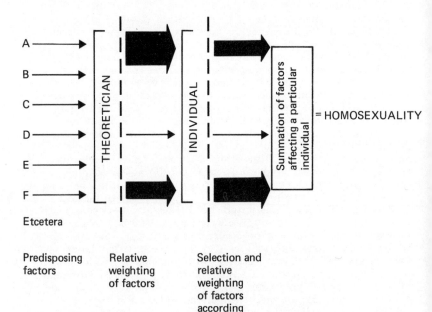

Figure 3.1 Multi-factorial additive model

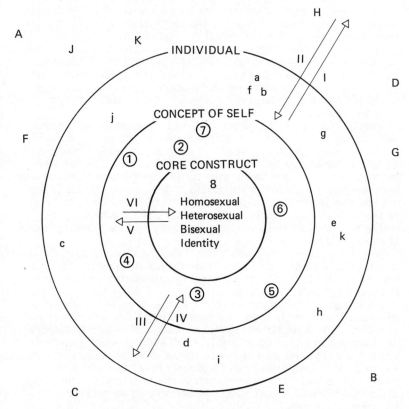

Figure 3.2 Representation of interacting processes involved in the development of sexual identity

The possible significance of such experiences for the development of a homosexual, heterosexual or bisexual identity derives
from the meanings the individual ascribes to A, B, C, etc.,
represented in the diagram by a, b, c, etc. Such meanings will
be influenced by the way in which the individual assimilates
how these factors are seen by the wider society in which s/he
lives, in interaction with the individual's personal experiences
of such factors and the way in which a, b, c, etc. interact
with each other.

The individual meanings we hold will, of course, influence
how we act on the world, and therefore the life experiences we
may encounter (A, B, C, etc.), which in turn may significantly
affect the meanings (a, b, c, etc.) such factors hold for us.
In other words, there is an ongoing two-way interactive process
between how we construe the world, which forms the basis for
our actions in that world (process I in Fig.3.2), and the
consequential experiences of that action, the assimilation of
which may in turn influence the way we view the world (process
II in Fig.3.2).

In this model we are postulating that the meaning an individual
ascribes to a particular factor is neither discrete nor static,
but rather is the result of an ongoing interactive process and
is therefore liable to change.

An important influence on the meanings a person ascribes to
life events will be the way in which an individual construes him
or herself (process III in Fig.3.2). Such self constructs are
represented in the diagram by 1, 2, 3, etc. We must recognize
again here that this is a two-way process, and that the way in
which an individual construes a given experience (A) and
ascribes meaning to it (a) may affect the constructs s/he holds
about her or himself and their relationship to each other
(process IV in Fig.3.2).

If we turn now specifically to sexual orientation, the
identification as homosexual, heterosexual or bisexual is one
such self construct (8). The holding of such a construct, indeed
any construct, may affect the relationships between the individual's other self constructs (process V in Fig.3.2). However,
this again is a two-way process, for the constructs a person
holds about her or himself (1, 2, 3, etc.), and their relationship
to each other, will influence the way s/he construes her or his
sexual orientation (process VI in Fig.3.2).

The maintenance of a self construct as homosexual, heterosexual or bisexual will be influenced therefore by the individual's
experience of the world (II), the way in which the meaning of
such experiences affects the individual's self-constructs (IV),
and also the relationship of sexual identity to the other constructs the individual has of her or himself (V and VI).

In this model, therefore, the stability of sexual identity will
depend upon all these interactions. Special notice must be
taken of the relationship of sexual identity to constructs which
are central to the individual's concept of self, and the way s/he

views the world in general.

Indeed, for most people the identification as either homosexual, heterosexual or bisexual is itself a core construct, as is the view that sexual orientation is a permanent characteristic. For many people, therefore, the possibility of change in sexual identity would represent a serious threat to their experience of social reality in general, and in particular to the fundamental ways in which they construe themselves and others. This is the explanation of why, for the majority of people in our society, sexual identity is experienced as stable.

This has important implications for the person who adopts a bisexual identity, as in Stuart's case. The likelihood is that other people will perceive one as being either heterosexual or homosexual, given, as we have already stated, that sexual orientation is seen by most people as being both polarized and permanent.

The individual's experience of this lack of affirmation of a bisexual identity, particularly from significant others, is likely to make the maintenance of such an identity relatively more difficult than either a heterosexual or a homosexual identity. This may be compounded by the kind of sexual and social relationships with either sex that the individual experiences. Indeed, to maintain a self construct as bisexual, rather than heterosexual or homosexual, it is likely that the individual will have to continue to engage in social and sexual relationships with both sexes.

We must also note that whilst how the individual construes the world will influence how s/he acts in that world, the assimilation of this experience may in turn affect the constructs s/he holds. In other words the perception of oneself as homosexual, heterosexual or bisexual, and the meanings related to such an identification for each person, will influence the kind of experiences the individual encounters. For instance, in our example of Janet one of the meanings of a homosexual identity for her was that she chose to have sexual relationships with women and not with men. The maintenance of such an identity will, of course, be influenced by the way in which such experiences are interpreted by the individual. In Janet's case the positive experience of sexual relationships with women and the lack of comparable experiences with men affirmed her identity as homosexual.

Identification as homosexual, heterosexual or bisexual has different meanings and significance for each individual. Such meanings and significances will derive from the relationship the construct of being homosexual, heterosexual or bisexual has with other constructs that the individual holds about self and others, and inasmuch as this relationship is a dynamic interactive process it may change over time. This has been illustrated in the previous case examples, where we have attempted to draw out some of the meanings associated with being homosexual, in Janet's case, or bisexual, in Stuart's.

These cases also illustrate how the meaning of being homosexual may for the individual take on a different significance over time.

It is of interest here to point out that sexual orientation is likely to be of more significance to those individuals who identify as homosexual or bisexual, given the stigmatization of same-sex relationships and the general assumption of a heterosexual orientation.

In conclusion let us summarize the important ways in which the model we have described differs from other models which have sought to 'explain' homosexuality. We have emphasized that the development, maintenance and meaning of a homosexual identity is unique for each person, and have attempted to describe the complex interactive process by which this occurs.

Within such a model the attempt to explain homosexuality by reference to specific etiological factors would be invalid on several counts. First, we would argue that it is not possible to generalize about a limited number of factors being influential in the development of a homosexual identity. Rather we would consider that for a given individual any number of factors may be significant.

Second, the importance of any one factor to the development of a homosexual identity will depend upon the meaning it holds for a particular individual. In this way factors which may have significance in the development of such an identity for one individual may, for someone else, have little or no relevance.

Third, we would emphasize that the concept of etiology, in its concern with causation, largely ignores the need to consider the process of maintaining a particular sexual identity. This, of course, rests on the assumption that a particular sexual orientation is a permanent characteristic of the individual. Our model, however, has described the various processes by which either stability or change of such an identity can occur.

Fourth, in this search for causation the individual is usually seen as a passive recipient of etiological influences. Our model focuses on the active role of the individual in selecting and ascribing meaning to factors which may, for that individual, be of significance in the development and maintenance of a homosexual identity.

Obviously, inasmuch as the concept of etiology has been important in many of the therapeutic approaches to homosexuality, our critique of the validity of this concept has important ramifications for therapy. This has already been discussed in chapters 1 and 2.

Finally, whilst we have chosen to focus on the development and maintenance of a homosexual identity, we would stress that the model we have presented in this Chapter is one which explains the development and maintenance of either a heterosexual, a homosexual or a bisexual identity. In other words, in contrast to many other models, rather than assuming a natural development we are here recognizing the need to explain the construction and maintenance of any sexual identity.

4 GOING GAY: identities life cycles and lifestyles in the male gay world

Kenneth Plummer

Until the 1970s, to talk of becoming a homosexual was to talk of etiological factors: chromosomes and heredity, strong mothers and weak fathers, Oedipal failure and faulty conditioning - these, and many others, have been variously invoked as the cause for homosexuality. In this Chapter my concern with what makes a person 'a homosexual' is very different. For whatever small contributory part such medical and psychological factors may play in establishing early preconditions, the path to becoming an adult 'homosexual' invariably involves a social dimension in later life; of learning, adapting to and creating homosexual meanings and incorporating these into one's life pattern. For a great many people, however, their responses to homosexual meanings may be very negative: they have a same-sex experience in some form (a sexual fantasy, a bonding with one's buddies, even direct physical contact), but they do not see it as homosexual - it is 'camaraderie', 'playing around', 'drunken foolery', 'macho' hustling. The wider cultural meanings that such experiences are homosexual can be kept firmly at bay by a series of rationalizations, and such men do not come to see themselves as 'gay' (Plummer, 1975, pp.137-41). Whilst such experiences are possibly widespread [1] they will not be my concern here; rather my interest lies in that group of men who 'go gay' - that is those men who do come to see themselves as homosexual, enter the organized world of homosexuality and adopt a gay lifestyle. It is only the iceberg tip of homosexual experience - a visible tip that can therefore be observed and discussed. The larger, concealed world of homosexual experience must await exploration.

It is helpful to tease this process of 'going gay' through three dimensions. First, there is the ontological, which examines the very categories 'gay' and 'homosexual' - what is this 'thing' that people are becoming? Second, there is the cultural-historical, which examines the specific historical and cultural themes giving distinctive shapes to homosexuality - how might development differ according to one's historical experiences? Third, there is the life-cycle dimension, which questions the stages encountered in 'going gay' - what are the recurrent life crises involved in becoming a homosexual? In what follows, I will make some tentative observations on each of these three dimensions.

ONTOLOGY: WHAT IS THIS THING CALLED HOMOSEXUALITY?

My first concern is with the category 'homosexual'. Clearly it
can be used simply as an adjective - to describe same-sex
experiences (behaviour, fantasies, feelings) without suggesting
a way of being. In this view, becoming a homosexual is no
different from becoming a tennis player, a good cook or a stamp
collector: it merely describes what people may do, and
signposts a particular preference they may have for the time
being, and suggests that such experiences are learnt in the
same way as everything else is learnt (Gagnon, 1977, p.2).
Nobody devises special theories to explain why people opt for
stamp collecting: why should they do so for homosexuality? To
do so is to engage in 'the tyranny of isness', of converting
doing into being (Sagarin, 1975; 1976).
    This view has virtues: it captures the experience of many
people who have homosexual experiences (sex, fantasies,
intimacies, emotional involvements) but who do not see themselves as homosexual, and it breaks down the significance
attributed to the sexual realm in this culture, by seeing it as
an ordinary learnt phenomenon. It is a view strongly endorsed
by Kinsey in 1948, and by the subsequent Kinsey researchers
who coined the term 'homosexualities' to refer to the myriad
ways of experiencing homosexuality (Bell and Weinberg, 1978).
    Yet despite this, and my own preference for the term as an
adjective, roughly since the start of this century many people
have come to use the term as a noun: 'the homosexual' refers
to a type, a species, a form of being, a condition or an
'essence' (Foucault, 1979; Plummer, 1981). Mere experience
is transformed into core being - the description becomes the
thing. Thus Humphreys (1979b) suggests that in this culture
homosexuality is not comparable to stamp collecting. Indeed,
homosexuality is likely to become a central identity because
it is condemned, and because it is so firmly connected (in this
culture, again) to those core identities of gender - masculinity
and femininity. (By implication, Humphreys does suggest that
if homosexuality was not stigmatized, and if it could be dis-
connected from its intimate link with gender, then it would lose
its current centrality.)
    Now it is important to distinguish this view (held mainly
by phenomenologists like Warren and Ponse, 1977) that
homosexuality is constructed as an essence from the view
(held by clinicians and sociologists like Whitam, 1977a and b,
1980) that homosexuality is an essence: the constructionists and
the essentialists respectively. Although they ultimately converge
on the idea of homosexuality as a noun, they do so from starkly
opposing angles.
    For the essentialist, homosexuality is a universal, a form
found across cultures and throughout history: and the
'homosexual' of ancient Greece is directly comparable to the
'homosexual' of modern London. Whitam, for example, views

it as a 'non-dominant, universal manifestation of human
sexuality' (Whitam, 1980,p.99), and in comparing three different
societies (United States, Guatemala and Brazil) concludes
that on at least six indicators (like playing with dolls as a child
and 'dressing up') homosexuals differed significantly from
heterosexuals in all three cultures. In contrast, for the
constructionist, homosexuality is not a universal essence.
Human gender and human sexuality is a diffuse open-ended
matrix of potential and possibility - to be narrowed down and
organized in specific ways by specific sociohistorical form-
ations (Kessler and McKenna, 1978). How we think, feel and
act out our 'sexualities' will depend on the ways that family
structures set boundaries to emotional development, and the
wider society sets boundaries to cognitive categories. (And,
of course, there is always the possibility that such boundaries
could be transcended!) These - as every anthropologist and
historian knows - are far from universally constant.

The very notion of 'the homosexual' as a type of being is
an invention of the mid-nineteenth century that has slowly
had profound implications for the way homosexual experiences
are patterned in our culture (Plummer, 1981).

Essentialists thus differ from constructionists on the way
people become homosexual. For the essentialist, people
develop an orientation early in life (through biology or
psychodynamics) and it stays with them, to define their real
underlying sexual being throughout life. Learning sexuality
entails discovering what one really is. People can be unaware
of this 'real' being - in which case they remain cases of
'latency'. For the constructionist, becoming sexual is a question of understanding how people develop on a vast matrix
of sexual and gender possibilities across time. Some indication of the variables involved is given in Table 4.1. Constructionists hold that there is no essential link between
these components; a biologically male person can behave
homosexually without seeing himself as homosexual, see himself as a woman without seeing himself as a homosexual, see
himself as a man whilst seeing himself as a homosexual or
see himself as a homosexual but not behave as one. The
permutations from this chart are clearly enormous, and it is
beyond my scope to discuss them here. The cornerstone of
this theory of becoming centres upon the way in which the
person's identity is socially created, socially bestowed and
socially maintained (Dank, 1971; Weinberg, 1978). In this
view, learning to become a homosexual is largely a matter of
learning to see oneself as a homosexual.

A paradox that emerges from this contrast is that ultimately,
despite widely differing sources, the two positions converge
on the idea of 'essence'. For the essentialist, homosexuality is
a form of being; for the constructionist, homosexuality
becomes a form of being once it is defined as such. Thus,
however, inadequate the term 'the homosexual', or 'the gay'

TABLE 4.1 Locating homosexuality on the sexual matrix

Level of analysis	Organic	Behavioural Acts Roles		Emotional Feelings Orientation		Cognitive Meaning Identities	
A Gender	1	2	3	4	5	6	7
B Sexuality	8	9	10	11	12	13	14

1. Key dimensions
   A Gender: all those matters pertaining to the male and the female.
   B Sexuality: all those matters pertaining to the potential. arousability and engorgement of the genitals (this is a very problematic definition).

2. Level of analysis
   A Organic: all those matters pertaining to bodily function and physiology.
   B Behaviour: all activity, and patterns of expectations surrounding activities (i.e. roles).
   C Emotional: internal feeling states.
   D Cognition: all those matters pertaining to the way we organize our thoughts.

Units
   1. Biological sex: a biological dichotomy between female and male chromosomally determined (e.g. the possession of a penis/vagina).
   2. Gender acts: momentary behaviours that are identifiable as distinctly masculine or feminine (e.g. the wearing of a dress).
   3. Gender roles: the constellation of expectations which indicate to others or to the self the degree that one is either male or female or ambivalent (e.g. the male role, the female role).
   4. Gender feelings: the emotions culturally associated with masculinity and femininity (e.g. aggression, for a man).
   5. Gender orientation: the underlying constellation of emotional feelings culturally associated with masculinity and femininity (e.g. activity for a man, passivity for a woman).
   6. Gender meanings: the meanings culturally identified with being a man or being a woman (e.g. intelligence for men, emotionality for women).
   7. Gender identities: 'The sameness, unity and persistence of one's individuality as male, female or ambivalent, in greater or lesser degree, especially as it is experienced in self-awareness and behaviour; gender identity is the private experience of gender role' (Money and Tucker, 1977, p.13).

Level of analysis	Organic	Behavioural Acts Roles		Emotional Feelings Orientation		Cognitive Meaning Identities	
A Gender	1	2	3	4	5	6	7
B Sexuality	8	9	10	11	12	13	14

8. Biological sexuality: the physiology of sexual and reproductive activity (e.g. the physiology of the orgasm - as
   discussed by Masters and Johnson, 1966).
9. Sexual activities: behaviour culturally defined as sexual
   (e.g. coitus, masturbation, fellatio).
10. Sexual role: the constellation of expectations culturally
    attached to certain forms of sexual activity (e.g. homosexual
    role, heterosexual role, sado-masochistic role).
11. Sexual feelings: momentary sexual excitements (e.g. 'fancy-
    ing' someone who is passing by).
12. Sexual orientation: a person's central object and the aim of
    sexual expression (e.g. paedophiliac, sado-masochistic,
    heterosexual).
13. Sexual meanings: whatever a person defines (momentarily)
    as sexual (e.g. a shoe, a dream).
14. Sexual identity: the sense a person holds of his or her
    sexual orientation (e.g. being a heterosexual, being a
    homosexual).

may be to social scientists, it does exist as a construct in the
wider world that many people can opt to identify with. In so
doing many people come to read their past as symptomatic of
a 'real gayness' that was there all along. The ironic spectre can
happen by which a sixty-year-old man - married with two grown-
up children - can come to negate sixty years of heterosexuality
by announcing that he was 'really gay' all the time. The past
is reread through the essentializing categories of the present.
Clearly, this makes it very difficult to decide whether homosexuality really is an essence or whether it is simply learnt to
be an essence, since on the surface they look the same. Yet one
'essence' flows from deep psychic necessity and the other from
social learning; one sees labelling as mirroring reality and the
other sees it as creating reality; one sees labelling as enabling
and the other as restricting and controlling. It is the latter view
of the constructionists that informs the remainder of this
discussion.

THE HISTORICAL AND CULTURAL MOMENT: SEXUAL STIGMA
AND THE HETEROSEXUAL ASSUMPTION

Central to the constructionist account of 'going gay' is the need
to locate development in a historical and cultural context. A
person never arrives out of the blue, but comes with a package
of collective historical experiences that have shaped and
influenced his or her life and while such experiences can be
'shaken off' they will normally leave a particular perspective
for viewing the world at later stages. The experience of homosexuality in the 1930s – criminal, sick and hidden as it was –
is not like that of the 1980s – decriminalized, demedicalized and
more visible as it is. Given the difficulties of being gay in the
1930s – bars were less common, 'cottaging' more prominent, gay
couples more open to harassment, self esteem more threatened,
gay organizations nonexistent, heterosexual marriage more
necessary – it is likely that these shared experiences will linger
with the older homosexual in the 1980s (Katz, 1976; Weeks, 1977).
Elderly gays may be more prone to being 'single', heterosexually
married and more fearful of gay meeting places and organizations because of their earlier experiences. Someone who has
lived through the 1930s will find it hard to grasp the slight
reductions in stigma that have occurred, and hence they will
probably find talk of 'coming out' in 1980 very threatening,
relating to their own 'cohort'. They may even feel angered and
frustrated by the young around them who seem to positively
flaunt their gayness; they will use the term 'queer' or at best
'homosexual' to describe themselves. In stark contrast, someone
who has known nothing but the post-liberation period of the
1970s may take bars, organizations, and couples for granted –
'carrying' these shared experiences with them into the twenty-
first century. Relating to their own cohort they may feel
irritated by the 'closetness', 'conservatism' and self oppression
of older gays and they will prefer the term 'gay' to apply to
themselves – with all the pride, anger, openness, visibility,
politics and health this implies (Morin, 1977; Kimmel, 1978, 1979).
    While these specific yet shared historical perspectives are
important, everyone living in the 1980s also has a common
cultural experience which generates some of the most central
problems of gay existence. This common experience centres
around a twin process: the first – the heterosexual assumption –
leads people to think in heterosexual terms; unless there are
very good reasons for thinking otherwise everybody in our
culture will be presumed to be heterosexual.[2] The second process – sexual stigma – leads homosexuality to become enmeshed
in a network of devaluation, hostility, fear, dread and even
outright loathing. This twin process is overwhelmingly important
because of the impact it will initially have upon any man who
believes that he may be homosexual, and because of the way it
may subsequently fashion gay lifestyles.
    The heterosexual assumption is the source of many gay

problems; it will, for instance, provide the routine expectation
that every adolescent will find a partner of the opposite sex,
settle down, get married, ultimately procreate and raise children. But such an expectation may lead some to get married who
will - in later life - come to wish they had chosen a gay lifestyle.
Many adult homosexuals are likely to have spent some time of
their earlier life in a marital situation - and this in turn generates a whole series of specific problems: of marital disharmony,
of spouses who reproach themselves for the relationship, of
divorce, of the problem of custody of wanted and unwanted
children and of gay parents (Miller, 1979).

Another crucial problem to flow from the heterosexual assumption occurs in many areas of social need, where professionals
are blinded to important problems. Thus, for instance, in the
area of residential care it will always be presumed that children,
the handicapped and the elderly (if it is assumed they are
sexual beings at all) are heterosexual. Discussions of elderly
gays in institutional care are nil: and yet somewhere between
3 per cent and 10 per cent of institutional populations are likely
to have homosexual interests. The same can be said for many
other social problems: homosexual racial minorities are not
discussed, yet given the traditional 'macho' West Indian culture
it is arguable that the problems of being gay within that culture
are much greater (Soares, 1979); likewise the homosexual 'poor'
are ignored - it is all very well to counsel homosexuals to become
involved in the gay scene, when the cost of membership,
entrance, travel, drinks and cosmetics are so high as to preclude those who live at or below the breadline. In all these areas
then, and many others, the heterosexual assumption is at work
quite strongly.

The other element of this twin process is sexual stigma. This
takes a number of forms: from the tangible operations of the
legal and medical professions who still have the power both to
criminalize homosexual experiences and medicalize them, to the
less tangible and more abstract sense that homosexuality is at
the very least 'odd'. This 'homosexual taboo' constitutes the
kernel of the homosexual's problems, if it can be reduced or
eliminated then the problems accruing to the homosexual experience will diminish too.

Two kinds of problems come with stigma: the objective and
the subjective. The first involves the constant risk of direct
physical exclusion from certain groups in society. Homosexuals
are still potentially liable to imprisonment and hospitalization;
they may still potentially be sacked from their places of employment; they may still potentially have their children taken away
from them; and they may still potentially be excommunicated
from their church, banished from their community or cut off
from their families (CHE, 1979). While not true of all experiences,
homosexuality is often regarded with such dread that it can
result in direct exclusion from participation in most avenues of
social life. Here, at the very least, real problems of civil

liberties are attendant. Even where the above direct forms of
discrimination are not practised, the subjective consequences of
stigma will still come into play. Once a man starts to contemplate
homosexuality it can be immediately accompanied by feelings of
guilt and shame; feelings which in turn lead to the need for
caution and secrecy; which in turn may lead to a profound sense
of being 'dirty and different'. Isolation grows, secrecy grows,
frustration grows - as one feels increasingly unable to satisfy
one's emotio-sexual needs. So too does the centrality of the
experience; it becomes pivotal, pressing and engulfing. This is
the core of the homosexual problem. Take the stigma away, and
the problems of guilt, secrecy, isolation, 'differentness and
dirtyness' and of gaining access to like-minded individuals
begin to wane. So many problems surrounding homosexuality
then could simply be removed if society eliminated its stigmatizing attitude.

Some homosexuals come to these kinds of problems very early
in life, resolve them and thereafter lead relatively unproblematic
lives. It is equally clear that some people cannot neutralize
this stigma: they live with it until they are sixty or seventy,
or until they usher their 'secret' into their grave. They wrestle
with it, fight against it, push themselves into all kinds of
unfulfilling avenues in order to fight off this dreadful affliction
that they think they possess. These are the homosexuals who
are likely to get caught up in the psychiatric nets - those who
cannot or will not come to terms with their homosexual experiences. The problems, however, can be resolved fairly quickly.
Once a man gains access to a non-stigmatizing, supportive gay
person; once a man can come to realize that there are many
other people in the same predicament who can lead good, useful,
positive lives; once a man can come to meet, talk and be friendly
with other homosexuals, then in many instances, if not most,
his problems recede.

THE GAY LIFE CYCLE: SOME TURNING POINTS

So far, I have been concerned with the importance of locating
the person's experience in history and culture. But each person's life also has a history: of growth, crisis and change. Until
recently, accounts of this history were notorious for focusing
upon the earliest years of life to the relative neglect of patterns
of adult development. Life seemed to end at five. More recently
there has been a growing interest in lifespan development
through which the predictable crises in adult life [3] are charted.
Through intensive studies of individual lives, portraits are
becoming established of critical turning points that most people
will encounter. Levinson (1978, p.58), for example, suggests
there may be an 'age thirty transition' which provides an
'opportunity to work on the flaws and limitations of the first adult
life structure, and to create the basis for a more satisfactory

structure with which to complete the era of early adulthood.[14]
With only a few exceptions, however, this work has been
dominated by the heterosexual assumption. Erikson's (1977,
p.239) celebrated account, [5] for example, highlights a sixth
stage – of intimacy versus isolation – where 'a mutuality of
orgasm *with a loved partner of the other sex*' (my emphasis)
becomes essential. Homosexuality is here defined out of the
model.

To avoid such devaluation, we need to analyse the specific
'turning points' – or crises – entailed in gay life cycles. Only
when we are clear about these should they be related to a
broader conception of development from womb to tomb. For the
time being, I would like to suggest two such crises: 'coming
out' and 'opting for a lifestyle'.

Coming out
The first, and usually most momentous, moments in any gay life
cycle are those involved in coming out. Given both the heterosexual assumption and the homosexual taboo, those who may
later in life 'go gay' will initially be socialized to believe that
they are heterosexual; nagging feelings of being different may
emerge very early in childhood or adolescence, but a clear
sense of being gay will only unfold later. Coming out refers to
this complex process of moving from a heterosexual (and confused) identity, given to one in childhood, to a strong, positive
and accepting sense of one's identity as gay being given to one
through awareness of the gay community. It is a momentous,
frequently painful, experience in any gay person's life –
comparable in impact perhaps to the birth of one's first child in
the heterosexual cycle. Experiencing it will dramatically reshape
one's life-route: life will never be the same again. Quite when
'coming out' will occur in any particular life is – as yet –
unpredictable; many will find it occurring during their first
heterosexual marriage, some may find it taking place in mid-
adolescence, and others can move through it during their
retirement. Most typically, though – in America during the
1970s – it seems to occur somewhere between the late teens and
early thirties (Dank, 1971; Crites, 1976; de Monteflores and
Schultz, 1978; Weinberg, 1978; Harry and DeVall, 1978).

Coming out is a complex business involving at least three
intertwined stages, which probably most people can never quite
complete. They are:

1 coming out to oneself – starting to see oneself as homosexual;
2 coming out in the gay world – starting to meet other gay
people;
3 coming out in the straight world – starting to be open to non-
gays about one's gayness.

The first step is often the hardest, since it usually has to be
taken alone without support from others: the whole weight of

cultural indoctrination has to be broken down. This, to engage
in understatement, is not easy. At home, at school, with one's
peers or confronting the media the message has insidiously been
the same: the only path is the heterosexual one, and 'queers'
are few and sick. How can you - in spite of your vague feelings
and fantasies - be one of that sick few? You can't - and even
if by some freak chance you were, it must be kept as a dark
and hidden secret to be carried quietly to your grave. Yet to
even start to have such ponderings is to set in motion the
spiral of signification by which the idea that you could indeed
be homosexual slowly becomes more and more central to your
life. At what point it breaks through - 'I am like that, I must
do something about it' - is largely unpredictable; but that
this breakthrough does happen - against all odds - is unmis-
takable (Harry and DeVall, 1978; Humphreys, 1979b). An open
mind, a liberal peer group, access to gay books, articles and
films, sight of a Gay Switchboard sticker, knowledge of a
homosexual person, etc. may all play their contributory roles
in facilitating this self awareness; but in the end it is only the
individual himself who can make the decision that he is gay and
act upon it.

These first tortured stages of coming out can usually be
circumvented speedily once the second stage - of meeting other
homosexuals - is reached. This involves gaining access to
homosexual role models that openly counterbalance the heterosexual role models of the preceding years (Riddle, 1978). The
earlier doubts - the guilt, identity confusions, secrecy and
sexual frustrations - can begin to fade once homosexuals are
met who, curiously enough, are 'glad to be gay', living reasonably contented and productive lives. The gay bar is extremely
important in this 'meeting' process, and more recently the
development of smaller, more intimate groups of gays have
strengthened this supportive process in coming out.[6]

The final stage in the coming out process centres around
relationships with the non-gay world: to tell others, and thereby
establish a continuity of identity between self and the world at
large; or to keep it a secret, and thereby live a marginally
dishonest, slightly dissonant existence. A whole range of people
could be told of one's gayness - family, neighbours, workmates,
spouse, children, community - and whom to tell and when to
tell can become significant issues for the gay person.[7]

In general, not coming out in this third sense does seem to be
linked to a less positive gay adjustment (Weinberg and Williams,
1974, p.186). On the other hand, more and more gays do seem
to be telling others; and although there are often initial traumas
(it is obviously hard for many non-gays to understand what
homosexuality is all about - they may never have thought about
it before), acceptance usually follows.[8] Often, indeed, it can
be positively beneficial to all parties - and in the long run it
can only serve to break down further the hostility and mythology which surround the whole subject. Coming out to the

straight world is often the first sign that the homosexual
person has successfully navigated his own problems and has
moved on to those of others. From an inward-looking perspective
to the gay world which has helped him find himself, he can now
look outward to the community which previously rejected him.

Opting for a lifestyle
The first set of turning points, then, are all concerned with
establishing a sense of who one really is - an identity which
ideally exists not just for oneself alone, but which is also at
home in the wider world. To summarize from Rainwater (1970,
p.375): 'A valid identity is one in which the individual finds
congruence between who he feels he is, who he announces himself to be, and where he feels his society places him.'
    In coming out to himself, to the gay community and to the
wider environment, the homosexual man can develop a consistent,
integrated sense of a self; a sense of self as gay which studies
suggest are most compatible with a reasonably well-adjusted
life (Bell and Weinberg, 1978).
    Knowing who one is, however, does not necessarily tell one
what to do or where to go. And here the second set of gay
turning points enter, which can be referred to as 'opting for
a lifestyle'. Although, arguably, the issue of choosing a lifestyle is increasingly an option for all people in capitalist cultures - gay and straight alike - it is still true that for most
heterosexuals there is little perceived choice: round about their
late teens and early twenties they are likely to be dragooned
into the 'rating-dating-going steady-engagement-marriage-
raising children' syndrome. Many people who become gay later
will initially move, more or less unthinkingly, into this pattern.
But this is most unlikely for those who have fully come out -
indeed it would usually be a contradiction of their gay identity.
    For many homosexual men, then, there is no obvious and
immediate lifestyle available: however dimly, it has to be reflected upon, and this can be a painful and prolonged search.
Confusion arises not from being gay - for that is clear and
accepted - but from not knowing how to incorporate gayness
into an overall life pattern. A host of questions will be pondered
upon, but three can be pulled out as particularly significant.
    First, the person will have to decide how far he wants to
become involved in the organized gay world: he may decide to
totally immerse himself in it and to sever contacts with non-gay
people, or he may decide to keep a great distance from all
organized gays. Second, the person will have to decide on the
kinds of gay relationships he wants: he may decide to imitate
the heterosexual world and establish a kind of psuedo-marriage
situation, he may decide to experiment with more diffuse, couple
relationships or he may decide to remain firmly single. Third,
the person will have to decide on the pattern and type of sexual
involvement he wants: he may decide to have a lot of sex
partners and to experiment with different activities, he may opt

for a monogamous partner, or he may decide to forgo sex and
remain celibate. These and many other questions may crowd
into the homosexual man's mind, and whether by default or
conscious choice, some outcome will have to be established. I
will comment on each of the three options mentioned above
briefly in turn.

The gay world   Since coming out will usually involve some contact with other gays, the most apparent initial lifestyle decision
concerns either staying with gays and maybe becoming more
and more immersed in the gay world, or else trying to disengage.
Most people, I suspect, will opt for the former route initially -
and will gain much security from it. For the gay world can
provide solutions to many of the homosexual's problems. Where
once he felt he was the only one, he is now provided with
visible evidence of thousands of similar people. Where once he
felt ashamed, he is now provided with an array of justification
and legitimations of homosexuality from others in the world.
Where once he felt confused and secretive, he is now confronted
with open guidelines - gay role models he can learn from. Where
once he was frustrated sexually he is now confronted with a
tangible pool of sexual and emotional possibility. The gay world
can become the gay man's 'haven in a heartless world'.
    What is this gay world? At its most general, it refers to all
those cultural forms which take male homosexuality as a key
concern - gay bars, discos, clubs, saunas and the like. Until
the 1970s such a world had existed in England and America, but
it was fairly restricted in scope, substantially hidden from sight,
and fairly culturally impoverished. While such small worlds
still exist in small communities,[9] it is perhaps now more appropriate to see larger cities as spawning 'satellite cultures'
(Humphreys, 1979a) where homosexuality comes to be a broadly
available and visible alternative culture for many, with its own
media and services. Within this embracing alternative culture
can be found a wide range of institutions (from varied gay bars
to baths, from varied churches to political organizations), a
range of special scenes and maybe even a gay ghetto - an urban
neighbourhood which 'contains gay institutions in number, a
conspicuous and locally dominated gay subculture that is socially
isolated from the larger community, and a residential population
that is substantially gay' (Levine, 1979, p.364).
    Since the early 1970s, especially, a new lifestyle option has
also evolved for many gays: that of working in and for gay
organizations. It is a much more feasible option in America,
where every large city has spawned its own gay community
centre and where the 'Gay Yellow Pages' lists every organization
in the land. But even in England, there is enough happening
for gay men to make a strong central commitment to gay causes:
working for the rights of other gays, through the Campaign for
Homosexual Equality; for the homosexual in the church, through
the Gay Christian Movement; for the commercial organization of

the gay community, through gay magazines, gay 'dating-services', gay products; for political change, through groups like Gay Left; for support and counselling, through groups like Gay Switchboard, Friend and Icebreakers; and for 'entertainment', through groups like Gay Sweatshop. Most of these organizations are significantly 'middle class' and have frequently attracted more youthful gays who have come out since the early 1970s.

Relationships Many diverse kinds of relationships and friend-ships are open to homosexual men, but probably the one which most men seek, many men find and relatively few sustain is that of the couple - a fairly permanent relationship between two men based upon a social, emotional and sexual foundation.[10] Most gay men at some point in their lives seem to seek such a relationship, and it is easy to see why. Brought up in a culture which high-lights the value and naturalness of 'coupling' - through the family of origin, through education, through religion, through the media - it is a difficult task for any individual to estrange himself from such concerns. A partner is a necessity - even if that means a heterosexual partner and all the later attendant problems of such 'mixed' marriages (Ross, 1971). Although it can be very difficult to find such a partner in the 'gay world' - partly because its institutions cater for people who have little in common but their gayness, partly because bars often establish expectations of 'casualness' in sexual relationships and partly because of continuing worrying doubts experienced by homosexual men because of social hostility - it is nevertheless the case that most 'out' gay men nowadays[11] seem to pass through a stable relationship for two or three years. Only a minority, however, seem to reach silver or diamond anniversaries. We cannot, of course, be sure of this - since gay couples largely constitute the unresearched and 'hidden segment' of the gay world: those who establish long-term relationships may simply vanish from sight into their havens of happiness (Tuller, 1978).
   The reasons for short-lived relationships are at least two-fold. On the most positive front, homosexual men can find after their first affair that the expectations of coupledom given to them by the 'straight world' are opposed to their personal growth and maturity: expectations of coupledom grounded upon male and female roles, procreation and childrearing in the straight world simply do not have the same relevance in the gay world. Couples are seen as restricting relationships, and the gay world is seen as providing the possibility of more variable patterns of stable friendships. What may be right for 'straights' is decidedly damaging to gays. On the more negative front, however, homosexual men who want their couple relationship to work may find themselves thwarted on all sides: not only are there most of the usual difficulties which any heterosexual couple faces - incompatibilities, misunderstandings, jealousies, practical housekeeping worries, sex, etc. - there are also many problems

which arise because of the lack of external validation given to their relationship. Social hostility to homosexual men, for example, may mean the relationship has to be hidden from family and workmates; it may mean difficulties in obtaining a joint mortgage, writing a mutual will or even visiting a sick partner in hospital; it may mean a general lack of support from others at times when the relationship is under severe stress. As hostility decreases, so these kinds of problems diminish - nevertheless they have played a paramount role in the past.

Despite such cautions, there is no doubt that large numbers of homosexual men do establish permanent relationships and more knowledge is needed of such relationships, comparable at least to that accumulated by marriage guidance counsellors for heterosexual couples. For instance, on the surface it appears that male gay couples have more egalitarian relationships than heterosexual couples - rigid role playing seems to be comparatively rare and that these are much more likely to allow, accept and even encourage non-monogamous experiences. Even more apparent is the fact that male homosexual couples do not usually have children to cement and give a focus to the relationship - although here there are signs of change as both 'gay fathers' and 'gay fostering' become possibilities (Miller, 1979). Such differences notwithstanding, however, the counsellor would probably be best served at present to presume that there are more similarities then differences between homosexual and heterosexual couples (Tripp, 1976).

Sexual experience A final, but highly significant, dimension out of which a gay lifestyle is assembled concerns sex. Whilst it is quite wrong to screen all understanding of homosexuality through sex, and to finally view all homosexuals as people obsessed with sex, it is equally wrong to minimize it. The cornerstone of homosexual experience has to be - by definition - an emotio-erotic relationship with one's own sex; and any gay lifestyle that denies (or minimizes) this must lead to hypocrisy or bad faith.

In the heterosexual world there are a number of avenues of sexual possibility, but the central route - of marriage - is clearly signposted. The times, of course, are changing, and increasingly extramarital sex - wife-swapping, serial monogamy, singles bars - are becoming acceptable: but marriage rolls on as the master plan. Likewise, in heterosexual relationships, coital sex is likely to remain the supreme goal - oral sex, masturbation and 'variations', while widely practised, usually take a subordinate role to the art of coitus: the final and most glorious act. In the gay world, neither of these seeming absolutes - marriage and coitus - hold. Alternatives have to be worked at.

The newcomer to the gay life does not know quite what gay sex is about; he will have his fantasies, it is true, but it is not uncommon for him to ponder aloud to the counsellor: 'Well, what

do gay men actually do?' Nobody tumbles out of the womb knowing about the arts of sexual conduct, and gay sex - like everything else - has to be learnt. The variety of gay sexual
practices is enormous; the newcomer will have to be exposed to
this range - through talk, reading or practice - until he is in
a position to know what forms of sexuality are preferred.
Ironically, for some it may be that sexual practices offer little -
it is the simple physical comfort of closeness to another man
that appeals. For others, though, there is a well-organized
network of diverse sex available through what Lee (1978,
pp.8-9) calls a 'gay ecosystem'; a system which

> supplies sex to the people involved, at any hour of the day
> or night, every day of the year. The supply is convenient
> and well organised. It is usually inexpensive. It is almost
> inexhaustible. It comes in an amazing variety of options. It
> is available to all seekers, the young and old, the beautiful
> and ugly, though naturally not in equal quantity or amount.
> The supply is generally free from serious risks to health
> and safety, provided that sensible precautions are taken.

Indeed, Lee goes so far as to suggest that this gay ecosystem
is 'better organized in the matter of getting sex' than the
heterosexual world, and that 'heterosexuals could learn from
this gay wisdom' (Lee, 1978, p.13). Lee's study is a detailed
catalogue of those parts of the gay world where sex is readily
available; certain streets, bars, baths, tearooms, discos,
beaches, classified ads and so on. Anybody, with enough
learnt self confidence and awareness of the rules of the game,
can find sex here.

Lee is not saying that all homosexual men want instant sex;
nor is he saying that it is the only thing that matters in their
lives. What he is saying is that for those men who do seek
casual sex, it is readily available. It is not without pitfalls,
but it is available.

IN CONCLUSION: THE PARADOX OF CATEGORIZATION

In this Chapter I have sketched three dimensions - the
ontological, the historical and the life cycle - involved in men
'going gay', of transforming marginal homosexual experiences
into full-blown gay identities and lifestyles. Especially in the
last two sections I hope to have provided 'non-gay' practitioners
with some very basic materials about gay development that may
enhance their practice. At base, the message is a very simple
one: since the wider culture - with its attendant 'heterosexual
assumption' and 'sexual stigma' - is the key creator of problems
for the homosexual experience, the main resolution lies with
reducing the impact of this stigmatizing culture by facilitating
access to the more supportive gay culture, with its gay role
models as sources for positive identities.

But life, of course, is not that easy, and problems not that

simply resolved; every 'answer' brings its own problems. To
facilitate access to a positive gay identity or a positive gay
lifestyle is potentially to provide security and the path to
psychological well being (Weinberg and Williams, 1974; Bell and
Weinberg, 1978); but it could also be a path which forecloses
diverse possibilities and openness. In the main, gay counselling
organizations would not see this as a dilemma. Their task is to
create conditions of positive support and thereby to usher their
client into a positive gay role - the role most conducive to
both personal happiness and political change. For them, the
entire process of 'going gay' that I have described is necessary
to counterbalance the tyranny of the dominant culture in
socializing the child to heterosexuality in its earlier years.
Nobody complains about the way in which such heterosexual
socialization forecloses possibilities and openness - it is presumed, part indeed of the heterosexual assumption. To worry
about such foreclosures of gay identity, therefore, is to lend
support to the ultimate superiority of heterosexuality.

I have much political sympathy with this view and counsellors
who worry about labelling somebody too quickly as homosexual
should be firmly reminded of the heterosexual assumption which
this harbours. Yet the 'paradox of categorization' does pose
very real practical problems.

On the one hand, labels are useful devices - they give order
to chaos, structure to openness, security to confusion. Knowing that one is gay is much more comforting than living with
the precariousness of confused sexual identities. On the other
hand, labels are destructive devices - they restrict where
other choices are possible, they control and limit possible
variety, they narrow human experimentation. In the short run,
labels are comforting; in the long run, they are destructive.

All this leads one back to the issue of ontology. The two views
that I raised earlier will take different stands on this dilemma.
For the essentialist the label homosexual identifies a real
essence, while for the constructionist the label is socially
created, socially bestowed and socially maintained. On the surface, therefore, it would seem that essentialists would accept
people labelled as homosexual, while constructionists would be
critical of labelling. But ironically this is not strictly true.

In the main, essentialists are clinicians who, whilst recognizing that homosexuality is an essence, would like to change
the homosexual back into a heterosexual: essentialism totters
towards absolutism, and in this case the absolutism is that of
heterosexuality. Likewise, constructionists are sociologists,
who - whilst recognizing that homosexuality is a historical
invention, agree that gay self-definitions have played a very
positive role: constructionism totters towards relativism, and
an openness to diversity in human experiences. Labels become
half-way houses towards further change and diversity: whilst
the label is needed now, it will ultimately be eliminated.

The task of practitioners is not an easy one: to label too soon may prematurely close possibilities, and to label too late may add to the weight of suffering. The uniting theme of theory and practice must be a constant sensitivity to the contradictions and paradoxes common to both.

NOTES

1. The classic source of 'incidence' figures is still Kinsey et al. (1948), with his contrast between a third of the male population who have orgasms with the same sex at some point in their life and the 4 per cent who become 'permanently' gay. I suspect that nearly all research has gravitated to the 4 per cent, and we know very little about the remaining 30 per cent!

2. These terms are also used by Morin (1977) and Ponse (1978). Ponse also suggests that once inside the gay world a new assumption becomes operative: the homosexual assumption – whereby all are presumed to be gay unless shown to be otherwise.

3. For a helpful review of this whole literature, see Kimmel (1980) and the studies mentioned therein. My quote comes from the popular study by Sheehy (1976). Most of this work is American – but for an English equivalent see Nicholson (1980).

4. The main exception to this is the case history of Poe to be found in Vaillant (1977) – a San Franciscan gay who appears at the end of this longitudinal study, and in a telling chapter challenges the author's heterosexual assumptions of development. Kimmel also includes a gay – George aged twenty-seven – as the first case history in the revised (1980) edition of his book.

5. In the 1950s Erikson published his celebrated discussion of the 'eight stages of man', tentatively outlining his view of life as a 'ground plan', out of which 'the parts arise, each having its time of special ascendancy, until all parts have arisen to form a functioning whole' (Erikson, 1968, p.92). These eight stages are well known, leading from the initial problems of trust and mistrust in the first few months of life to the problems of integrity and despair in later life. Erikson's work was deeply influential – in part because it simply lacked any rivals! – but at the same time it raised many problems. Formally, the stages posited were deemed necessary, universal and linear; and although Erikson is rightly credited with both historical and cultural interests, he ultimately presents a model which reduces such interests to timeless human need. Likewise, substantively, while acknowledging the variations across culture, he tacitly sides with specific features of his own culture and prejudice. For discussions of Erikson's work, see especially Roazen (1978), and for a feminist critique Millett (1970).

6. See Dank's (1971) discussion for a consideration of the different contexts of coming out.
7. A preliminary guide to issues to be considered in coming out may be found in Berzon (1979, pp.88-100). On coming out to the family, see especially Silverstein (1977) and Fairchild (1979).
8. These generalizations here and throughout are culled from American studies like Spada (1979) and Jay and Young (1979).
9. For a useful discussion on the optimum size of a town to generate gay bars, see the discussion in Harry and DeVall (1978).
10. On the diverse kinds of relationships, see Sonenschein's (1968) typology. In the Spada (1979, p.200) sample, only eleven (4 per cent) said they would not like to have a lover; 88 per cent said that they wanted one. In an English survey of 2,000 male homosexuals, about a quarter were unsure of whether they wanted such a relationship and 10 per cent were quite sure that they didn't (Plummer, 1978, p.182). In general, samples of gays in the community suggest that between 40 and 60 per cent of gay men are currently in such relationships (Plummer, 1978, p.176; Spada, 1979, p.332; Jay and Young, 1979, p.339). Bell and Weinberg (1978, p.86) remark of their sample that 'Virtually all of the male respondents had been involved in at least one ... "relatively steady relationship" with another man during the course of their lives.' For definition of couples and a discussion of the possible infrequency of such relationships, see Plummer (1978). A good general account is Tripp (1976).
11. I discuss this much more fully in Plummer (1978). Note too the work of the Gay Christian Movement in trying to establish religious validation for gay marriage ceremonies. See GCM (1980).

5 LESBIAN IDENTITIES

Diane Richardson

INTRODUCTION

The process whereby a person develops and maintains an identification as homosexual has received very little attention in the literature. This is hardly surprising, however, given the kind of theoretical assumptions that have been prevalent in conceptualizations about homosexuality. Three major influences can be identified as being especially important in this respect.

1 The view of homosexuality as a permanent characteristic, the result of particular etiological factors occurring relatively early on in life.
2 The definition of homosexuality largely in terms of sexual orientation and sexual acts, coupled with the failure to distinguish between same-sex acts and an identification as homosexual. This has fostered a unidimensional view of homosexuals as sexual creatures, in which a homogeneity of motivating influences and a certain personality type have been assumed.
3 The predominance of personal pathological models in which homosexuality is viewed as a 'condition' of the individual.

In this way, lesbianism has been seen primarily as a permanent and inherent quality of the individual. The emphasis, therefore, has been upon the development of such a state of being, of the homosexual 'condition', rather than on the development of a lesbian identity per se. However, as Plummer (1975, p.135) points out:
> One cannot see the individual 'automatically' and 'intrinsically' 'knowing' that he is a homosexual - as the simple interpretation of prior elements. Rather, we must analyse the social situations and interaction styles that lead to an individual building up a particular series of sexual meanings, a particular sexual identity.

I would further add that we must also consider how a homosexual identity is maintained, the assumed fixity of sexual orientation having resulted in a lack of attention to this question.

In this Chapter it will be argued, then, that it is both inadequate and highly oversimplified to consider identification as a lesbian as an inherent quality of the individual. Rather we need to view lesbian identities as socially constructed and maintained via the process of social interaction. In this way,

the process whereby a woman identifies as lesbian or not, and
(if she does) the meaning and significance such an identification
will have for her, will be influenced by the wider social meanings ascribed to lesbianism that she encounters, as well as the
specific responses of significant others to this information.

LESBIAN IMAGES

The imagery associated with lesbianism prevalent in both
scientific and popular accounts of homosexuality affects homosexual women both by informing public and professional opinion,
thus influencing how lesbians are perceived and treated within
society, and also by directly influencing how lesbians see themselves. Indeed, whether the individual introjects or rejects such
images she must still take them into account in the individual
meaning she ascribes to her identification as lesbian.

Ironically the lack of such imagery, due to the fact that
lesbians have been 'hidden from history', has been just as
significant in both these respects. Certainly, in contrast with
male homosexuality, lesbianism has been largely ignored by
the church, the law, the media and the scientific literature.
Whilst this social invisibility may have made easier the process
of publically passing as heterosexual whilst privately identifying as homosexual, the lack of available role models with which
to identify may, on the other hand, have consolidated feelings
of uniqueness and isolation for many lesbians. Interestingly,
similar feelings may also be elicited as a response to the imagery
of lesbianism which does exist, inasmuch as the individual may
feel unable to see any common identification between herself and
such stereotypes.

How then is the lesbian seen within society? Four major
commonalities can be recognized in the way that lesbianism has
been portrayed, at the level both of theoretical analysis and
of fictional accounts and representation within the media.

The lesbian as a 'pseudo-male'
It is generally assumed that gender identity, gender-role orientation, sexual object choice and sexual identity have a necessary
and covarying relationship with each other. Ponse (1978) has
termed this the 'principle of consistency', whereby, 'once one
of the above elements is given, the rest are presumed to follow
or co-occur' (Ponse, 1978, p.27). In keeping with this principle,
a 'deviation' in sexual object choice and sexual identity will
typically lead to assumptions about gender-role orientation and
gender identity. On this basis, then, a woman who identifies
as a lesbian is likely to be construed as masculine and as 'wanting to be like a man'. Such a view is echoed in the sterotype
of the butch lesbian, or dyke, as someone with close cropped
hair, mannish in manner and dress, with traditionally defined
masculine interests.

This portrayal of the lesbian has also been influential in the way in which sexual acts between women have been interpreted as a mimicry of heterosexual intercourse. Irrespective of the fact that the majority of lesbians do not experience themselves as suffering from penile deprivation, it is common mythology that lovemaking between women usually involves the use of penile substitutes such as dildos. In addition, lesbians have been described as suffering from feelings of 'virile inferiority' and wishing for a penis of their own.

These kind of stereotypic beliefs and assumptions about lesbians must be set in the context of the relative positions of men and women within society. This is reflected in a phallocratic view of sexuality, whereby primacy is placed on the phallus and the act of penetration. Lesbian sexuality has been interpreted within such a framework. Certainly to acknowledge that the majority of lesbians engage in mutuality in lovemaking rather than role playing, in which penetration may be of little or no importance, would be far more threatening to society's view of male and female sexuality. It is interesting to note in this respect, that whilst the downfall of the 'myth of the vaginal orgasm' in the 1960s severely shook the assumption that sexual satisfaction in women depended on a penis or penile substitute, it did not seriously challenge the equally prevalent myth of the 'dildo wielding dyke'.

To interpret the lesbian as a pseudo-male is to not only defuse the potential threat to the structure of society which lesbianism poses, but also to underline the inauthenticity, the invalidity of her choice as a woman to relate sexually and emotionally to other women.

De Beauvoir (1953, p.428) comments on this when she says of women:

Whenever she behaves as a human being, she is declared to be identifying herself with the male. Her activities in sports, politics, and intellectual matters, her sexual desire for other women, are all interpreted as a 'masculine protest'; the common refusal to take account of the values towards which she aims, or transcends herself, evidently leads to the conclusion that she is, as subject, making an inauthentic choice.

It is the portrayal of the lesbian as pseudo-male which has been the most potent influence in society's image of lesbianism. Bearing this in mind, however, the notion of the traditionally feminine or 'femme' lesbian has not been totally overlooked. Indeed the stereotype of the masculine lesbian demands there be a partner who will adopt the 'femme' role. In this way lesbian relationships, as well as lesbian sexuality, have been interpreted in terms of traditional assumptions about heterosexual relationships. Thus whilst the image of a feminine lesbian is potentially much more threatening than that of the masculine lesbian, it is contained by the assumption that such women are attracted to, and form relationships with, masculine women. The concept of two feminine or, for that matter, two masculine lesbians forming such a relationship would, on the other hand, be an extremely powerful threat to the way in which lesbians have been seen, and to the traditional view of heterosexual relationships upon which such stereotypes have been based.

Lesbianism as a sorry state to be in
With very few exceptions, the images of lesbians and lesbianism presented in the media, in literary accounts and in theoretical explanations of homosexuality are negativistic.

In novels, for instance, lesbians are usually portrayed as sick and unhappy individuals, engaged in relationships that are doomed to failure. In the final analysis such characters usually follow one of two courses of action. They either come to a tragic end as lesbians, often by committing suicide, or alternatively they are 'saved', usually by falling in love with a man and getting married. It is only with the rise of the women's and gay movements that literary treatments of lesbianism have begun to include descriptions of lesbian relationships as intrinsically fulfilling and positively preferable to heterosexual relationships. Such positive characterizations, however, are few and far between in comparison with the plethora of negative accounts of lesbianism that are available. It is perhaps not so surprising therefore to find that many lesbians have introjected such images and have a negative view of themselves.

This relative difference is all the more significant when such negative images are voiced by 'informed' and powerful institutions in society, for instance, the law, the church and 'scientific' opinion. Even though lesbians have tended to be beneath, rather than outside, the consideration of the law and the church, secular and legal attitudes towards homosexuality in general have been influential in the view of lesbianism as sinful and immoral. This position was undermined to some extent by explanations of homosexuality in terms of biological and/or psychological abnormalities (see Chapter 1), whereby, rather than being seen as a sin, lesbianism was considered to be a sickness: a pathological 'condition'. In addition, most theoretical explanations of homosexuality, although differing in the emphasis placed on particular etiological factors, have tended to assume a naturalness about a heterosexual orientation and identity, and in so doing have described homosexuality as 'atypical', 'abnormal' or as an 'immature' form of development. Such views must be set not only against notions of the 'naturalness' of heterosexuality, but also against the primacy, particularly for women, placed on marriage and the nuclear family.

The following quote from 'Sexual Deviation' by Anthony Storr (1964, pp. 79–80), first published in 1964 and still widely read, exemplifies this:

lesbians who protest that, for them, this kind of relationship is better than any possible intimacy with a man do not know what they are really missing. There is no doubt that for women who, for whatever reason, have been unable to get

married, a homosexual partnership may be a happier way
of life than a frustrated loneliness, but this is not to say
that it can ever be fully satisfying.
It is just such assumptions which are being challenged by an
increasing number of lesbians, who in coming out as openly gay
are asserting and affirming the view of homosexuality as a
positive preference for same-sex relationships rather than as a
negative outcome due to an inability to form relationships with
men.
    An attempt has been made to defuse the challenge to tradi-
tional assumptions about homosexuality which this poses by
incorporating it within the negativistic framework already outlined. For instance, by describing being open about one's
homosexuality as psychopathological: 'Most lesbian women are
content to keep their homosexual inclinations hidden from
general view and it is only the most psychopathic among these
who make a show of their abnormality' (Munro and McCulloch,
1969, p.157). Similarly, the rejection of the negative imagery
associated with lesbianism and the assertion of the positive
aspects of lesbian relationships and lifestyles may be described
as a 'defense mechanism against the emptiness, the coldness and
the futility of their lives' (Romm, 1965, p.291).

Lesbian sexuality
Gagnon and Simon (1967) point out that the sexual aspect of
most social roles is usually ignored, even in those cases where
an assumption of sexual activity can normally be safely made
(e.g. the roles of husband and wife). However, where sexual
activity is identified with a particular role they suggest that
rather than being ignored, the sexual component tends to be
emphasized and exaggerated. Certainly this would seem to be
the case with lesbianism, where the sexual aspects of such an
identity and social role have tended to dominate the way in
which lesbians have been perceived. Other, non-sexual, aspects
of such an identification and lifestyle have received relatively
little or no attention. In this sense, then, lesbians are 'doubly
deviant': not only are they seen as having adopted a 'deviant'
sexual object choice, but in contrast to the traditional view of
female sexuality they are seen as sexually active and independent of men. An attempt to contain the potential threat lesbian
sexuality poses to the view of women as passive sexual objects
for men has been to place lesbian acts within a pornographic
framework. In this way sexual acts between women have been
interpreted as erotic stimuli for others.
    The image of lesbians as primarily sexual beings underlies
yet another important element of the general mythology surrounding lesbianism, that of the morally dangerous person. This
aspect of the lesbian stereotype is made particularly apparent
in the kind of concerns expressed about the relationships lesbians have with children, for instance in the case of the employment of lesbians who work with children, or alternatively of

children who are living in a lesbian household. Such concerns
are compounded by the tendency to confuse homosexuality and
paedophilia, as well as the prevalence of seduction and contagion
theories of homosexuality (see pp.27-8).

In direct contrast to the view of lesbians as 'compulsively
preoccupied with sexuality in general and sexual practices in
particular' (Wilbur, 1965, pp.278-9) is the emphasis on the
emotional rather than the sexual aspects of lesbian relationships.
Storr (1964, p.76), for instance, states that

> the homosexual woman is generally looking for a mother as
> well as for a sexual partner: and, in many instances, the
> mutual dependence of the couple upon each other is more
> important than the sexual satisfaction which each may obtain
> from the other.

This view of homosexual relationships between women as
re-enactments of the mother-child relationship has been heavily
coloured by psychoanalytic theories of female homosexuality
(Socarides, 1963). Also influential in this desexualization of
lesbian relationships is the little notice that is taken of female
sexuality in general other than where women are seen as sexual
objects for men.

Lesbianism as a permanent condition
Central to scientific and popular explanations of homosexuality,
as well as the attitude of the church and the law, has been the
belief that sexual identity is a permanent characteristic which
is assumed to remain stable over the lifespan, or at least after
the period of adolescence and early adulthood. A lesbian identity
in this sense then is seen as an immutable quality of the self;
as an essence.

Such a view has been extremely important in the way that
homosexuals have been perceived and treated by society at large.
Campaigners for social reform, for example, have often underlined the permanency of the homosexual 'condition' in arguing
for an end to legal and social discrimination of homosexuals. An
appeal for social justice on the basis of 'they can't help it and
are incapable of change'. In addition the belief in the permanency
of sexual identity has reinforced the polarization of lesbian and
heterosexual identities, and their associated meanings.

We should note here, however, the emergence of theories
which view sexual identity as socially constructed and maintained,
and thus open to the possibility of change. Such models raise
rather different questions about social acceptability. It is one
thing to accept someone as homosexual on the basis that they
are 'incapable of changing', and quite another to accept them as
homosexual if heterosexuality is seen as a possibility. In addition, to question the assumption that sexual identity is a fixed
entity, stable throughout one's life, is to acknowledge that a
person may identify as homosexual at any stage of the life
cycle (though we should note here that a major redefinition of
self may become increasingly more difficult with age).

It is also important to recognize that the predominance of a belief in the essentiality of a lesbian identity has been significant not merely at the level of how mainstream society has perceived and reacted towards lesbianism, but also in the meanings ascribed to such an identification by lesbians themselves. Many homosexual women do define lesbianism as an immutable characteristic of their personality, and it is a core-construct of their self identity. Even where this is contra-indicated by a previous identification as heterosexual, and a prior absence of feelings of attraction to the same sex, the individual may selectively reinterpret the past in keeping with her present identification as homosexual, and therefore the notion of essentiality is preserved. For example, this process of reconstruction may take the form that she was 'really gay all along' and that it was just a case of her 'real self' having been suppressed up until the time she identified as a lesbian.

I have so far focused on the kinds of assumptions about lesbianism which are prevalent in society, pointing out that such imagery will be significant in the meanings lesbians themselves ascribe to their sexual identity. The introjection of such beliefs may result in a variety of negative responses to their identification as lesbian. These may include feelings of alienation, guilt, loneliness and isolation, a lack of self worth and self esteem, worries, for some women, about whether they are 'unfeminine' or not and a sense of uniqueness. The latter may also, of course, be experienced as a positive aspect of such an identity.

On the other hand the individual may reject, rather than introject, the beliefs and values commonly associated with lesbianism; although this would seem to be very much dependent on the availability of alternative role models which affirm the validity of a lesbian identity and lifestyle. This is unlikely to happen whilst the individual's identification remains secret and privatized. Indeed, it is this group who are likely to be most 'at risk' of introjecting society's negative view of homosexuality.

The person who chooses to disclose that she is a lesbian, however, immediately widens the source of social meanings of lesbianism available to her, even if, as is usually the case, she initially tells only a few highly selected individuals. Bearing in mind that a lesbian identity is not a static entity but an ongoing process, this may in turn result in a change in the meaning and significance such an identification holds for her. More specifically it is likely to be the reactions she encounters from significant others, as well as her experience of the homosexual subculture, which will be most important in this respect.

COMING OUT

The expression 'coming out' will be used here to refer not, as has sometimes been implied in the literature, to a single event (e.g. Hooker, 1967) but to an ongoing developmental process.

This process begins with a person questioning whether or not they are heterosexual and/or with the ascription of the label homosexual to themselves. The process of the formation of a lesbian identity may both begin and end at this point. That is, the individual may see their attraction to the same sex as an entirely privatized aspect of their self image.

For the majority, however, the next step will be to inform particular individuals of their identification as lesbian, e.g. their best friend or parents, or someone at the other end of a telephone self-help service. The decision of who to tell will of course be dependent on the perceived costs and benefits involved in such a disclosure for each individual, as well as the knowledge of homosexual self-help organizations. In each case the response the individual encounters will modify the developmental path that the process of identity formation is likely to take.

Consider, for instance, a young woman still living at home who decides to tell her parents that she is a lesbian. They respond by suggesting she see a psychiatrist. Contrast this with a similar case where the woman contacts a homosexual organization or self-help group for advice. They respond in an accepting and friendly manner, and act as a liaison in her introduction to the homosexual world. The former response reinforces the negative image of homosexuality as a sickness, which the individual is already likely to have encountered. The latter response, however, whilst acknowledging the problems a person may have in coming out as openly homosexual, is both supportive and accepting of her identity as a lesbian.

Apart from the influence the different meanings of lesbianism implicit in these two responses may have on the meaning the individual imputes to her identification as lesbian, we must also note the repercussions of disclosure in each case. They too will have an influence on the development of that identity. Particularly important in this respect is whether entry into the homosexual subculture is prevented, hindered or facilitated.

IDENTITY AND THE LESBIAN SUBCULTURE

The separation of the homosexual and heterosexual worlds has resulted in the development of a complex and diverse homosexual subculture which has developed its own meanings of lesbianism and lesbian identities. These have not, however, developed independently of the way in which lesbians have been perceived and treated by mainstream society. Indeed it must be pointed out that whilst there are important discontinuities in the meanings ascribed to lesbianism in the two worlds, certain continuities are manifestly apparent. For instance there exists in the homosexual world as well as in 'straight' society a strong belief in the essentiality of identity and the expectation of a consistency between sexual object choice and sexual identity. In the homosexual world, therefore, a woman who states that she finds

other women sexually attractive, and/or who engages in homosexual relationships, will be expected to adopt a lesbian identity.
This expectation is compounded by the 'homosexual assumption',
whereby within a homosexual context a person will be ascribed
the label homosexual unless they give off cues to the contrary
(e.g. by continually remaining in the exclusive and close
company of males rather than females in homosexual settings).

On initially encountering the lesbian world, therefore, the
individual is likely to encounter validation of her emerging
lesbian identity. However, in the majority of cases in order for
her to be accepted within this subculture she must continue to
maintain such an identity. In other words the social norms of
the homosexual world serve to both affirm and confirm an
individual's identification as lesbian.

Apart from its role in the process of identity formation and
maintenance, the homosexual subculture as a source of social
meanings of lesbianism is also influential in its effect on the
content of lesbian identities.

Important in this respect is the diversity of role models which
the individual encounters on entering the lesbian world, in
stark contrast to the stereotypic characterization of lesbians as
either 'butch' or 'femme' which she is likely to have previously
heard of or read about. Indeed, in actuality it is only a minority
who do conform to these roles.

The availability of role models with which the individual feels
able to identify is particularly important at the initial stages of
the development of a lesbian identity. The scarcity of available
role models may lead to the experience of a lack of congruence
between what the individual 'knows' about lesbians and the
kind of person she feels herself to be. This conflict may occur
not only outside of but within the homosexual subculture if the
individual feels she has little in common with the other lesbians
she meets. The chances of this happening are increased by the
fact that the homosexual world tends to be male dominated. This
can mean that lesbians may have to face hostility and ostracism
from homosexual clubs, bars or organizations as a result of
male sexism. Coupled with the lack of alternative social settings
which cater specifically for homosexual women, at least in
Britain, this means that there are likely to be far fewer lesbians
within the homosexual subculture than there are homosexual
men. In addition it should not be forgotten that being homosexual is in any case a low common denominator, sexual identity
being only one aspect of a person's self identity.

The significance of a lesbian identity and its relationship
to other dimensions of a person's identity and lifestyle will, of
course, vary from individual to individual, depending on the
particular meaning ascribed to such an identification in each
case. Bearing in mind such individual differences, we can also
observe some important commonalities, or group identities,
within the lesbian world.

Ettorre (1980, p.98) distinguishes two main 'types' of

lesbians; the 'sick, but not sorry', and the 'sorry, but not sick'. The former group, she suggests, view
their lesbianism as an 'entity' or 'object of human nature.' Believing that 'it' is a purely sexual 'thing', these lesbians manifest the 'sick, but not sorry' syndrome. Having emerged from the isolation of the past, they, in varying degrees, placidly accept traditional images of lesbians as sick, gene- tically inferior, hormonally imbalanced, and so on. As a result, sick but not sorry types have a tendency to feel that they are 'born lesbians'.
Although this group are described as more or less accepting of traditional models of homosexuality, this does not include acceptance of the stigmatization of lesbianism within society. The need for social change in this direction was characterized as a desire for an alteration in attitudes towards homosexuality leading to social tolerance.
The 'sorry but not sick' group, on the other hand, are described as rejecting of society's stereotypes of lesbianism, in particular the notion of homosexuality as personal pathology. Lesbianism is seen instead as a relative choice, influenced by a variety of factors other than sexual attraction. In taking into account social, emotional and political reasons for such an identification, lesbianism becomes not so much a matter of a privatized aspect of the individual's personality but part of her view of society as a whole. Lesbianism in this sense is a way of life rather than merely a sexual preference. This view is re- flected in the characterization of the demands for social change as an attack on the existing social structure, in particular the position of women within society.
It is important to recognize here that same-sex sexual acts are just one criterion for imparting a homosexual identity to oneself and/or others, and that in many cases engaging in homosexual acts does not necessarily lead to the adoption of a homosexual identity. In such instances the individual ascribes a meaning to her homosexual relationships which is compatible with the maintenance of her identity as heterosexual or bisexual. For instance she may rationalize such experiences by saying, 'I must have been drunk at the time,' or that 'This is just a stage I am going through.' Alternatively, a person may describe her relationship with a person of the same sex as a unique and individualized one: 'I fell in love with this particular person who just happens to be a woman.' We should, of course, note here that not to adopt an identity as lesbian whilst continuing to engage in lesbian acts and/or relationships will, for each individual, depend on a variety of interacting factors. These may include the sexual identity of their partner(s), the way they are viewed by significant others, their involvement with the homosexual subculture and their sexual and social exper- iences with both men and women.
A lesbian identification may, on the other hand, precede lesbian acts. In such instances the motivating influence for the

adoption of such an identity may not be sexual at all, e.g. the
need for validation and acceptance within the homosexual subculture.

The meanings attached to lesbianism and a lesbian identity by
the group with which the individual mixes will be influential
not only in the development of her identity, but also in its
maintenance. In other words the meaning of a lesbian identity
will, for each individual, affect the strength with which it is
held. In this respect lesbians who believe that they are 'born
like it', and those who identify as gay for political reasons may
both have a very strong and stable identity as lesbian, although
for entirely different reasons.

We must be careful here in employing the notion of lesbian
'types'. This is particularly so given the tendency in the literature to ignore individual differences in the meaning and
significance of a lesbian identity, and instead to emphasize the
homogeneity of lesbians as a social group.

A study by Ponse (1978) of seventy-five homosexual women
is less open to such criticism than is Ettorre's, in describing
two kinds of lesbian groups, rather than lesbian 'types', which
provide different kinds of support for lesbian identities. These
are termed the 'secretive' and the 'activist', each representing
different concerns with the issue of identity. In secretive
groups the emphasis is upon the maintenance of secrecy about
the lesbian identities of the members, whereas within activist
groups concern is said to be focused on the content or meaning
of a lesbian identity.

In their emphasis on traditional explanations of homosexuality
and their view of lesbianism as a sexual preference rather than
as a lifestyle, secretive groups come close to the 'sick, but not
sorry' types described by Ettorre (1980). Activist groups, on
the other hand, overlap with the 'sorry, but not sick' types,
whereby self determination in identity formation, a rejection of
traditional imagery of lesbians, and lesbianism as a social and
political choice, are emphasized.

The two kinds of groups are also described by Ponse (1980,
p.97) as differing in their ideological justification of lesbianism:

> The ideology of the secretive group emphasizes accommodation
> by gays to a minority status and stresses not disrupting
> relations with the heterosexual world. In contrast, the ideo-
> logy of the activist group rejects the minority status of gays
> by openly challenging the legitimacy of the heterosexual
> order.

In secretive groups, therefore, there is an emphasis on social
conformity and a tendency for individual members to conceal
their identity as lesbian by 'passing' as heterosexual outside of
the homosexual subculture. Activist groups, on the other hand,
tend to view such secrecy as oppressive, and instead have
emphasized the social and political importance of being open
about one's lesbianism.

The rise of the women's movement has, of course, been most

significant in the emergence of a political analysis of lesbianism as a positive choice, which any woman can make, between non-sexist sexual and emotional relationships with women and sexist relationships with men. Not only has it provided ideological bases, but in very real terms it has fostered group support for lesbian identities. The lack of a widespread men's movement at the present time deprives the majority of homosexual men not only of such support networks, but of an ideological 'justific-ation' of their homosexuality, such that their identity as gay men can be seen in terms of a political statement about male and female gender-roles, rather than merely as sexual attraction to men

At the individual level a decision about whether or not to disclose one's lesbian identity will depend on an evaluation of the costs and benefits involved in any given situation. In each case the decision made will influence the process of identity formation and maintenance.

SECRECY VERSUS DISCLOSURE, AND THEIR RELATIONSHIP TO IDENTITY

The majority of lesbians are engaged in a dynamic and continual process of moving between coming out as openly homosexual and passing as heterosexual; depending on their individual con-structions of the particular social situations in which they find themselves. Passing in this sense involves the presentation of a public identity which is incongruous with the individual's sense of personal identity. All lesbians have experience of this, and indeed it is only a minority who achieve personal authen-ticity by publicly identifying as gay to the world at large.

It should be noted, however, that even where the individuals usually construe themselves as being 'out' about their lesbian-ism to the world at large, there may still be circumstances where they choose to 'pass' rather than disclose their gay identity, e.g. in the company of an aged and wealthy grand-mother at Christmas.

In considering the possible effects of secrecy or disclosure on identity formation and maintenance let us first of all examine what is the majority experience: that of being open about one's lesbian identity in only a restricted range of social environments and of passing as heterosexual for the rest of the time.

The management of such a double identity and lifestyle is facilitated by a variety of influences which serve to make dis-covery of a lesbian identity unlikely. These include:

1 The heterosexual assumption: the assumption that outside of a homosexual setting a person is heterosexual unless proved otherwise.
2 The separate and separatist nature of the homosexual and heterosexual worlds.
3 The social invisibility of lesbianism. In this respect it may be

easier for lesbians to pass than homosexual men, given that
it is relatively easier for women to live together or to remain
unmarried without eliciting questions about sexual orientation.
4 The privatization of sexuality, which means that many of our
  interactions with others can be conducted without needing to
  refer to sexual orientation.

In addition to this, lesbians may themselves facilitate the
process of passing by employing various strategies such as an
avoidance of situations where homosexuality may be discussed,
a conscious monitoring of the presentation of self and bodily
image and the invention of a social life in keeping with a heterosexual identity. (For a fuller discussion see Plummer, 1975;
Musgrove, 1977; Ponse, 1978.) However, whilst it may not be
too difficult for a lesbian to pass socially as heterosexual, we
must consider the psychological sequela of such a process.

Interestingly, the public emergence of more and more lesbians
who have openly declared themselves as gay has meant that
attention is focused on the problems of coming out rather than
the psychological strains involved in passing. The latter may
include feelings of self denial, dishonesty and loneliness, a
sense of alienation from both oneself and others, anxiety at the
thought of discovery and an acute sense of self-consciousness
resulting from the continual monitoring of one's public image.
Additionally, the individual may experience a sense of conflict;
between two separate identities and social realities, between
what is felt to be the true and the false self.

The process of passing is likely to both perpetuate and
accentuate such feelings. This is due to the fact that in order
to maintain secrecy about a 'true' identity as a lesbian, the
individual will be engaged in a continual process of categorization of other persons and situations as homosexual and thus
safe, or heterosexual and potentially threatening.

Secrecy, therefore, serves to underline the importance of the
sexual identity of both self and others, thereby increasing both
the significance of, and commitment to, a lesbian identity.

The social and psychological strains of secrecy can also
predispose the individual to disclosure of the secret, in this
case their lesbian identity. The effect this may have on such
an identification will, of course, very much depend on the kind
of responses to disclosure encountered by the individual, and
the meanings she ascribes to these. In this respect the process
of coming out within a homosexual setting is likely to have rather
different implications for sexual identity than would coming out
within a heterosexual milieu. Ponse (1978, p.86), for instance,
states that within the homosexual subculture

Such disclosure not only provides entry and promotes the
informal forms of friendship and sociability available in the
lesbian world; it also allows the discussion and elaboration
of this identity with a validating and positive audience of
others like the self.

Disclosure in heterosexual contexts, on the other hand, may elicit either social acceptance, or rejection and hostility. Ironically this latter response may well be indirectly supportive of a lesbian identity, inasmuch as it serves to increase group solidarity and commitment and the positive assertion of a choice to be gay in the face of oppression.

Coming out in either homosexual or heterosexual contexts, therefore, is likely to be supportive, either directly or indirectly as the case may be, of a lesbian identity; resulting in a strengthening of commitment to such an identification both within the lesbian community and for the individual herself.

CONCLUSION

In this Chapter I have discussed both mainstream society and the homosexual subculture as sources of social meanings of lesbianism which the individual may introject or reject in coming to identify as homosexual. In addition, it has been pointed out that sexual identity is not a static entity whose meaning and significance to the individual remains the same, but rather that it is an ongoing developmental process, which may occur at any point in the life cycle. In this respect the processes of coming out and passing are seen as being of prime significance in the development and maintenance of a lesbian identity.

Part three

PRESENTING PROBLEMS

To introduce this Part we would acknowledge that in the past homosexuality has been seen as a problem, and that homosexuals have consequently been characterized as lonely, miserable, unhappy and neurotic. Furthermore such problems were seen as being located in the individual, rather than as a result of society's attitude towards homosexuality. In this Part we recognize that homosexual women and men may have particular problems associated with their sexual orientation, and have concentrated on the crucial areas where problems are likely to arise.

We have included here consideration of the existence of legal discrimination against homosexuals (Charles Dodd). Such legal discrimination is one factor, along with stereotypic views about both lesbianism and motherhood, in attitudes towards lesbian mothers. This we have discussed separately. The state of the law is also important in helping young homosexuals, where fears of corruption are often manifested. In addition to these legal concerns we have also discussed the social and emotional needs of young people, who are often an isolated group (Rose Robertson). This is also frequently true of elderly homosexual women and men, whose needs are often neglected (Jeffrey Weeks).

The specific problems of isolation we deal with in the sub-section which also looks at the strains that may be involved in leading a 'double life' as a married homosexual. This emphasizes the point that we should be careful of stereotypes which see marriage as an insurance policy against loneliness and/or sexual difference, contrasted with the image of homosexual relationships as transient and unstable. The subsection on sexual and emotional problems reminds us that relationships between members of the same sex, including longlasting coupledom, can involve similar amounts of commitment, problems and reward as do heterosexual relationships. It is only recently, however, that sexual dysfunction has been recognized to be no respecter of sexual orientation, and this is also discussed (Glenys Parry and Ray Lightbown).

A feature of recent years in coping with and redefining the problems of homosexual women and men has been the use of self-help groups. We recognize this, and place such provision alongside the professional facilities which may be available, suggesting a synthesis of the two forms is needed.

6 SELF AND PROFESSIONAL HELP

John Hart

To discuss the merits and possibilities of self help and professional help for homosexuals, we have first to ask quite
simply, 'What problems do homosexuals have?' We can then take
a cool look at the types of help which are (a) required, and
(b) available. It is possible that in this way we can evaluate
not only the available help (and examples of this are detailed
elsewhere in this book), but also what different sorts of help
are effective with particular problems. We will then, hopefully,
be in a position to observe the gaps where need is not at
present met, and to consider how this might be remedied. This
will have moved us on from over-generalized prescriptions such
as, 'S/he requires professional help because of problems of
sexual orientation,' or, 'What s/he wants is a self-help group
to help with social integration.'
   In assessing why and when it is that homosexual people have
needs for social or psychological help outside of their circle of
friends or family, I do not want to separate social needs from
the recognition of political rights. To give an example: the
obvious and ordinary needs of homosexual teenagers for
relationships with their peers will probably not be fully recognized until they have legal equality with heterosexuals. Hence
questions of legal reform, and the development of counselling
and social facilities for young homosexuals cannot be considered
separately. I would also wish to emphasize the importance of
understanding the psychological effect on homosexual people of
being outside (for homosexual men), and beneath (for homosexual women), the law. On questions of legal and social
inequality, it is tempting to assume that campaigning organizations such as the Gay Activists Alliance (GAA), the Campaign
for Homosexual Equality (CHE) or, at a casework level, Gay
Legal Advice (GLAD) are the organizations which should be the
'primary helpers'. This would, however, be to ignore the fact
that we live in a society where the employees of large welfare
bureaucracies do have, and use, discretion whilst working
within a statutory framework. Of course, these workers have
to abide by the laws of our society, but in practice they, like
the police, exercise discretion, especially when dealing with
'victimless crimes'. In 'Gay News' (no.174, 6-19 September
1979), the police were reported to be implying that they would
'turn a blind eye' to 'people's minor misdemeanours' in their
search for information from gay people in a hunt for a man who
had already murdered two gay men. The point I am trying to

make is that discretion can be a powerful aid to the homosexual person legally discriminated against, but it does place her or him in a powerless position vis-à-vis an individual professional case decision.

My own research (Hart, 1979) uncovered examples of probation officers/social workers acting very differently when faced with similar client behaviour. This variation was not necessarily related to the individual needs of, or response to, the client, but rather to the worker's own moral stance, relationship to the agency, and knowledge relating to sexuality. For example: on hearing about a teenage boy having an affair with an older man, one worker might threaten either of the pair with the police, or with parental involvement, whilst another would offer supportive counselling and/or advice about teenage and/or other gay groups, so that both partners were aware of a social network in addition to the important relationship they were enjoying. I know of a lesbian woman with children who during her career as the client of social workers has faced both morally disapproving workers, with traditional ideas about the primacy of the heterosexual married unit in bringing up children, and a black feminist social worker whose attitude was one of advocacy for her client's legal and social needs. In short, we cannot know what these judgments about sexual orientation will be based on, in advance of getting into an individual 'helping' relationship. We might, however, anticipate a negative response. This places the potential client of the professional in a vulnerable position without legal rights or the protection of any ethical code of practice which could offer effective protection from the undisclosed nature of the moral judgments and actions of the worker. We may conclude that professionals, operating within and sometimes outside legal prescriptions related to sexual behaviour, vitally effect the personal wellbeing of everyone whose sexuality is not 100 per cent heterosexual – for a detailed discussion of this see 'The Law and Sexuality' (Cohen et al., 1978).

We can now perhaps see that any consideration of personal problems is here intimately bound up with a political struggle, and in this area of our concern it is the legal framework which has to be one focus for the helping person. The attitude of social workers, judges and parliament in, for example, lesbian custody cases, and on the age of consent for male homosexuals, is vital in creating a living environment which is conducive, or not, to the homosexual person's self image, available lifestyle and emotional health. The effects are not just felt by homosexual people, but by their children, parents, other relatives and friends. The organizations mentioned so far are offering self help for legal/political rights on either a national campaigning level or in individual case situations. I have also implied that the way professional helpers in welfare organizations and police departments interpret and use their discretion is also to be considered as contributing to how homosexual people can live

integrated lives in our present society. It is something to which
organizations like the British Association of Social Workers
(BASW) and the Royal College of Psychiatrists (like their
American counterpart) could turn their attention. The fact that
professional helpers are not always positive in their approach
to gay lifestyle problems is something we shall return to later
in this Chapter, and elsewhere in this book.

To divide self-help groups (or even professionals) in the
arena of sexual politics as either (a) seeking to achieve the
social integration of their members/clients, or (b) seeking to
change the society from which they are differentiated, is I
believe, a naive enterprise. Clearly, both aims are attempted
during the lifespan of any of these groups or professional
organizations.

Civil rights advocacy is not the total life story of a minority
or oppressed group. Prejudicial attitudes affecting individuals
in a society are slow to change, and the results of these
discriminations are often internalized by the person who is
stigmatized. If we consider the psychosocial needs of such
individuals, we see that the development of a positive self image
requires that they meet with others who can help them achieve
a different analysis of their sexual orientation. As Powell (1975)
writes: 'In place of groups whose ideas, ideals, and modes of
conduct support the problematic condition, the objective is to
substitute a group frame of reference that will support a more
constructive resolution of the problem.' Such an approach is
potentially an adult counter-socialization and cannot be provided
solely in a one to one therapeutic relationship. At best we are
referring to self help in a total caring community, and 'in the
meantime' we are making do with self-help groups which probably meet once a week. The needs to be met may be characterized as a re-ordering of the individual's personal constructs
- that is in the way s/he see her or himself as a homosexual
person in this society. This process is often described as
'coming out'.

Once this process begins, the individual can find her or
himself with more and more time available, having been released
from previous (often exhausting) ways of socially organizing
a 'double' life. The opportunities for enjoying an alternative
lifestyle do thereby increase considerably. Of course, this does
place a high demand on 'a caring gay community'. The opportunities in such a community could be wide ranging, with
abundant role models, consciousness-raising groups, entertainment, social and sexual relationships, accommodation sharing.
Before I continue, it is perhaps necessary to inform readers
who have not recently been in touch with the gay scene that
they cannot assume that a call to a gay switchboard will automatically ensure such opportunities are their's - or their clients'.

Especially for the non-gay referee we must consider what is
the likely availability of a positive milieu for the previously
isolated homosexual person in search of a new analysis of their

sexuality. The need to do this was impressed upon me when a
well-known theorist on social work told me that when as a social
work practitioner he had been faced with a homosexual person,
'I would just refer them to the gay community.' Such a
unidimensional approach runs the risk of pushing people in at
the deep end, who then find the water only six inches deep.
We have elsewhere addressed ourselves to providing alternative
responses for counsellors (see Richardson and Hart, 1980).

What are the realities of local social provision for homosexual
people? As the 'Gay News' fortnightly guide shows plainly, the
commercial and social facilities available in London have a
diversity and comprehensiveness for homosexuals as well as
heterosexuals which no other centre in Britain can match.
Although outside London it is not possible to generalize, it is
salutory to consider the likely availability of social facilities in
a town of, let us say, half a million people and, using the
'one in twenty' statistic, a consequent homosexual population
of 25,000. Assuming that there are places of higher education
there will usually be a polytechnic or university gaysoc. The
potential size of a gaysoc in terms of numbers of students is
probably hundreds, but this will not be reflected in the actual
attendance at meetings. It may still be difficult to come out in
a hall of residence or on a course, but probably less so than
if you are an apprentice electrician.

Gaysocs are likely to be small in membership, often male
dominated and are not necessarily confined to students. They
can provide for some a signpost to parties, social and sexual
companionship, and also an alternative political analysis of
homosexuality for the young person who may still be struggling
with a pathological view of her or his sexuality derived from
labels like 'poof' or 'butch' at school, and 'sex education' which
characterized homosexuality as immaturity or sickness. These
groups may well seem too 'heavy' or male dominated for some,
and for women the local women's group may prove to be more
appropriate. However, as Donnison (1978) indicates, women's
consciousness-raising groups may tend to be middle-class
dominated and, as such, of limited interest to a working-class
woman. Here I am reduced to generalizations, and I should add
therefore that my experience is that gay groups in higher
education and women's gay groups can and do integrate non-
students, and that an intellectual approach to a gay identity is
not the exclusive province of middle-class people. Some may
find in gaysocs or women's groups a more accepting atmosphere
than at a local CHE meeting.

The problem here is one shared by any gay organization;
what/where after sexuality is the common denominator? Some
elements do seem constant - the need for discos, political campaigning, finding partners. After this, what happens depends
upon the individual charisma of group members. So, what will
the prospective new member find? Maybe a group obsessed with
committee procedure, in-fighting or how to pass for 'straight'.

Perhaps a new member may only be made welcome on the
strength of a pretty face. Equally likely, they may find an
atmosphere of welcome, a new network of friends and, in effect,
a reconstruction of their social lives. We should not individualize
the blame/responsibility for these variations. It is possible to
take the structural view that a gay community is an impossibility
in our society. Unlike certain locations in North America geared
to service industries, the gay consumer/employee in Britain is
not seen as being of great importance to the economy, further,
homosexuals are distributed throughout the social classes;
hence the lack of a common identity, voice and power base,
and the consequent appearance of homosexuals with very
different lifestyles, with diverse political allegiances and familial
and gender-role affiliations. This is especially important in
considering the differences between homosexual women and men,
who may see themselves as having very separate identities
(see Hart and Richardson, 1980).

Perhaps most often people are not visible on the 'gay scene'
because of the ineffectiveness of sexual orientation in providing
a focus for people's social or political aspirations. Of course
individual 'political gays' do exist, and their influence is felt
in the middle-class 'talking shops' which provide a useful social
support for a minority. Coming out at college is obviously
comparatively safe, whilst the whole area of manual workers and
trade unionism is as yet underdeveloped. Possibly the pressure
on young working-class homosexuals to be married is lessening,
and therefore they may feel more able to explore their sexual
orientation.

We can, in a search for a common denominator for homosexual
people, see the commercial gay scene as the lowest. In any town
there is likely to be one or two often very crummy pubs and
clubs where homosexuals can find varying degrees of tolerance,
occasional police harassment and the possibility of social/sexual
contact. Hooker (1965, p.99) wrote of the American scene:
'Bars also serve as induction, training and integration centres'.
Some years on in Britain this still seems an overstatement of
most people's experience north of Watford and south of Croydon.
All one can state for certain is that they are not the places to
go to on your own for the first time when you may feel very
uncertain of how to get to know other gay people.

As for other more structured ways into the gay scene, there
are the 'signpost'-type organizations such as Lesbian Line,
Icebreakers and Friend, the latter providing a counselling and
befriending service with chosen volunteers operating in about
twenty groups in England and Wales. Often a phone referral/
information service is also offered by local gay groups. The
befriending service will obviously be marked by differences
in the abilities of the individual people involved. For the professional or other potential referee, the task is a simple one,
but with profound implications for professionals: to get to know
and form working relationships with local self-help groups. I am

aware that the need for this is not confined to the area of
sexuality. Although by now many professional people would
claim to 'accept' homosexuality as one permissible sexual
orientation, rather than see it as a type of mental illness, there
are often severe limits to this acceptance. This is highlighted
in one of the frequently expressed fears that I hear from both
heterosexual and homosexual people, including counsellors,
that by introducing someone to the kind of groups and organizations referred to in this Chapter, their client will be 'pushed
into' sexual situations and an identity for which they are not
yet ready or to which they are not fully committed. It is therefore important to directly face the fears behind such questioning. Partly it is an 'etiological question', and we discuss in
chapters 1 and 2 of this book theories about the causation of
homosexuality and their practice implications. Also echoed in
such fears is the value assumption about the preference for
heterosexual lifestyles, acts and identities over that of homosexual lifestyles, acts and identities. Each person must face
these questions for her or himself, and separately with each
client. The question of encouraging 'the uncommitted' is another
version of the contagion theory also referred to elsewhere in
this book. It does seem to me that, given the heterosexual
assumptions of our society, any young person who chooses a
homosexual lifestyle and identity is making that choice on the
basis of having been fully exposed to the alternative 'mainstream' sexuality.

I have so far dealt with the legal framework and the available
social outlets for homosexual people, and have implied that
there are roles for both the professional and the self-help
group in being concerned about both the legal framework, and
also the social environment for homosexuals. Indeed I believe
that the resources of self helpers and professionals and consideration of legal and social problems should all be assessed
by the individuals involved as being interdependent. The professional often has a referring role, but at the same time has a
professional responsibility to become familiar with the 'local
scene' so that individual befriending especially is not an ill-
thought-out act or gesture, but rather a decision based on
knowledge of each other for either 'client', social worker/
counsellor, gay befriender or group contact. The professional
can also lend support to combat legal and social harassment,
and this is a potentially new focus to their approach to helping
people; clearly training courses need to explore such unknown
territory.
     A new, still to be developed area for professional helpers is
that of viewing themselves as just part of the totality of their
client's world. With this perspective their interventions would
be to facilitate the potential social network resources which the
client can draw upon, including her or his own, for reciprocity
is vital in maintaining the self esteem of the helped person. To

act as a link between self-help groups and larger social movements, and to facilitate supportive relationships and exhanges
between self-help groups and other helping networks, are all
roles available for professional helpers (see Gartner and Riessman, 1977). Discussing working with sexuality is a useful model
for social intervention in general, with the self-help network
being helpfully labelled as such. For a more general discussion
on bringing people together as resources for each other within
a network, see Sarason and Lorentz (1979). I have emphasized
so far the resources available in the gay community, and I want
now to consider the contribution professionals themselves might
make beyond acting as advocates, or as referees and facilitators.

It is obvious that homosexual people are at the receiving end
of a number of negative messages from society, and that for
some individuals the ensuing psychological damage of legal
discrimination and social stigma are too great for a remedy to
be achieved by the counter-socialization available in most self-
help groups. In my counselling work with homosexuals I have
encountered certain individuals who have internalized society's
fears about sexuality as self hatred. The picture that emerges
is what the ego-psychologists so nicely term as 'identification
with the aggressor': 'camp' mannerisms, self oppressive remarks,
a belief that they are destined to face a lonely old age which
will begin by the time they get to thirty. Of equal concern are
those people who make only fleeting appearances at pubs, clubs
and self-help groups, or who even refuse to consider the
possibility of appearing 'on the scene', restricting their homosexual acts to pornographic magazines, responding to personal
advertisements in gay publications or occasional sexual encounters in public conveniences - 'cottaging'. There may also
be neurotic features to their behaviour, such as depression -
including suicide attempts, especially by isolated young people
who see themselves as unbearably 'different'. Other manifestations of psychological problems may be very restricted social
functioning because of a high anxiety level, an obsession with
a lack of physical attributes, or in sexual dysfunctioning.
Alcoholism may also feature; indeed because of the emphasis on
bars as meeting or socializing places, excessive drinking may
frequently be in evidence. It is important alongside the consideration of individual therapy to know of the existence of
Alcoholics Anonymous gay groups.

When considering relationship problems of homosexual people,
a common theme which can be heard - with all three ears! - is
what I term 'the stylus has got stuck'. It is the repetition of
behaviour patterns which result in the woman or man ending up
on the losing side. I encountered a young man who had spent
four years unemployed at home drooling over Starsky and Hutch;
on entry into the gay scene he devoted his attention to searching for, and immediately falling in love with, men who most
closely resembled Hutch. The result, however, of his obsession
was repeated disappointment and rejection. The task was to

help him see that his quest was the extension of his masturbatory fantasy, developed during a time when he was escaping
from the realities of social interaction. This involved encouraging him to attend a gay social group and later going through
with him his maladjusted (or underdeveloped) ways of socially
interacting. For example, at first he would attend meetings
without saying a word to anyone, hoping that someone would
come over and give him 'a hug or a grope'. When this did not
happen and people appeared preoccupied with the discussion,
he would feel very depressed and on one occasion after a meeting he wept for a long time, during which he told me of his
previous unsuccessful attempts to make friends. This involved
him in going into town and trying to talk to people on the bus
or in shops. Of course his social passivity extended to all areas
of his life, including some sexual dysfunction, and I used video
recording and playback to increase his confidence in face to
face, and especially job interview, situations. The task of helping with his sexual dysfunction involved encouraging him to
worry less about his own erections, which had previously been
associated with solitary masturbation fantasies, and to get him
to concentrate on the sexual arousal of the person he was with.

Such problem behaviour often comes in more sophisticated
or disguised forms, and in many people develops into usual ways
of responding; individual help is needed if they want to identify the patterns of such self denigrating behaviour and learn
alternative ways of interacting. The alternatives may be,
especially for men, a continual reinforcement of their experience
by 'one night stands', of the sort depicted in the British movie
'Nighthawks' (a film by Ron Peck and Paul Hallam, 1978). I am
not here suggesting that one night stands are in themselves to
be evaluated as unsatisfactory acts - rather that an obsession
with such acts to the exclusion of other social contacts may lead
to a person feeling 'empty' or isolated. In such instances it will
be obvious that the sexual orientation of the counsellor and the
client is not necessarily the primary concern. The client's
sexuality is just one factor to be taken into account when
assessing the need for a particular form of therapeutic intervention (see Richardson and Hart, 1980). Often what is required
is both individual counselling and social group support.

Having looked at some of the ways in which need is met by both
professionals and self helpers, we shall now consider where
resources do not meet needs.

On a macro level, campaigning organizations aim to change
the legal framework for homosexuals and end discrimination at
work. There is also a middle-range educational task which is
well represented by the CHE teaching kit of tapes, slides and
booklets called 'Homosexuality - A Fact of Life', aimed at
educating students and teachers about sexual diversity. On a
micro level, I have had the experience of a fourteen-year-old
boy, who was quite sure he was gay, wanting my help in finding

him a boyfriend. Although such requests are not uncommon from any age group, my usual negative response to such specific demands was made very difficult in this instance because of the boy's very restricted opportunities for meeting other gay people (in that no social group in the area would accept someone of that age), and my awareness that the alternatives were the commercial scene or 'cottaging' (both outlets being frequently used by under-aged males). My subsequent counselling, based on little more than 'wait until you are older like the rest of the young gays I know', was grounded more on my own self protection than what I assumed were his needs, although I was also concerned that he was at risk of being exploited in some social situations. All this relates very importantly to the unmet needs of homosexual teenagers and the way the law makes counselling work in this area hazardous for both self and professional helpers. Nevertheless, gay teenage groups do exist and are gaining a voice via the Joint Council for Gay Teenagers and the Gay Youth Movement. The education of professionals, such as probation officers, about homosexuality is being undertaken by a number of gay organizations in addition to their work in public relations - giving 'an opinion on' a range of issues connected with homosexuality on local radio stations and newspapers.

The task for professionals is, as I have earlier and elsewhere (Hart, 1979) documented, a more open discussion (and therefore an influence on public attitudes) of their moral stances and subsequent behaviour working within the statutory framework. We may therefore conclude that in providing for the needs of homosexual people in the legal and social area, both self and professional help have a place, and that the 'helpers' may not ever meet individual beneficiaries. In situations of unmet need, I would not agree with Henry (1978) that 'the responsibility for non-member sufferers must fall on professionals'. Such a prescription ignores (i) the diversity of the needs of gay people; (ii) the limitations of one to one counselling for what may be in some instances lifestyle discrimination rather than psychological disturbance; (iii) the attitudinal, knowledge and availability limitations of professional counsellors; (iv) the problems attendant on professional hegemony.

When we consider what precisely are the unmet needs of homosexual people, we encounter similar problems of bias as those of existing surveys. We just do not know what would emerge from a genuinely random sample of homosexual people in Great Britain. Perhaps the 'unmet needs' are primarily in the minds of writers on the subject. However, it would seem logical that it is the less vulnerable person who is likely to emerge 'on the scene' whilst others remain hidden within a heterosexual society with only their fears and conflicts for company. It remains an unanswered question (to which we address ourselves in Chapter 3) as to how such people, having only minimal contact with other homosexuals (as certainly is often the case in my experience), come to define themselves as homosexual. The search for appropriate help for homosexual people in need will have to continue. Whose responsibility is this?

In this Chapter I am proposing a negation of divisions between types of helping agencies, and have seen such separateness as based on prejudice rather than a realistic assessment of the needs of individuals, although different skills may be needed in subsequent helping. What does this imply - for both groups? First, some radical changes in both knowledge and attitudes in professional education - in social work, counselling, psychology and psychiatry. This book is intended to provide alternative theoretical approaches to homosexual acts, lifestyles and iden- tities, to enable the worker to move from a pathological view, through acceptance, to a positive affirmation of gay lifestyles. This in itself can provide a basis for attitude change. From this should emanate a willingness to share perceptions, skills and knowledge with non-professional people. An example of this could be making video available to non-professional helpers as well as instructions in its use, in social skills training or in community education. In gay groups, individuals can tune pro- fessionals in to the feelings involved in leading a double life (it is easy to confuse one's own elitist, liberated social life with the experience of the majority of gays, which is of a hostile world). Equally, the exclusiveness of lack of warmth in some gay groups can be changed by an articulate outsider sharing their perception of this. How salutary it is when non-gay people at gay meetings become very concerned at the energy wasted on 'in-fighting'. Gay groups do also need to move beyond any stereotype of the professional as obsessed with 'curing their sexual deviation' (which some may well have experienced), to seeing certain professionals as being able sympathetically to offer help to the psychologically disturbed, whom the group may sometimes reject or exclude for a period, or someone who has a specific relationship or sexual problem. I have myself coun- selled homosexual people who could not discuss problems in their group of friends because they felt they were all too personally involved. Publicity by professionals, the media and gay groups themselves of successful self-help or positive therapy experience, will hopefully encourage isolated homosexuals to become involved in a social network and this is therefore the best hope of providing for unmet needs.

All this may seem too idealistic a search for integration of the personal and the political, of professionals and the gay com- munity - and impossible given the structure of society. What does, in my view, make what I have advocated sometimes within our grasp is the emergence of gay people who are themselves professional counsellers, who are involved with the law or social welfare (a good example being GLAD referred to elsewhere in this book). Many of these gay women and men have been 'at the receiving end', labelled as having, and/or having felt that they have, personal problems related to their sexual orientation.

Their experience of deliberately crossing the boundaries of helper and helped can make available more energy for working towards legal, social and psychological change, and in this process they can begin to offer a model of how the barriers between self and professional help can be lowered. A more symmetrical relationship between helper and helped is not just applicable to working with a group of people who happen to be homosexual. In helping to change their own personal situation, openly gay people are drawn into helping achieve some small change, by providing positive models, in the social and legal position of millions of homosexual people in Britain, the majority of whom will probably never feel the need for specific self or professional help.

7 THE LEGAL PROBLEMS OF HOMOSEXUALS

Charles Dodd

To understand the legal problems faced by homosexuals in
Britain it is not sufficient to consider only the criminal law,
even though this exerts a powerful impact on many homosexuals.
To do so would be to under-emphasize the legal problems of
lesbians, about which the criminal law has little to say, and it
would ignore other major areas of life where homosexuals can be
penalized because of their sexuality.

In what follows I have made use of the body of knowledge
acquired by Gay Legal Advice (GLAD), a group of homosexuals
professionally involved with the law, who offer skilled help and
understanding to other homosexuals with legal problems by
means of a telephone service. I have also drawn on existing
publications on sexual law, law reports and newspaper articles.
The criminal law in Scotland and Northern Ireland differs from
that in England and Wales and, to provide a geographically
more balanced picture, I have drawn attention to the special
problems experienced in those parts of the United Kingdom.

THE CRIMINAL LAW

It has never been a crime to be homosexual, but certain homosexual acts have been and still are punishable at law. The
position in England and Wales following the passage of the Sexual
Offences Act of 1967 is that homosexual acts between two males
are not criminal provided that both parties are over twenty-one,
consent, commit their acts in private and are not members of
the armed forces or merchant navy. We may say that this piece
of legislation, though often lauded as a liberal measure legalizing
homosexuality, only exempted certain homosexual acts from
criminal penalties. This is an important distinction. Homosexuality is still not seen as fully lawful and is often seen as
immoral.

1 The age of majority is eighteen, the age of consent for
heterosexuals sixteen, for homosexual males twenty-one. A
working paper on the age of consent has, however, recommended that it should not be more than eighteen for homosexual males (Policy Advisory Committee on Sexual Offences,
1979).
2 To be within the law, sexual acts between consenting adult
males must be committed in private. The presence of a third

party specifically renders the act unlawful; no such restriction exists for heterosexual relations.
3 A man breaks the law if he persistently importunes another
man in a public place for an immoral purpose, i.e. homosexual
activity. It is, though, within the law for a man to solicit a
female, e.g. by kerb crawling.
4 The maximum penalty for indecent assault by a male on a
female is two years' imprisonment (five years if the girl is
under thirteen); the maximum penalty for indecent assault on
a male of any age by another male is ten years' imprisonment.
5 All homosexual acts between males are against the law in
Northern Ireland, and they are likewise illegal between merchant seaman on board a United Kingdom merchant ship. (See
p.143 for the situation in Scotland.)
6 Members of the armed forces are subject to military law rather
than the provisions of the 1967 Act. 'Disgraceful conduct of
an indecent or unnatural kind' can lead to a maximum of two
years' imprisonment and a dishonourable discharge, even if
the acts committed would have been within the law under
the 1967 Act.

THE CRIMINAL LAW IN OPERATION

To state the law as printed is one thing; to be clear about what
the law is in practice is another. Courts have spent much time
interpreting the legislation. The word 'private' is open to much
speculation even though public toilets are specifically not private
places within the meaning of the 1967 Act, and an act is not
committed in private if more than two males are present. It is
wise advice to encourage a defendant to plead not guilty and
to consider trial by jury whenever there is a dispute over
whether or not an act was committed in private, for it is then
up to the jury to consider the circumstances of the particular
case. In one incident known to the writer, sexual activity was
admitted by the two defendant males, but the jury acquitted,
presumably because they felt the particular circumstances (the
incident occurred in the early hours of the morning in secluded,
open parkland with no other parties present until the arrival
of the police) rendered the act 'committed in private'.
    Importuning for an immoral purpose is another important
concern. For the activity to be against the law, it must be
ongoing, involving approaches to more than one person, or to
the same person on more than one occasion (Dale vs Smith,
1967). The layman's definition may differ from the strictly legal,
and the boundary between sociable and criminal activity can be
imprecise. That the conduct contemplated would have been
lawful under the 1967 Act is no defence to the charge of
importuning (R. vs Ford, 1977).
    More legal problems are created by the age of consent being
fixed at twenty-one. The law holds that young people must be

protected even from themselves (R. vs Willis, 1974). Yet the
Policy Advisory Committee on Sexual Offences (1979) noted that
the majority medical view was that a male's sexual orientation
is in most cases fixed by the age of sixteen, and found also that
prosecutions for consensual sexual acts involving young men
aged between eighteen and twenty-one are rare, implying the
law in this area has ceased to be enforced.

'Gross indecency' - in essence acts involving bodily contact
between two men - is an emotive issue, often regarded as a
distasteful nuisance by the police and the court. Considerable
concern has been expressed by solicitors and social workers in
many parts of Britain by what they believe to be the nature of
police activity in certain open spaces and public conveniences -
the use of spy holes in urinal broom cupboards for instance.
More modest charges may also be preferred against homosexual
males. Two men walking arm in arm along a London street in the
early hours of the morning were charged with a breach of the
peace but were subsequently acquitted ('Gay News' no. 134,
12-25 January 1978). In Manchester, the owners and patrons
of a homosexual club were reminded of the provision of a City
Corporation Act of 1882 which prohibited licentious dancing,
interpreted in this instance as homosexual males dancing
together.

One of the implications of the above is that homosexuals must
be aware of their basic rights at law, and of the essential nature
of any charges laid against them. For most people this will
necessitate legal advice before a plea is taken, even though the
pressures and temptations to plead guilty in such circumstances
can be strong, for many homosexuals remain vulnerable and
afraid of publicity. It is the prosecution's responsibility to
prove that a homosexual act occurred without consent, was not
performed in private or involved someone under the age of
consent.

Of at least as much importance for homosexuals is not how
the laws are interpreted by the court, but how homosexual
behaviour is viewed by significant others, including the police.
It is disturbing when the police appear to act as agents pro-
vocateurs, encouraging offences and then arresting the victims.
In one case the defendant saw a smiling young man outside a
public house frequented by homosexuals, and a conversation
developed during which it was alleged the other man said, 'Do
you want to come back to my place?' As they walked along the
road, a uniformed policeman arrived and arrested the defendant,
the other man then identifying himself as a plainclothes police
officer. The defendant was subsequently acquitted of importuning; entrapment, though, is no defence in law ('Gay News'
no. 162, Sneddon vs Stevenson, 1967).

Uncertainty and inequity are present if police practice varies
geographically. Walmsley (1978) considered the offence of
indecency between males from 1967 to 1973 and found that
offences known to the police doubled, the number of persons

prosecuted trebled, but prosecution rates varied greatly between different police areas. In 1973 the rate ranged from 100 per cent to less than 20 per cent. He found the most likely hypothesis to explain the rise in criminal activity to be the 1967 Act itself, which made clear that acts committed in public remained illegal but introduced summary trial, making the prosecution process easier. A greater likelihood of conviction together with simplicity of processing explain the increase in offences, whilst the prosecution rate is highest where the processing procedure is simplest. These offenders can then be dealt with as simply as drunks. Yet a homosexual conviction has very different implications, on the life of the person and on the severity of the sentence imposed, from a conviction for drunkenness.

Walmsley and White (1979) looked at the police caution, and found it was used mainly for heterosexual offences. The offence of unlawful sexual intercourse with a girl under sixteen more frequently resulted in a caution than that of indecency between males, though both involve consensual behaviour and are victimless crimes. Cautioning for homosexual offences, according to this research, is the exception.

Uncertainty and anxiety can be heightened by the need for the police to refer homosexual cases where one or both of the males are under twenty-one to the Director of Public Prosecutions for a decision regarding whether or not to prosecute. The Director has published certain of his guidelines which help us understand the processes involved, and say something about his perceptions of homosexuality. In all cases referred to him he adopts the 50 per cent test - if there is a prosecution, is there a greater than 50 per cent chance of conviction? Then, looking specifically at sexual offences, the relative age of offender and victim are considered, taking into account the presence or absence of corruption and consent.

'I do not prosecute a man of twenty-two for a homosexual offence against a man of nineteen, although if, for instance, the older went into a public toilet intent on finding a partner and the younger was or might become a male prostitute, I would probably decide to prosecute both' ('Observer', 7 January 1979).

The Director has another part to play in influencing legal pressures on homosexuals, and this relates to the law of conspiracy. He authorized the prosecution of the magazine 'International Times' for corrupting public morals by publishing contact advertisements for male homosexuals, and it was convicted of the charge. In essence, however, a new offence had been created, whilst the proceedings helped reveal legal attitudes towards homosexuality and the limitations of the 1967 Act. A distinction was drawn between exempting certain conduct from criminal penalties and making it lawful in the full sense, and Lord Reid said he could find nothing in the 1967 Act 'to indicate that Parliament thought or intended to lay down that indulgence

in these practices is not corrupting' (Knuller vs DPP, 1973).
The decision in Knuller poses difficulties for social workers
and counsellors assisting homosexuals. A worker in contact with
a homosexual male under twenty-one who turns a blind eye to
the latter's sexual relationships could find a charge of corrupting public morals being laid against her or him, and her or his
organization. It was this sort of sentiment that enabled the
Charity Commission in 1978 to refuse to grant charitable status
to the theatre group Gay Sweatshop; because one of its aims
was to educate the public regarding homosexuals and their
status in society. Libraries and booksellers have refused to
stock publications such as 'Gay News' on similar grounds. Lynch
has considered the position of agencies which counsel homosexuals, and feels that if counsellors see themselves as, and
work towards, reducing psychological problems encountered by
homosexuals, then their activities are lawful because the element
of mens rea of conspiracy is lacking. But he cannot be dogmatic
or confident as 'the conflicting social attitudes that exist, and
the ambiguity of some of the relevant authorities, forbid such
certainty' (Lynch, 1979).

Prior to 1967 the law relating to homosexual activity was
often held to provide a charter for blackmailers, yet if social
disapprobation continues and is given support, implicit or
explicit, by the law, it is hardly surprising to find that blackmail remains a problem for homosexuals today. One informal
study learnt of thirteen cases of blackmail reaching the criminal
courts over a ten month period (Campaign for Homosexual
Equality, 1979).

What has been said so far has been wholly male focused.
Lesbianism per se, unlike male homosexuality, has never been
against the law, and indeed one could say that lesbians have
been seen as beneath the law's consideration. It is possible,
though, for indecent assault charges to be brought against a
woman in respect of an act with another woman, whilst lesbians
kissing or holding hands in public, like their male counterparts,
could be held to have committed a breach of the peace and be
required to enter into a recognizance to keep the peace and be
of good behaviour.

Scotland (legal situation until February 1981)
In Scotland the relevant legislation is contained within the 1885
Criminal Law (Amendment) (Scotland) Act, codified and consolidated in the Sexual Offences (Scotland) Act 1976. All male
acts of gross indecency are criminal acts whatever the circumstances in which they are committed, whilst acts of 'shameless
indecency' may be prosecuted at common law, and these can
involve lesbian acts, whether in private or public. However,
those homosexual acts between males which would have been
lawful if committed in England or Wales are not prosecuted at
Scots law following a discretionary policy adopted by the Lord
Advocate, but each Lord Advocate must renew the discretion on

taking office. He is not bound to do so, nor can he bind a successor. The sanction therefore remains, though there are no prosecutions and Scottish male homosexuals have no clear idea of where they stand and are dependent on the continuity of existing political decisions. Reform of the law was considered unlikely by many commentators, but in July 1980 the Commons, during the course of a debate on the Criminal Justice (Scotland) Bill, voted to bring the law in Scotland into line with that in England and Wales. This took effect on 1 February 1981.

Northern Ireland
The 1861 Offences Against the Person Act, with its mention of the 'abominable crime of buggery', for which the penalty is life imprisonment, still applies in Northern Ireland, as does the 1885 Criminal Law (Amendment) Act. For many years the 1885 Act was rigorously applied, but in the 1970s a campaign for legislative change became noticeable. The Northern Ireland Standing Commission on Human Rights reported in 1977 that public opinion favoured an extension of the 1967 Act to the Province, and a draft law was published in the summer of 1978 which would have brought the law into line with that in England and Wales. Political and religious forces combined together to campaign against these reforms and proposals, under the emotive title 'Save Ulster from Sodomy', and this, helped by the presence of a minority government in Westminster, led to a retreat from the official reformist stance; in July 1979 the Secretary of State for Northern Ireland announced that plans for legal reform were to be dropped. It was felt that the law should be less liberal than in England and Wales because of the higher moral standards and church attendance in the province, together with the opposition of most churches to the possibility of reform.
    At the same time however a Belfast male homosexual had laid a complaint with the European Human Rights Commission that the United Kingdom government, by virtue of its treatment of Northern Ireland homosexuals, was breaching Articles of the European Human Rights Convention relating to privacy and discrimination. In 1980 the Commission ruled that Great Britain was violating human rights relating to domestic privacy of homosexuals in the province, though it also held that male homosexuals there were not discriminated against compared with homosexual men in other parts of the United Kingdom.

FAMILY LAW

There is a strong belief that homosexuality is the preserve of the single person, but those who practise in the criminal and domestic courts will know that this is not the case. The problems of homosexual parents wishing to maintain contact with their children after the break-up of their marriage were little thought

of until the early 1970s, and even now interest focuses mainly
on the position of lesbian mothers. Action for Lesbian Parents
and GLAD have been consulted by a number of homosexual
people anxious for advice on matters of custody and access to
children. Courts have held that a spouse's homosexuality is
unreasonable behaviour, providing grounds for divorce, and a
homosexual parent's fight for access to, or custody of, their
children can be a long drawn out and, often, a fruitless
experience.

Sometimes strict conditions are imposed, as when a lesbian
mother was permitted access to her son on condition that
homosexuality was not to be mentioned during the access
periods, and that she would not sleep with her lover at such
times ('Guardian', 7 August 1975). In 1976 Mrs W., a lesbian,
was granted custody of her eleven-year-old twin daughters by
the Appeal Court, but it was stressed that the decision had
nothing to do with sexuality, but all to do with bricks and
mortar - the father was unable to provide suitable accommodation
for the children ('Guardian', 5 November 1976). One case with
disturbing implications for homosexual parents comes from the
field of adoption. The mother of a boy, D., divorced his father
on the grounds that his homosexuality constituted unreasonable
behaviour, and she was given custody of D. She and her
second husband later sought to adopt D., but his father
objected. It was held by the House of Lords that the father's
consent to the adoption was being unreasonably withheld and
could be dispensed with, permitting the adoption to proceed.
No reasons other than the father's homosexuality and the
possibility of the boy being introduced to undesirable ways of
life were put forward as justifying the dispensing of consent,
and it was felt the father had nothing to offer his son in the
future (Re D., 1977).

EMPLOYMENT

In the area of criminal law, although much uncertainty and
discretion were present, there did exist the printed law and
stated Appeal Court decisions. In family law there is more scope
for less objective factors coming into play, and this is true also
of employment issues. The main areas are the refusal to offer
someone employment on the grounds of their homosexuality
and the dismissal of someone from their employment on similar
grounds.

Looking at the first issue, it is often difficult to establish
that a person was not offered employment because of their
homosexuality, but issues are most clear wherever children
or vulnerable groups are involved or where there are issues
of national security. One survey found a reluctance on the part
of certain Social Services Departments to employ homosexuals
(National Council for Civil Liberties, 1977), while the Department

of Education and Science maintains a 'black list' of teachers
with convictions for sexual offences. In certain sections of the
Civil Service, homosexuality would be a barrier to obtaining
positive vetting, without which access to confidential and classified material is denied. The argument here is that homosexuality renders one liable to blackmail. Overall it appears that
the onus is frequently on the homosexual person to prove that
her or his sexuality will not affect adversely the performance
of duties or put potential employers at risk.

The rights homosexuals have in the second instance relate to
proving unfair dismissal under the Employment Protection Act
1975, provided they have been employed in a post for at least
twelve months. One of the problems they face is that Industrial
Tribunals, rather like Justices of the Peace, are inconsistent
and do not have to follow decisions set by their colleagues elsewhere, though they would have to take account of decisions
of the Employment Appeals Tribunal.

One case is particularly worrying for homosexuals, given its
potentially wide implications and its endorsement by an Appeal
Tribunal. After two and a half years' employment, James
Saunders, a handyman at a Scottish youth camp, was dismissed
at the end of 1979 when it was discovered he was homosexual.
He had been of good character and there were no allegations
of homosexual behaviour by him towards the children of the
camp. An Industrial Tribunal upheld his employers' decision,
arguing it was reasonable to assume a risk to children and
therefore to dismiss.'This in the Tribunal's opinion was fair
and reasonable, even if the Tribunal itself would not have made
the same decision' ('Gay News', 29 November-12 December
1980). The Appeal Tribunal, in confirming the decision, accepted
that there was a lack of scientific evidence suggesting that
homosexuals posed a greater threat to children than heterosexuals, but ruled there was no doubt that such a view existed.
In other words homosexuality itself, or rather the fantasies and
prejudice associated with it, can be sufficient reason for dis-
missing someone from their employment. It follows that homosexuals who in the course of their employment are in contact,
direct or indirect, with young people may now find themselves
placed in a highly vulnerable position.

To some extent homosexual employees can be protected by
representations and activities on their behalf by their trade
unions. Strike action by the National Association of Local
Government Officers (NALGO) was influential in persuading a
local authority to abide by an Industrial Tribunal decision that
one of its social workers had been unfairly dismissed following
a conviction for gross indecency (National Council for Civil
Liberties, 1977). NALGO and certain other unions are opposed
to discrimination on the grounds of sexual orientation, but this
attitude is not widespread and the General Secretary of the
National Association of School Masters/Union of Women Teachers
has expressed the view that homosexuals in the teaching

profession produce a lowering of confidence on the part of the
public towards teachers generally.

INTERNATIONAL MOVEMENT

Under this heading we must consider the difficulties experienced
both by homosexual foreigners trying to enter this country on
a permanent basis and by British homosexuals trying to enter
another country. The 1971 Immigration Act introduced the notion
of patrials, people who cannot be excluded from Britain and
can live here lawfully. Apart from birth and blood ties, length
of residence in Britain provides a criterion for patrial status.
Working here for four years with the permission of the authorities is one way to be considered settled which can apply to
homosexuals, but otherwise there is a great emphasis on lawful
marriage. The attitude to marriages of convenience has been
sharpened appreciably in recent times, and hence it is that
much harder for homosexuals to achieve patrial status. The
immigration rules suggest that homosexuals do not have the
same right to bring in their foreign lovers to this country as do
single heterosexual males.
    Nor is getting to another country an easy task as Carl Hill,
a British citizen, found in the summer of 1979 when he arrived
at San Francisco airport wearing a Gay Pride badge. Exclusion
proceedings were commenced against him under a 1952 American
Law which bans entry to the United States to 'sexual deviants'.
Homosexuals, or rather persons who are openly gay are rendered illegal aliens. Being seen to be openly gay renders one
liable to discrimination and encourages homosexuals to keep
their sexuality a secret.

FINANCIAL PROBLEMS

One of the themes that has emerged above is the great importance society attaches to the family unit. Many of the financial
problems homosexuals encounter arise from this emphasis. A
major area of difficulty for homosexuals relates to wills. It has
been estimated that some 30 per cent of the population do not
make a will, but when one dies intestate one's property descends
to one's next of kin in an order specified by the intestacy rules.
These rules make no provision for lovers of the same sex. Thus
the deceased's spouse, if there were one, could claim over the
head of the homosexual lover, and the deceased's children and
near relatives, who may have strongly opposed the homosexual
relationship, may also claim property over the head of the
lover. It is therefore vital for homosexuals to leave a will making
clear their intentions.
    Homosexuals are also at a disadvantage in the field of tax.
Homosexual couples living together are taxed separately and

would each receive a single person's allowance, which in total would be some hundreds of pounds less than the total allowances available to a husband and wife. Such a bias is reflected throughout tax law. For example, all interspousal transfers of wealth are exempt from Capital Transfer Tax, but if one homosexual person gives her or his lover wealth, no such exemption applies.

THE LEGAL PROBLEMS OF HOMOSEXUALS

Homosexuality and homosexuals are still perceived negatively in society and by many who administer the laws of society. To refer to someone as homosexual during the course of a criminal trial can be held to be an attack on their good character (R. vs Bishop, 1975). It is worth remembering too that whilst racial minority groups and women generally are to some extent protected from discrimination by the law, the same is not true for homosexuals of either sex.

Over the years a passive response to the legal pressures encountered tended to exist, epitomized in the phrase well known in the criminal courts, 'plead guilty and get it all over with'. Now, however, there are signs of change and a growth of activism within the gay community generally. There is a greater awareness of the rights provided by the law and a willingness to make use of them and, where appropriate, to challenge and contest. This new spirit was well caught by John Saunders ('Gay News', no. 182 10-23 January 1980) after his dismissal from work:

I've never been part of the organised gay movement. I suppose I am a loner by temperament, but this is important to me and I can see how important it is for everyone who is gay and therefore at risk. It's like they always say - you never believe it's going to happen to you. When it does, you have to make up your mind whether to take it meekly or fight.
And I'm going to fight.

CASES REFERRED TO

Dale vs Smith, 1967: 2 All ER 1133.
Knuller vs DPP, 1973: AC 435.
Re D., 1977: 1 All ER 145.
R. vs Bishop, 1975: 2QB 274.
R. vs Ford, 1977: 1WLR 1083.
R. vs Willis: *The Times*, 18 December 1974.
Sneddon vs Stevenson, 1962: 2 All ER 1277.

8 LESBIAN MOTHERS

Diane Richardson

The debate surrounding homosexuality and parenthood has
focused primarily on lesbians rather than on homosexual men,
contrary to the usual male bias which exists in the literature.
This can be seen as a reflection of the traditional association of
childrearing with women, whereby it is likely that many more
homosexual women than men will have children, and be engaged
in bringing them up. Bell and Weinberg (1978), for instance,
found that at least a fifth of the group of homosexual women
they studied had children, compared to only a tenth of the male
homosexual sample. Even so, whilst there exists a substantial
body of research into possible parental factors in the etiology
of homosexuality, relatively little has been written about children whose mothers are homosexual and the possible effects on a
child of being brought up in a lesbian household. This is in
part a reflection of the social invisibility of lesbians within
society. In addition, given that motherhood is an explicit
representation of previous heterosexual involvement, and as
such decreases the likelihood of a woman being seen as homosexual, this neglect has been compounded by the assumption
that lesbians do not in any case become mothers, or, perhaps
more significantly, that mothers do not become lesbians.
    The rise of the women's and the gay movements has provided
a supportive framework in which women have openly declared
themselves as gay. It is the public recognition of lesbian mothers
that has elicited a considerable amount of concern as to whether
or not being brought up in a lesbian household is likely to be
detrimental to a child's future growth and development. More
specifically, there are three major areas of concern which can be
identified:

1 That the child will grow up to be homosexual and/or develop
  an atypical gender-role orientation;
2 that the child is in 'moral danger';
3 that the child will suffer social isolation from her or his peers
  and significant others as a result of the stigmatization of
  lesbian relationships in society.

    Before examining each of these points in detail, let us first
consider at a rather more general level why it is that concerns
about the 'adequacy' of lesbians as parents have arisen, and
the possible implications of such concerns for lesbian mothers
and their children.

We should note that singling out lesbian mothers in this way is in itself highly significant, given that the majority of women who become mothers do so without any questions being asked. The complex culturally and socially determined hierarchy of beliefs about what constitutes the ideal family unit in our society is particularly relevant here. It is expected, and regarded as desirable, that those who want to have children will get married. The stigmatization of unmarried mothers and their children is a reflection of this. Similarly, ideas and beliefs about optimum family size, sexual composition and spacing of the children and age of conception, are all contributory factors in the formation of a popular stereotype of the nuclear family. Faced with families who are in some way seen to contravene this 'ideal', the question of whether such a home environment is conducive or not to the child's growth and development becomes a matter for concern. Quite apart from scientific knowledge and values, then, popular stereotypes of the family will be influential in questioning the adequacy of certain individuals as parents. A lesbian home environment obviously challenges such traditional stereotypes, based, as they are, on the sexual and economic relationships between men and women. In discussing lesbian mothers, therefore, it is important to recognize the potential threat which lesbianism poses to the structure of society (Ettorre, 1980).

We should be careful to note also that concerns about child welfare are frequently based not only in the ideology of the family and popular beliefs about homosexuality, but also upon certain rather deterministic assumptions about the effects of early socialization experiences. Whilst it may be possible to make probabilistic statements about the effects of certain environmental factors in a developmental sense, any discussion of how a particular environment affects a child must take into account the fact that there exists a complex two-way interaction between the individual qualities of the child and the environment. Different children will respond to similar home environments in quite different ways. It is therefore impossible to make large scale generalizations about the possible effects of a certain type of home environment which will be applicable to all children. In a similar vein, we should not necessarily take at face value the assumption that the early socialization experiences which a child encounters are necessarily going to have far-reaching effects in later life.

Having stressed the fact that in discussing the effects of a lesbian home environment upon the child we must be careful to avoid simplistic models of socialization, there is another conceptual point which needs mentioning. This is the assumption that we can, in any case, talk sensibly about the effects of a 'lesbian home environment' upon the child.

The theoretical models of homosexuality prevalent in the literature in the past have been influential in fostering a unidimensional view of homosexual women (and men) as a homogeneous group, whereas more recently the enormous diversity amongst homosexual women and men has begun to be recognized (Bell and Weinberg, 1978). Bearing this in mind, we cannot talk about how adequate lesbians are as mothers as if they constituted a homogeneous group. They will come from a variety of social and ethnic backgrounds, hold a wide range of beliefs and attitudes about child rearing, and will have a diversity of identities and lifestyles. We cannot, therefore, assume that just because homosexual women share a similar sexual orientation we can treat them as equivalent as far as parenting is concerned. This is as nonsensical as trying to argue that heterosexual women can similarly be considered as a uniform group when we come to look at how they are bringing up their children. This might be clarified if we posed the question, 'Do heterosexual women make good parents?'

Having suggested that homosexual women constitute a diverse group, the polarization between lesbian and non-lesbian mothers must also be questioned. Indeed, Goodman (1973) states that the similarities of motherhood for both lesbian and non-lesbian mothers far exceed the differences, and where differences do occur it would seem that they are linked to social roles, discrimination and oppression in regard to homosexuality, rather than to sexual preference per se. This is an important point to make, given the tendency in the literature to emphasize the differences rather than the similarities in the socialization of homosexual and heterosexual women. In this respect it is important to note that for all women there is a prime emphasis placed on marriage and motherhood.

In going on to discuss the sort of family environment a lesbian mother might provide for a child, then, we must be careful not to imply that we have a homogeneous and distinct group of women. However, given the sort of social typifications about both homosexuality and the family which exist, there may be a homogeneity of a sort, in that they represent a stigmatized group within society.

This is obviously extremely important as a contextual background in which to set some of the comments made about lesbians and their adequacy as parents. For example, viewing lesbianism as some kind of psychological abnormality raises a whole set of questions concerned with mental health and parenting, mental health having always been seen as a fundamental criterion in how responsible a person is thought to be in bringing up and caring for a child.

Adoption is quite an interesting example of how many of the social and cultural beliefs about child rearing and the family come into play in selecting for parenthood. In this respect we might ask what the likelihood is of a lesbian couple being able to adopt.

In the first place only married couples can adopt, so that a child could only be placed with one member of a lesbian couple. This would also apply for a heterosexual couple who were living together in 'common law' marriage. Adoption by a single person, however, has always been a fairly rare event. In 1975, for example, out of a total of 21,299 adoptions only 149 were by sole adopters. Compounding this is the fact that as waiting lists for children increase, and the actual number of children available decreases, ideas about who is 'best qualified for parenting' become crucial. (Figures are for England and Wales.)

One other area where traditional assumptions about mothering have played an important role in decisions about child welfare, and which has direct relevance to the debate surrounding lesbian mothers, is child custody. In the majority of custody cases, both uncontested and contested, it would seem that custody is usually awarded to the mother (Wolfson, 1971). However, where custody is contested and the mother is known to be homosexual a rather different picture emerges; it appears that in such cases it is the father who will be granted custody. Cohen et al. (1978) report only three cases where a lesbian mother has won a contested court case over custody or access, and in each case the judge was concerned that the decision should not be seen as sanctioning lesbian parenthood. Brophy (1979, pp.58-9) examined four contested custody cases where the mother was known to be homosexual. She states that

In none of the cases discussed was the mother's 'fitness' for her role as a mother – in her nurturing capacity – seriously called into question; in no case had the child welfare or social services been involved at any stage in the child's development. In all cases, except one, the judge made reference to the good quality of care which the mother had provided prior to marital breakdown. In all cases the children were in the mother's possession at the time of the hearing ... in all cases the mother did have some adequate accommodation to which she proposed to take the child. In most cases it was at least matched (materially) with the father's proposals, and in one case it was seen by the Court as, in certain aspects, superior.

In each of these instances, however, it was considered in the 'best interests of the child' that custody be awarded to the father. Brophy (1979, p.60) tentatively concludes that the usual presumption in favour of the mother was overruled by justifications based upon 'the mother's choice of sexual partner and the lifestyle which that choice represents to the judiciary'. In response to the discriminatory attitude of the courts in custody cases involving lesbian mothers, the group Action for Lesbian Parents was set up. They have produced an advisory pamphlet for lesbian mothers entitled 'Care and Control', as well as a list of barristers and solicitors well equipped to deal with such cases. They also offer support and advice throughout custody hearings.

The general picture described above would seem to be paralleled in America, despite the American Psychological Association's passing a resolution in 1976 that sexual orientation of natural or prospective adoptive or foster parents should not be the sole

or primary variable considered in custody or placement cases.
Such a situation is all the more significant given the traditional assumptions about the importance of the mother-child
relationship, and the association of child care with women,
which normally plays a significant role in custody decisions.
Indeed, it highlights the essential contradiction which exists
between 'innate' theories of mothering and the expectancy that
maternal 'instincts' will be expressed only in particular social
organizations, i.e. the nuclear family.

Let us now consider the three major areas of concern that
have been voiced and the scant research literature pertaining
to each of these.

PSYCHOSEXUAL DEVELOPMENT

It is perhaps hardly surprising that it is the area of psychosexual development which has received most attention in the
literature on children with homosexual mothers. What studies do
exist tend to be either psychoanalytical and focused on the
individual case example (e.g. Osman, 1972; Weeks et al., 1975),
or preliminary reports from small scale studies (e.g. Kirkpatrick
et al., 1976; Green, 1978). Before discussing these, however,
it may be useful to consider the theoretical assumptions upon
which such studies are based.

Both psychoanalytical and social learning theories of psychosexual development have argued that identification and imitation
of the same-sex parent in the early years of life is crucial in
terms of gender identity and gender-role development. In the
case of boys being brought up in a lesbian home environment,
then, it might be argued that because they lack an 'appropriate
identification object' they are likely to have more difficulty in
establishing a masculine gender-role orientation than if a same-
sex role model were present.

Most of the research that has been carried out on the effects
of father absence on gender-role development in boys has been
concerned with situations where the father is absent because of
cultural mores or occupational obligations; or, alternatively,
where he is permanently absent due to death, desertion or
divorce. The case of father absence in a lesbian home environment
may not be adequately covered by any of these categories.
Indeed under certain situations it may be more instructive to
think about paternal privation than paternal deprivation (e.g.
lesbians who conceive as a result of artificial insemination). In
addition, where a lesbian couple are bringing up a child together
it is not merely father absence, but the additon of another
'mother' figure which is involved.

Bearing this in mind it is perhaps of some relevance to note
that whilst certain studies have supported the view that boys
in father absent families tend to be less 'masculine' on various
measures of sex-typing than are their father present counter-

parts (e.g. Burton and Whiting, 1961), others have claimed
no significant differences on measures of sex-typing between
father absent and father present groups (e.g. Santroch and
Wohlford, 1970).

Quite clearly the outcome of such studies will depend on many
variables, such as socioeconomic status, type, length and cause
of absence, the developmental stage of the child, the child's
sex, the child's relationship with the remaining parent, the
effects of father absence on the mother's relationship to the
child and so forth. Without adequate controls for such factors
as these, coupled with a variety of methodological problems
involved in measuring gender-role orientation, reflected by the
fact that many of the measures have low intercorrelation, it is
understandable that a clear-cut picture does not emerge.

With girls there is not quite the same sort of concern as there
is with boys about the effects living in a lesbian home environment may have on psychosexual development. In this case, given
that there is a same-sex model available for identification and
imitation, the focus tends to be upon how 'adequate' a role model
a lesbian mother may or may not be. It has been suggested, for
example, that ambivalence may be created in the child's developing psychosexual identity (Weeks et al., 1975). With boys also,
though not with specific reference to lesbian mothers, some
psychoanalysts have implied that without a father present
'sexual inversion' may occur as a result of the guilt engendered
by the apparent fulfilment of Oedipal fantasies and wishes.

These kinds of concerns about psychosexual development are
related to the assumption that the child's acceptance or rejection
of a particular gender role is related to the value the parents
ascribe to that role, and to the model the parent actually offers.
However, we must be careful to recognize that the genesis of
gender-role development is still an area which is not clearly
understood, and that it is likely to be influenced by many other
factors besides role models within the family. Certainly, the
concept of identification with the same-sex parent as the key to
understanding gender identity and gender-role development
would seem to be far too simplistic an explanatory concept.
Mothers, for instance, play a significant role in the psychosexual
development of their sons, as well as fathers with their daughters (Kagan, 1964). Nor, of course, should the effect of siblings
and peers be neglected, although once again the data is somewhat inconclusive as to the exact nature of this effect. We must
also bear in mind that different aspects of a child's gender-
role development may not be affected in the same way.

It should also be pointed out that concern about the possible
effects of father absence on a child will be influenced to some
extent by the perceived social justification for that absence. For
instance, the rights to parenthood of seamen who, because of
the nature of their work, have to leave their families for long
periods of time in order to 'provide for the family', are rarely
questioned. Lesbian mothers, on the other hand, represent a

group of women who have chosen to rear their children without a 'father'. There is no apparent social justification for this, and coupled with the negative attitudes which exist towards homosexuality in our society, it is not surprising to find a lack of public acceptance of lesbian parenthood.

Let us now examine the scant literature on children raised in specifically lesbian households, bearing in mind the problems involved in conducting research in this area given the social invisibility of lesbianism, and the possible risks which may be involved for lesbian mothers in participating in such studies.

Kirkpatrick et al. (1976) interviewed, and gave a battery of tests to, a group of twenty children, aged five to twelve, whose mothers were homosexual. In the majority of cases the mothers were living with a female partner. On the basis of their findings, the report suggests that these children were no more likely than other children to adopt atypical gender-role behaviours or become homosexual themselves.

A preliminary report of a study by Green (1978) of children living either in lesbian households or in families where one of the natural parents had had a 'sex-change' operation, came to similar conclusions.

Gender identity, gender-role orientation and sexual partner preference (in the case of the older children), were assessed in a total of twenty-one children who were living in a lesbian household. The age range of this group was five to fourteen years, whereas the number of years they had lived in such an environment ranged from two to six years. In the majority of such cases the children were aware that their mother was homosexual. Measures of assessment used included toy and game preference, peer group composition, the kind of clothes they liked to wear, roles played in fantasy games, vocational aspirations and the draw-a-person test. The adolescents in the group were also asked about their erotic fantasies as well as actual sexual behaviour. According to Green most of the children had a preference for toys, games, clothing, friends, etc. which were 'typical' for children of their age and sex. In addition, those old enough to describe their sexual feelings and desires were reported to be heterosexually orientated. In conclusion Green (1978, pp. 696-7) tentatively suggests that children being raised by female homosexual parents 'do not differ appreciably from children raised in more conventional family settings on macroscopic measures of sexual identity'.

In an attempt to explain this Green suggests that parental lifestyle is only one factor to be considered in psychosexual development, and that the exposure of such children to conventional family styles and sexual identities outside the home is also likely to be important (e.g. in the mass media, at school, via the peer group and their families).

Whilst this study would suggest that being brought up in a lesbian household does not seem to result in atypical psychosexual development, it must be acknowledged that Green is

cautious about drawing too many firm conclusions from the
data presented. Indeed, he stresses that it is a preliminary
report based on only a few families, with no control group and
only a brief follow-up period.

Green's study does, however, raise some important theoretical,
methodological and moral questions pertinent to research in this
area. Theoretically this type of study adopts a certain model of
psychosexual development, which suggests that early experience
is particularly important in the development of sexual identity,
in particular homosexuality. Such a model of homosexuality we
have criticized earlier in the book.

Similarly we may also question the validity of the measures
employed by Green as indicators of sexual preference and
gender-role orientation. In addition, to use research which
shows that children raised by lesbian mothers do not necessarily
grow up to be homosexual or have an atypical gender-role
orientation, as an argument for the acceptability of lesbian
parenthood is to adopt a particular moral stance towards homosexuality. It is to implicitly accept a view of homosexuality as
a negative outcome of development. As one mother commented in
talking about her two children:

It's terrible really when I think about it, in order to keep my
children I've had to agree to bring them up to be heterosexual,
whatever that means, and I ask myself what does that say
about being gay, which I am. And what happens if my kids do
decide to have gay relationships? It's not on, is it? Not seen
as a viable option.

The view of a homosexual identity as a viable developmental
option (Morin and Schultz, 1978), as well as the positive effects
of exposure to homosexual role models during childhood (Riddle,
1978) has, then, been largely ignored in the debate surrounding
lesbian parenthood.

At the Institute of Psychiatry in London, Susan Golombok,
working with Professor Michael Rutter, has studied forty children being brought up in lesbian households, compared with a
group of forty children living with single unmarried mothers. In
the 'Guardian', 16 January 1978, she tentatively suggested that
'so far we have not yet found any children who appear to have
been harmed by being brought up by lesbian mothers. There
seems not to be any harmful effect upon children's psychosexual
development.'

DANGER TO CHILDREN

One assumption which is highly relevant to any discussion of
homosexuality and children is that homosexual men and women
pose some sort of sexual threat to children, either directly or
indirectly, by influencing their later sexual orientation. Such
fears are grounded not only in the confusion of paedophilia and
homosexuality, but also in the emphasis placed on sexual acts,

and contagion and seduction theories of homosexuality.
At the level of a direct sexual threat to children, there are
virtually no cases of female paedophilia, homosexual or otherwise, reported in the literature. This may well reflect the
different social meanings for sexual behaviour that exist for
men and women within our society, plus the fact that physical
intimacy and contact between women and children, given the
traditional association of women with the maternal role as well
as the perceived 'passivity' of female sexuality, seems less likely
to be viewed in sexual terms than if the same actions were
carried out by a man. Despite this, however, the notion of
lesbians being a sexual threat to children does seem to have
some currency. This is an instance where the traditional perception of female-child relationships are overshadowed by
stereotypic beliefs about homosexuality. In such instances
'deviance is greater than conformity' (Gagnon and Simon, 1973).

This sexual concern may make itself known in the treatment
lesbians receive in custody cases. On one occasion where a
judge did grant a lesbian mother access to her child, this was
on condition that every time her little girl had to use the lava-
tory the mother's lover had to go to the other end of the house
('Guardian', 16 January 1978).

SOCIAL ISOLATION

The final area of concern that has been expressed about children
who are living in lesbian households is that they will suffer on
account of society's stigmatization of homosexuals. It has been
suggested, for example, that this may lead to feelings of
embarrassment, shame and guilt in the child, who may experience
being teased or isolated from her or his peer group.

We must bear in mind that there are, as yet, no systematic
studies which have looked at the feelings of children themselves
who are living in lesbian households. Green (1978), however,
did include some qualitative information about whether or not the
children in the families he investigated had been teased or not.
Out of a total of twenty-one children only three recalled being
teased, and in each case these were isolated experiences. In
addition we should note that it is unlikely that a child will be
stigmatized by all of her or his peers, or that all occasions of
teasing will have serious consequences for the child in terms
of his self esteem and social relationships. The possible effects
of teasing will obviously depend on many factors, such as the
form the teasing takes, how often and under what circumstances
it occurs and who does it, as well as the particular personality
of the individual child concerned.

We might in any case want to question the emphasis placed
on the stigma which the children of lesbian mothers might face,
particularly when it is used as a justification for the removal
of a child from such a home environment. Children are

stigmatized for all sorts of reasons, for instance, if they are
mentally or physically handicapped, illegitimate, from an ethnic
minority group, too fat, too thin, too small, too tall, if they
speak with a different accent and so on.

CONCLUSION

In this chapter I have outlined the major concerns that have been
expressed about children whose mothers happen to be homosexual. In the absence of any substantive evidence that a
'lesbian home environment' is in itself a potentially damaging one
for a child, these would seem to derive mainly from sociocultural
beliefs about both homosexuality and the family (Richardson,
1978). In this respect concerns about the effects lesbian mothers
may have on their children are essentially moral concerns. This
is reflected in both the way lesbian mothers have, as a group,
been singled out as potentially 'dangerous' to their children, as
well as in the way researchers have chosen to assess their
'adequacy' as parents.

9 PRESENTING PROBLEMS OF GAY PEOPLE SEEKING HELP

Glenys Parry and
Ray Lightbown

We must state at the outset that it is our belief that being
homosexual in itself has nothing to do with personality disorder,
developmental arrest or underlying pathology. Indeed, after
many years working in a number of different counselling and
therapeutic settings, we are not even sure that there are any
forms of presenting problem specific to homosexual people.

In essence, many of the problems we face are by virtue of
being human, and we believe that certain fundamental issues
should be considered. These include, crucially, making sense
of the world we are born into, developing a stable, cohesive
and realistically valued self concept in relation to that world
and dealing with the challenges posed by intimate relationships
with others. In these general terms, we wish to emphasize the
common psychological ground between homosexual people and
everyone else.

Having stressed commonalities, it is possible to turn to the
ways in which working with homosexual clients may be different
from working with heterosexuals. Our remarks are addressed
mainly to workers who have not spent much thought on this
topic, and who are not in touch, either through friends or
colleagues, with gay lifestyles. We will outline some of the
issues homosexual people face which may be unfamiliar. We will
include problems relating to self concept, coming out, gaining
a gay identity late in life, bereavement and sexual problems
within homosexual relationships.

What homosexual people have in common is that they have
entered, and grown up homosexual within, a world dominated
by the cultural myths of exclusive heterosexuality, where
homosexuality is feared and vilified; a deviant social category.
Throughout our lives we are aware of the world-view of
homosexuality as sinful, sick, sordid or at least immature or
second rate. These beliefs are part of the social fabric, part of
the way that our 'received' reality is structured. It requires
considerable personal resources to come to challenge the prevailing ideology. The process of 'making sense' of these beliefs
may take many years, and it may prove difficult to escape a
legacy of self depreciation. The developmental task of achieving
a cohesive and valued self concept, when set in this context,
assumes a new dimension. Problems concerning self esteem will
certainly be an important part of the counsellor's work.

At the same time as people become aware of their attraction
to the same sex, they are also living in an anti-gay world, or

more accurately a world which does not acknowledge the validity
or even the reality of non-heterosexual lifestyles. Most of us do
not wish to lose the approval of our parents or our peers, and
so a tension is set up between our personal external world (and
the face we present to it) and our personal inner world of
emotions, thoughts and fantasy. People differ greatly in the
degree to which they are aware of this tension, and may
experience it as a vague sense of something being 'different'
about them, without knowing what it is. What happens after
this depends on a great number of factors, including whether
we are able to meet or hear about homosexual people, the attitudes of our parents and to a large extent our own inner
resources, for this is a very lonely time for anyone. A remark-
able number of people succeed in constructing a personal understanding of their homosexuality and accept it as part of their
self image. Some, however, are not able to understand what is
happening to them in these terms, or to tolerate the awareness
of their homosexual feelings. Common strategies used in an
attempt to hold on to a self image which is acceptable in the
individual's terms are denial and splitting. The 'homosexual'
part of the self is associated with 'badness' and is split off from
the rest of the self. After this it is literally disowned, and
homosexual feelings and fantasies begin to be perceived as alien,
unpleasant. Characteristically, though, they may assume a
compulsive form, so that the person in the denial of these feelings comes ironically to be dominated by them.

The counsellor's job in such a situation is very clear. Through
her or his patient, warm and empathic tolerance of the client,
including homosexual feelings, the client can begin to discover
and own what has previously been split off and disowned. How
difficult this process is depends on how profound is the client's
anxieties about their homosexual feelings. Simple acceptance
and a positive attitude to the client's homosexuality and
encouragement to begin or continue expressing it may be all
that is required. Beyond that it is necessary to make an intuitive
formulation about the depth of the client's self loathing. If this
is very great, any simple affirming stance will be violently
rejected by the client, who may demand indignantly some 'real'
help, and may beg to be given aversion therapy or some other
so-called 'cure' for homosexual feelings. It is here that the
counsellor's own faith that there is nothing intrinsically pathological about homosexuality becomes so important.

In the past, many therapists have colluded with the client's
formulation of 'the problem', and have embarked upon re-
orientative therapy. Leaving aside the ethical issues for the
moment, such a course of action is misguided because it misses
the point. It leaves unchallenged the client's desperate avowal
that 'there is nothing wrong with me except these homosexual
impulses, and if I could get rid of them, I would be perfectly
OK.' In going along with this, the therapist has failed the client,
above all by failing to see the seriousness of her or his

predicament and the depth of the distress. We have found that
a concerned and caring stance, coupled with a firm refusal to
join the client in her or his desperate attempt to deny a wider
problem, is what helps in the long run. Of course, in taking
this position it is essential to respect the client's 'truth' whilst
being very honest with the client about one's own beliefs. We
might use some statement like, 'No, I can't agree to help you
get rid of these homosexual feelings, because I do not believe
in the methods you speak of. I will try to help you in a different
way. If, after one session, you still feel you dislike my approach,
I will put you in touch with someone else.' When a mutually
satisfactory 'contract' has been negotiated, the most important
skills in the counsellor are the general ones which apply to
any client. Certain further issues will be encountered, however,
and we will attempt to review some of them.

   There are a number of practical problems encountered after
the client has accepted her or his homosexuality and begun to
explore 'being gay' within the counselling relationship. There
comes a point where the client has to 'come out' as gay to friends
and family. We might expect that a client has made contact with
other homosexual people before wishing to tackle the task of
coming out to heterosexual friends or family, but quite often
people confide in a close friend first. There are quite a number
of specific skills involved in telling people about oneself. It
requires accurate judgment of the realistic consequences of the
action, and this is not always easy. It is possible either to
underestimate negative consequences or overestimate them.
Generally speaking, we find that people more often overestimate
(or catastrophize) the consequences. Once the decision has
been made to come out to, say, parents, the counsellor can give
a great deal of practical help and support. It is best if such an
important event should be planned for in advance and rehearsed.
We all know that, however good our intentions, when speaking
with parents in the heat of the moment it is all too easy to be
overwhelmed by pain, anger or anxiety. It helps to avoid this
by role playing the event with the client, to give them a chance
to test out the different ways they can handle the situation and
their feelings within it. Role playing is valuable for another
reason. One of the commonest reasons people do not live open
and relaxed gay lives may be that they have no idea about what
being openly gay would feel like. It has no meaning for the
client if it is unreal in its implications. One way to reach towards
making this a personal reality for the client is by following the
process 'imagine, act, become'. Role play provides a bridge
between imagination and action. Furthermore clients have found
assertive training and social skills training useful in giving
them specific strategies for coping with negative reactions to
coming out, whether these are an attempt by confused parents
to manipulate the client's guilt, or subtle 'Why do you need to
flaunt it?' put-downs from employers.

   It is clear from our remarks that we take a positive attitude to

coming out. Indeed, we see it as an essential part of building
a positive and integrated self concept, and reducing the tension
between 'me as others see me' and 'me as I see myself'. The gay
person who says, 'I accept my homosexuality, but I don't see
why I should tell anyone else about it, it's my own business,'
is likely, in our experience, to be whistling in the dark. Such
a statement may reflect considerable uncertainty about whether
one is deep down lovable, basically OK. The person whose self
esteem is so fragile as to be threatened by the thought of others
'knowing' is likely to be acting from a basis of self depreciation,
not trusting her or his own experience of her or himself. In
these circumstances, it is very easy to find oneself in a collusive
misalliance, but, for the reasons outlined previously, it is
important to avoid this. However, there is an equal danger at
this stage of feeling that the client needs to 'get on with it'
and to show impatience, or even to become persecutory: e.g.
'Have you told them yet?' Respect for the client's deeper
feelings and bad fantasies about the consequences of being open
is essential, and it is often helpful to use a construct theory
approach, including repertory grid explorations of how 'openly
gay' is construed by the client.

We should add that we are aware that there are situations
where coming out can have serious and unwelcome consequences,
such as losing one's job or losing custody of one's children. We
are not advocating coming out to all people at all times whatever
the cost. Rather, in the interests of establishing an integrated
self concept, it is important to be honest with those who give
us our identity by their knowledge of us.

Prevailing attitudes to homosexual relationships may not have
altered profoundly, yet many of those growing up in, say, the
1920s and 1930s speak with regret about the difficulties they
face in finding personal fulfilment. Inevitably, there are
casualties. It is not uncommon for an older woman or man, who
has only recently felt able to identify as gay, to seek help.
This work can be very distressing, as the counsellor may feel
very helpless in the face of the client's need. The local gay
scene may offer little, and the client may become depressed
when the full sense of what they have missed dawns upon them.
Staying with this pain and sharing it is a considerable challenge,
and yet ultimately it is worthwhile. Sharing the client's sadness
and anger validates her or his gay identity, and initiates a
process of working through that which can otherwise become
'frozen' into a lifelong and entrenched bitterness.

Ageing and the tragedy of missed opportunities is a ubiquitous
human concern, which may take special forms in homosexual
counselling. The same can be said of bereavement. It is unlikely
that the process of mourning after the loss of a loved partner
is any different for homosexual people. What is different, often,
is the context within which the grieving takes place. Many
bereaved people report their feelings of social isolation, even
to the point of being shunned by friends and acquaintances.

This experience is even keener for the average homosexual person, for in many cases their relationship is not socially recognized, let alone sanctioned. The bereaved homosexual woman or man may not be invited to the funeral, and if no will was made may have to face the ordeal of their dead lover's family sharing out savings or possessions. Then the process of mourning begins, and if, as in many cases we have worked with, there is a total lack of social support, this can become blocked and a 'pathological grief reaction' may follow. The role of the counsellor is again very clear. By giving wholehearted warm approval to the love relationship and sincere recognition of the enormity of the loss, the ground is prepared for grief work to begin. In addition to psychotherapeutic work, local gay befrienders, if available, can support the client and per- haps introduce new social ties.

As with the other topics covered, our discussion of helping homosexuals with sexual problems is a very general one. We assume a working knowledge of the causes and mechanisms of sexual dysfunctions and their treatment as applied to hetero- sexual couples. If this is not the case, Masters and Johnson (1979) and Kaplan (1974) will provide background information.

Clearly, in order to feel confident in applying these methods with homosexual people, the counsellor must not only build up a broad-based knowledge of human sexuality but also feel entirely comfortable in saying and hearing explicit sexual des- criptions or words relating to homosexual lovemaking. It is also important to be clear what patterns of sexual behaviour are typical, and what are the common problems encountered.

Between men, initial activities often include kissing and mutual masturbation, either simultaneously or sequentially. With increasing experience, differentiated preferences arise. Preliminaries may include fondling, massaging, open mouth kissing and other sexually arousing acts. This could be follow- ed by mutual masturbation, body rubbing, fellatio, anal intercourse or any combination of these. Between women, kis- sing, fondling, massage, stimulation of the breasts and nipples may be followed by manual masturbation, cunnilingus or rubbing against the partner's thigh.

In general terms, problems can arise, as with heterosexual couples, through either ignorance or inexperience or a more deep-seated sexual dysfunction. Of course, the extent to which sexual problems are merely symptomatic of covert hostilities in the relationship should be assessed, and more general coun- selling offered if this is the case. The problems of ignorance and inexperience may be compounded in a homosexual couple by lingering feelings of guilt or shame. Sexual behaviour, like most human behaviour, is learned, and the conditions associated with good learning (low performance anxiety and positive role models) are perhaps more conspicuously absent for homosexual people.

For both sexes, learning to give and receive pleasure in an

intimate relationship takes time and practice. For example, masturbating someone else is an acquired skill, even between people of the same sex, for different people have different preferences in terms of, for men, dry or lubricated glans, speed of stroke, type of grip and firmness of grip, or, for women, whether simultaneous vaginal stimulation is enjoyed, which part of the clitoris is most sensitive and so on.

Common problems found amongst men include: dislike of fellatio, gagging or retching; problems associated with anal intercourse including a fear of penetration, or inability to relax leading to premature ejaculation, delayed ejaculation or impotence. Among women, problems may include lack of sexual desire by one partner, dislike of cunnilingus and anorgasmia, whether caused by poor technique or by intrapsychic processes.

In the great majority of cases of sexual dysfunction, the solution is easily achieved by straightforward application of standard sex therapy techniques within a warm, accepting and good humoured counselling relationship. The counsellor's attitude is crucial, to role model the open, communicative and unembarrassed style so necessary to progress. Here the depth of the counsellor's acceptance of homosexuality will be tested, and if s/he has not worked through her or his own homosexuality, problems can arise.

In this brief essay, we have attempted to set our topic in perspective. The references at the end of this Part include some useful books and articles for the worker new to counselling homosexual men and women (Heiman et al., 1976; Harris and Sisley, 1977; Silverstein, 1977; Walker, 1977; Leiblum and Pervin, 1980; Richardson and Hart, 1980).

10 MARRIED AND ISOLATED HOMOSEXUALS

Diane Richardson and
John Hart

The problems of people who are married or isolated are here
considered together because they may have the similar experience of living a lifestyle which is not congruent with their
identification as homosexual. In using the expression 'married'
homosexuals we wish to include all those who are in long-term
heterosexual relationships.

There are of course many reasons why someone may feel
isolated as a homosexual in our society, and being married is
just one of these. We will first discuss some of the other reasons
for isolation, before looking in particular at the experience of
being married and homosexual.

The fact that in our society people are assumed to be heterosexual unless shown to be otherwise leads almost invariably to
the common initial experience in identifying as homosexual,
that one is different and alone. This is reinforced by the unlike-
lihood of the person knowing anyone else who is homosexual,
given that the majority of homosexual men and women pass as
heterosexual outside of a gay milieu.

In addition, the images of homosexuals that are available
are likely to be stereotypic, e.g. the 'camp' homosexual man
and the 'butch' lesbian, and the individual may feel s/he
cannot identify with these. The effects of such intrapsychic
isolation may include loneliness, alienation from peers and
significant others, a personal pathological view of one's
sexuality and the psychological strains involved in not reveal-
ing part of one's self identity. The latter may include fears
of discovery, having to continually present a facade, a sense
of falsity and superficiality in relationships with others and a lack
of self worth. Such painful experiences, in conjunction with a
lack of awareness of the possibilities of a positive view of
homosexuality, may result in the individual seeing the only way
out as 'cure'. An extreme reaction for some individuals to such
a view of their homosexuality may be the development of various
manifestations of psychological disturbance, which may include
suicidal gestures and attempts.

For the socially isolated person there is the task of knowing
who to tell and/or contacting 'someone else like them'. Given
the general lack of information which exists about homosexual
organizations and self-help groups, s/he may have to decide
on whether to tell family and friends. Of course, involved in
such a decision will be an evaluation of the possibly dangerous
implications of parents or close friends having this knowledge:

for example, a young person could be made the subject of statutory child care. People may also face extremely hostile and violent reactions and/or social ostracism. The only other alternative may be to refer her or himself to a 'professional helper', for example a GP, priest, agony columnist or organization such as the Samaritans. The advice s/he receives will obviously vary tremendously, depending upon the helper's attitude, and may by no means guarantee an introduction to local homosexual organizations, either because of the helper's lack of knowledge of these, or their theoretical/moral stance.

This mention of self-help groups leads us to recognize that the availability of these and other social facilities for homosexual women and men (e.g. clubs, discos, bars) will vary according to geographical location. A lack of such facilities in Britain is particularly apparent outside the major metropolitan areas. For the many homosexual women and men who do not live within easy reach of such areas, the lack of immediately available and regular social contact with other homosexuals may not lead to any substantial change in their experience of being isolated.

In discussing the availability of social facilities we should note that because the gay milieu tends to be male dominated, the problems of social isolation may be greater for homosexual women (Hart and Richardson, 1980). Age as well as gender can also be an influencing factor here, in that most self-help and commercial organizations do not cater for adolescents, nor for those beyond middle age.

Certainly if the person is able to meet other homosexuals this may diminish feelings of social isolation. We must also recognize that such occasions may enable the individual to make and develop a particular relationship with another person. Involvement in a long-term relationship does of course offer some protection against the isolation which may be experienced by an individual. An emphasis on such a couple relationship may, however, lead to the pair seeing no further need of a homosexual social network, and a detachment from such interactions. The consequences of this, in terms of social isolation, are clearly apparent when such a partnership ends, either through death or separation. Indeed as Bell and Weinberg (1978, p.216) point out:

> Suicidal ideation and suicide attempts are apt to occur at the time of the breakdown or dissolution of a significant 'couple' relationship. Such extreme reactions on the part of those involved need not lead us to conclude that homosexual adults have some special deficit in their personalities. Rather, homosexual partnerships may involve more mutual interdependence than is found among heterosexual couples and, for that reason alone, their disruption may be more debilitating for those involved.

We must also consider the amount of investment the individual feels able to make in living a homosexual lifestyle. Obviously the woman or man who sees it as necessary to pass for heterosexual the majority of the time, and is only openly homosexual in restricted environments, will be more at risk of social isolation than someone who has a greater involvement in the homosexual subculture. In addition, someone who is open about her or his homosexuality in a majority of situations is far less likely to feel alienated from either self or others.

Clearly, helping the isolated homosexual person requires an assessment of the reasons why s/he is isolated, and to what extent this has social/psychological components. In addition, in advising in such a situation account should be taken of the possible problems which may arise for each individual in managing a homosexual identity. This may involve a discussion of the costs and benefits of being open or secretive about homosexuality in relation to particular people and situations. Assessment of local social facilities for homosexuals may require the advisor to directly facilitate the setting up of self-help groups if these are not available.

If we now turn to 'married' homosexuals we are obviously dealing with a diverse group of people who are likely to have the common experience of conflict in the commitment they feel able to make to living a homosexual lifestyle, in addition to being involved in a heterosexual married lifestyle. Marriage has sometimes been recommended as a 'treatment' for people who have difficulty in accepting their same-sex interests. The reality has usually been, however, that marriage has for such people, led to a compounding of their problems.

Married homosexuals form a larger group than one might first anticipate, given that homosexuality is frequently seen as precluding cross-sex relationships, marriage and children. Bell and Weinberg (1978) quote a number of studies which found that approximately 20 per cent of homosexual men, and even more lesbians, have been married at least once. Their own study reports that more than a third of the homosexual women and less than a fifth of the homosexual men had been married. (Most of the black male and female homosexual respondents who had been married, and about half of their white counterparts, had children.) One of the many reasons for this reported higher frequency of marriage among homosexual women is that marriage may be seen as a preferable alternative to a life career of low paid, low status employment.

What are then some of the common experiences of being married and homosexual?

We first need to recognize that some individuals will have identified as homosexual before getting married, whilst others will have come to such an awareness during their married relationship. In either case they must make a choice whether or not to share this knowledge with their spouse, and if they have children, with them. In addition a decision must also be made whether or not to seek, outside of their marriage, same-sex relationships.

If the homosexual woman or man chooses not to tell her or his spouse that they identify as homosexual, then there are likely to be problems of alienation and feelings of emotional distance from the partner, as well as fears of discovery. On the other hand, if s/he does explain the way s/he feels s/he may encounter a range of hostile reactions which include rejection, violence, disbelief and the risk of separation and loss of the children. If this is the first time the person has revealed a homosexual identity, such a negative response may be particularly damaging to her or his self image. Alternatively, the spouse may be understanding, although this may include the suggestion that some sort of psychiatric help is needed.

Clearly these reactions will partly depend upon the current state of the couple's emotional and sexual relationship. Another important factor will be whether the partner is already involved in a same-sex relationship or expresses the need to seek such a relationship. This may seem to be related to open and closed marriages, where the conflicts are usually seen as being attached to the status of monogamy. However, we would emphasize that for the married homosexual and their partner there are additional problems to be faced related to the separate, and in many instances separatist, social worlds of homosexual and heterosexual women and men. The homosexual partner will also have to face the additional stigma that is involved in having relationships with the same sex. We must be aware, however, that being married reduces the likelihood, and hence the stigma, of being seen as homosexual. This may be beneficial in situations where the individual wishes to pass as heterosexual. Within a gay milieu, however, this may be dysfunctional, in that the married homosexual may have to face distrust and/or suspicion from other homosexuals, who may take the view that such a person is not 'really homosexual'. In addition, relationships with married homosexuals are frequently seen by possible partners as being too problematic in terms of the dual commitments of the married person.

In discussing the experience of being married and homosexual we should, of course, take note of possible sex differences. For example, women are more at risk of experiencing a violent response from their husbands to a declaration of their homosexual interests than are homosexual men from their wives. On the other hand, a man may be at risk from his wife's actions because of the potential illegality of his homosexual experiences. Also we should note that, irrespective of sexual orientation, all women and men are liable to be subject to the double standard of morality which exists in our society concerning extramarital relationships. In this respect non-monogamous relationships, with either sex, are generally viewed as more acceptable for men than women. In addition, given the greater social and financial independence of most men in our society, the opportunities to engage in homosexual relationships are generally more available for men than women. Also, having the responsibility of caring for children may be another reason why homosexual women find it difficult to make contacts outside the home. Social facilities for homosexuals reflect and reinforce this disparity; they tend to be both male-orientated and dominated. It is also easier for homosexual men than women to have casual sexual contacts if they so wish, in that known public places for such encounters (e.g. lavatories, public parks, etc.) do not exist for women.

Clearly the married homosexual in facing her or his homosexual identity will have some important life decisions to make. A number of choices are available. These include wishing to continue the married relationship whilst identifying as homosexual but choosing not to engage in same-sex acts, having an 'open' marriage which does include the possibility of such relationships or dissolving the marriage. Alternatively, s/he may choose to remain married and seek treatment for homosexual feelings.

Certain problems exist for married homosexuals in each of these adaptations. If they decide to remain in a monogamous relationship with their spouses, there may be problems such as feelings of lost opportunities and a lack of validation of their identities as homosexual. In addition, their partners may feel guilty about restricting their choice. Where the homosexual man or woman does operationalize her or his homosexuality whilst continuing with the marriage, the problems, as we have already suggested, may be centred on the management of two separate lifestyles. We may note here that in thinking about the couple it is more likely to be the female spouse who suffers more discomfort, because of the ability of the married male homosexual to pursue a homosexual lifestyle at the expense of his wife and children. The corollary to this is that married female homosexuals may have less opportunity, energy, time or finance to involve themselves in a lifestyle outside the home.

Where separation or divorce is seen as the solution then there may be problems of decisions over custody and access of the children, financial and property settlements and social and emotional dependency needs. The latter may of course take different forms for men and women.

Finally, where the married homosexual seeks treatment as a solution, an assessment needs to be made of the meanings of her or his homosexual identity, for both self and spouse. Masters and Johnson (1979) have shown that it is possible to help homosexual people who wish to increase their ability to enjoy heterosexual relationships. Such procedures, however, may not be applicable to people who see no dissatisfaction with their heterosexual or homosexual relationships, and/or who view their problem as being related to the management of two separate lifestyles. In offering help the adviser should, of course, also be aware of the self-help groups which cater specifically for the problems of married homosexuals and their partners (see p.189).

11 YOUNG GAYS

Rose Robertson

Most of the literature on homosexuality in the past has assumed the difficulties connected with this sexual orientation are the prerogative of adulthood. But the experience of all counselling and supportive agencies concerned with male homosexuals and lesbians has been that questions about sexual orientation in fact begin in adolescence.

The legal problems of male homosexuals under the age of twenty-one are dealt with in this Part by Charles Dodd (pp.139-43). In the total absence of legislation for women one could assume a nominal age of consent of sixteen for lesbians, this being the age set for heterosexuals. But in view of the prejudice against lesbians of all ages, this is quite academic.

With such a legal situation the problems and the dangers of offering a counselling service, befriending service or support group to the teenage homosexual immediately become apparent. Forming a youth group which gives young people the opportunity to meet and socialize together could be construed as corrupting them. Relationships formed between young males and those who are over twenty-one, could also be open to legal prosecution. We should note here that there is no distinction in law between a loving, caring relationship formed between two people of differing age groups and the same sex, and those where self gratification by the older person is the only motive. Both could be presumed as being of criminal intent.

Starting in the early 1960s public opinion on many social issues appeared to undergo massive change. Sexual liberation was seen as very much a part of this liberalization. Abortion was comparatively easier to obtain, the pill became readily available, sex and settled relationships outside marriage became widely accepted after generations of disapproval and unfrenzied discussion of sexual matters in the mass media became common.

However, most sex education in schools remained concerned purely with the clinical, mechanical act of sex culminating in procreation. Almost invariably it neglected the range of sexuality in all human beings; and it neglected almost entirely the emotional response of one person to another. Therefore, young people were growing up in a society that inevitably made them aware of themselves and others as sexual beings at a very early age, yet left them quite unequipped for their emotional responses to sexual situations. In this environment, also, were young people who were developing a predominantly homosexual orientation. However confused and conflicting society's guide-

lines about heterosexuality were, they did at least exist.
Homosexual young people, however, develop their identity
in a heterosexual environment in which they feel alienated. The
only role models likely to be available are the stereotypes offered
by the media: for males the exaggerated gestures, the limp
wrists, the mincing walk; for females the butch, manly PE
teacher. Virtually all young persons who feel themselves to be
homosexual cannot identify themselves with this caricature of
the homosexual. These problems of identity can create a stunt-
ing of emotional and psychological growth, the consequences
of which may carry over into adult life.
Anyone who has been involved in dealing with the young
homosexual over the past decade will, whatever their previously
held beliefs, have been confronted with repeated evidence that
homosexuality is not a deliberate decision, but an orientation
of which the young person becomes aware, which develops as
s/he becomes more emotionally and sexually aware.
Young people often describe a feeling of uneasiness about
themselves, an awareness of being different, but an inability
to define or put a label on that difference. They frequently feel
alienated and isolated from their peer group. At this stage
they may not identify themselves as homosexual, although their
fantasies during masturbation may centre around the same sex.
During this period of development, and particularly when
these young people are trying to come to terms with themselves,
it should be emphasized that there are no patterns or guidelines
with which they can identify.
A comparison with the experience of young heterosexuals may
highlight and emphasize the difficulties of the young homosexual.
Boys and girls at an early age, certainly by thirteen, have a
variety of ways of learning about their sexuality. Discos are
open to them, youth clubs are readily available, advice centres
abound. More important than all this, however, is the general
approval of society and the support of family and friends. These
circumstances combine to give teenagers the opportunity of
trying out heterosexual relationships, thereby allowing them to
gain knowledge of themselves and be aware of their preferences.
This learning process is denied the young homosexual. Even
if, despite the many difficulties confronting them, they have
accepted themselves, they then have to confront a number of
ensuing difficulties. Should they tell parents? How? Will their
parents reject them, and what will they then do? Do they
confide in friends, in brothers and sisters? Do they produce,
for the benefit of the family and others, girl friends or boy
friends, real or imaginary? And where can they meet, socialize
and exchange confidences with other young homosexual people?
Young people living in large towns or cities may have available to them, through citizens advice bureaus, doctors, social
workers, samaritans and other helping agencies, information
about counselling and social groups concerned with their
particular needs. However, this does not make it any easier

for those young people who are homosexual to go in and ask for relevant information. Nevertheless, amongst homosexual young people these are the luckier ones. Workers in this field will be aware of the absolute despair of young people in isolated small towns and villages who feel themselves to be homosexual. They may feel afraid to approach a family doctor because he is a family friend, unable to tell a minister of religion because of fear of chastisement, unable to approach a teacher because the education given, particularly the sex education, leads them to assume that those teaching do not accept other ways of relating than heterosexual.

It should therefore surprise no one that breakdown, depression and attempted suicide are often the end product of pressures that become unendurable.

Counselling to avert these situations is thus best started whilst the person is young, and before s/he has become set into a pattern of stunted growth and repeated depression. Ideally, such counselling should involve the family so that a reconciliation can be attempted between what the young person sees as normal family life, and her or his sexuality.

While the young person may have had some years to come to terms with her or his orientation, parents are usually completely unprepared for this development. They have been totally unaware that the child growing up in their family may not in future fulfil the role they assumed s/he would. With parents feelings of guilt are predominant; they feel they have somehow gone wrong in the upbringing of the child, and that their mistakes have led to this result.

The belief is also strongly held by parents that the young person does not know her or his own mind. It is felt that they have not tried sufficiently hard to make contact with the opposite sex, and that if contact were only established and continued, they would change. The following statements, often made by parents, give a clear indication of their acceptance and belief in a universal stereotyped homosexual person:

'S/he cannot be gay; they don't look gay.'

'He has never used make up.'

'S/he gets on so well with boys/girls, and has many friends of the opposite sex.'

'He likes football, and has always been the manly type.'

'She is so feminine and pretty and has always been popular with boys.'

'We have always tried to be good parents; why are you punishing us?'

There is, on the part of these parents, a feeling of alienation from their children. They have found something entirely unexpected in someone they had good reason to feel they knew better than anyone else. It is as though they have now entered a strange, subterranean world, some secret and threatening society to which they have no part; the shock is immense, although violent reactions are rare. Where these do occur they

may be the result of initial shock, and/or deep problems in
one of the parents or the marriage, often of a sexual nature.
A parent with sexual difficulties of any kind will tend to assume
that this has been the cause of the child's homosexuality. Careful and patient counselling is essential in these cases, and
frequently leads into areas of difficulty for the parents far
removed from the original issue, the young person's homosexuality.

Again a comparison with the heterosexual situation may
delineate the difficulties for the parent with a homosexual child.
If young people show signs of exploring relationships with the
opposite sex at what the parents consider too early an age,
parents have mechanisms to cope with this. Although they may
feel out of their depth, or uneasy about the apparent sophistication shown by sons or daughters about sexual matters,
they can at least share these worries to a greater or lesser
extent with other parents, relatives, friends or neighbours.
They can strike a posture, real or otherwise, of righteous
indignation or parental understanding.

Parents who become aware of a homosexual orientation in
their children have none of these safety valves. The sharing
of confidences, learning how other families are coping, the
normal ways of making a problem bearable and possibly understandable, are denied to the parents of the homosexual young
person. They fear exposure, ridicule, and prejudice for their
children and themselves.

Even the most understanding parents have difficulties with
the knowledge that their child is homosexual. Many believe,
wrongly, that all homosexual people are attracted to very young
children; others, that there cannot be lasting relationships
between homosexuals. Many others subscribe to the belief that
homosexuality means only a series of sexual affairs without
emotion and without love. They therefore see their child's future
life as lonely, unhappy and loveless. None of this is any more
inevitable for the homosexual than it is for the heterosexual.
However, in the absence of such knowledge, the fact that very
few programmes on the media show the positive and fulfilling
nature of a stable homosexual relationship becomes very
significant. Virtually no programmes have shown that homosexual
relationships range from the totally satisfactory to the quite
unstable, in exactly the same manner as do heterosexual
relationships. Instead, the media usually paint a bleak and
depressing picture of the difficulties and prejudices likely to
be met.

Parents have fears concerning other members of their family.
Will brothers and sisters be homosexual too? Should a brother
or sister previously sharing the same room be separated?
Should brothers and sisters be told about a homosexual sibling?
If they allow the boy or girl to mix with other homosexuals,
will this encourage their child to become 'more gay'? A homosexual orientation is, on occasions, found in more than one

member of the same family, but this is very much the exception
rather than the rule. To separate without explanation, and for
no logical reason, two brothers or two sisters who have previously shared a bedroom is unnecessary and wrong. The homosexual brother or sister will inevitably feel rejected by and
under suspicion from their own family.

In the experience of the writer, it does great damage to
family relationships if the siblings of the family are aware that
something is causing unhappiness to parents and a loved brother
or sister, and yet are kept in ignorance of the cause. They feel
uneasy, resentful and angry that they are not trusted sufficiently to share a family problem. When siblings are of an age
to be able to understand and absorb an explanation of sexuality,
giving them this knowledge not only strengthens family ties
but may pre-empt many of the sexual fears and worries they
may have had about themselves.

There is no doubt that parents generally are reluctant to
allow homosexual young people to mix with others of a similar
orientation and are particularly fearful and suspicious of
relationships between younger and older homosexuals. They feel
that by allowing a young person to join a gay youth group -
should such a group be available to them - they will be
encouraging them to be homosexual.

Behind this thinking, of course, is the hope that if they can
segregate their young son or daughter, keep them away from
any contact with other homosexuals, somehow they will become
heterosexual, and the whole episode can be forgotten. This
grasping at straws by so many parents is significant. It demon-
strates clearly the still widely held belief that all young people
are heterosexual and can only be 'corrupted' into homosexuality
by contact with homosexuals. The rules of logic cannot be
applied to human emotions and reactions in a traumatic situation.
If they could the logical answer would be that the heterosexual
is the corrupter of the young homosexual because of the attempt
to force her or him into a way of life, a pattern of relating,
which s/he does not want because of her or his emotional and
sexual feelings and desires.

When counselling the young homosexual it should always be
remembered that her or his identity may have been challenged
for many years. The young person is not helped by a counsellor
expressing doubts about the ability of the client to decide
where her or his predominant orientation lies. Neither is it of
help to suggest psychiatric treatment. Healthy young homosexuals, male or female, need practical and sensible suggestions
as to how best they can fit their homosexuality into the rest of
their lives. Bearing in mind that they will live and work in a
largely heterosexual environment, being at ease and accepting
of themselves is of prime importance.

There will, however, be people of all ages seeking help and
presenting homosexuality as being the sole cause of all their
difficulties. In many cases this will prove not to be true.

Careful questioning brings out factors in the background, signs of emotional disturbance which are deep rooted and quite distinct from a developing homosexual orientation.

This distinction can best be illustrated by quoting a factual case history.

Derek was sixteen years old, one of many homosexual teenagers who come for counselling ostensibly because they are homosexual and cannot accept themselves. His parents separated when he was four years old, later divorced and subsequently both remarried. Derek lived with his father and his new wife from choice, until he was eight. He made regular weekly visits to his mother but showed no interest in the two children she had borne to her new husband. It was after one of these weekly visits he quite unexpectedly expressed the wish to live with his mother. He appeared to feel very strongly about this and the necessary arrangements were made. Six months after the move he began truanting from school, quarrelling violently with his mother and being disruptive both at home and at school. He was referred to a child guidance clinic and, with his mother, made regular visits for the next twelve months.

At the age of fourteen years he made his first suicide attempt and was seen by a psychiatrist. Derek told him he was a 'queer' and that his parents would never accept him as such, that if they were told he would make sure that the next time 'he would do the job properly'.

He gave no further details of what exactly he meant by 'queer', and the psychiatrist felt himself to be on too uncertain ground to follow up with detailed questioning. With this impasse, and the boy coming to feel his problem was being ignored, the sessions fizzled out. However, feeling the pressure to be unbearable, the boy next contacted an agency that dealt exclusively with young people's sexual difficulties. Here, under painstaking and slow questioning, it emerged that what he in fact was doing was cross-dressing: that is, putting on various articles of women's clothing - his mother's in this case - when privacy permitted. His sexual fantasies, however, remained strictly based on girls. Derek had assumed that such wearing of women's clothing meant he was homosexual.

As the pressures of his situation mounted, and as the professional attention he was receiving failed to diagnose his problem correctly, he began cross-dressing almost blatantly, virtually inviting discovery. He began to take items of his mother's clothing that he knew she was currently wearing. Discovery inevitably followed. Meanwhile, he remained ultra-sensitive and hostile towards any questioning of his sexuality by the psychiatrist.

Here, indeed, the professional is as much a victim of the general ignorance of sexual matters as is a young person such as Derek. Anything but the right sort of careful questioning, and then the correct evaluation of information received, is doomed in such a case. Here the psychiatrist's lack of information on the issues of homosexuality and transvestism, and his evident unease with sexual matters on which he was under-informed, fed the young person's own unease with these matters, and widened the gulf between professional and client.

Under similar circumstances of lack of recognition, young people will often behave publicly in what is socially seen as a conspicuously gay manner, while clamming up tightly in private discussion if they feel the agency they are dealing with is at a loss to understand what they are facing.

There is no supportive lifestyle for the young isolated homosexual. Correct diagnosis of her or his surface difficulties, and understanding of the deeper pressures involved, is the beginning of bringing her or him back into the fullness of society.

12 THE PROBLEMS OF OLDER HOMOSEXUALS

Jeffrey Weeks

Despite its inevitability, there is a dearth of both theoretical work and empirical information on the ageing process of homosexuals. As Plummer (1975, p.152) has put it, 'the process of "reaching middle age" and "becoming old" as a homosexual are two areas where little is known and much needs to be known.' Since these words were written little has happened to alleviate the situation. The major organizations concerned with the social needs of older people have displayed little interest in the specific problems of older homosexuals. A pamphlet published by the organization Age Concern in the early 1970s on the sexual difficulties of older people failed even to mention homosexuals at all (West, 1977, p.165). Even the growth of empirical research into the lifestyles of gay people has revealed little about older homosexuals. A recent comprehensive survey of the field could find only five empirical studies dealing with the theme between 1967 and 1978, and all of these concentrated on male homosexuals and used small samples (Kimmel, 1978, who himself used fourteen male respondents for his research). Because of the long-standing oppressive regulation of homosexuality there is little evidence that can be deployed systematically about the ageing processes of homosexuals in the past (though see autobiographies such as Ackerley, 1968 or Driberg, 1977). And though the stigma has eased over the past decade or so, there are still few respondents who can sufficiently cast off a lifetime of discretion to talk freely about their intimate experiences and feelings to researchers, however sympathetic the latter may be.

A considerable amount of generalizations are still based upon samples drawn from prison populations or psychiatric case books. The ever-growing evidence of homosexuals well integrated into the gay community, while presenting a different position, is probably in a way also unrepresentative, for a high proportion of homosexually inclined people still live secretive and furtive sexual lives. The result is that we know more about the publicly stigmatized or the open and guilt-free than about the isolated. Moreover, the information so far available relates overwhelmingly to men, this reflecting not so much a male bias in research interest as the lower social profile, hitherto, of lesbian identities and subcultures (see Faraday 1981).

The empirical material in this paper comes from a series of interviews conducted with twenty-five homosexual men over sixty in 1978 and 1979.[1] The interviews were largely unstructured in form, and the information gathered constitutes brief life histories rather than a series of readily accessible answers on the 'problem of ageing'. The sample, obtained from personal contacts, through gay self-help organizations and from advertising in both the gay and non-gay press, is by its nature 'unrepresentative' in a formal sense. Those who agreed to be interviewed obviously had a relatively high degree of self confidence and a willingness to talk freely about their lives, which is perhaps not yet characteristic of the homosexually inclined population as a whole. No lesbians were interviewed, the project being explicitly related to male homosexual subcultures, so the data obtained pertains clearly to male homosexuals only, and this no doubt will bias some of the points made here. In particular, the concern with casual sex and regular subcultural involvement, which plays a major part in male homosexual lifestyles, is a less obvious factor in the lesbian way of life (for a discussion of the consequent research problem see Faraday, 1981). But despite these obvious limitations the interview material is very useful because it enables us to test some of the prevailing myths against the lived experiences of self-defined homosexuals. And in the relaxed atmosphere encouraged by the form of the free-ranging interview it was possible for the respondents to talk freely about their lives.

It needs no underlining that heterosexuals and homosexuals share most of the general social and physical characteristics of getting old in our culture. But the point we need to bear in mind when talking about ageing is that it is not a simple or unproblematic process, with preordained effects. It is, on the contrary, a complex biosocial process structured by a variety of historical factors. 'Ageing', as an experience, changes through time; an obvious enough point, perhaps, but one frequently overlooked when sweeping generalizations are offered about the problems of ageing, especially in this context, among homosexuals. As a corollary of this point, we need also to remember that we can no longer regard 'being homosexual' as constituting a single experience (Bell and Weinberg, 1978). There is now abundant evidence for the social variations in homosexual roles, identities and behaviour (Weeks, 1981), and it is easier to be an older homosexual person in the more relaxed ambience of New York or San Francisco than in a South Wales mining village. It is also easier to live a homosexual life if you are male, though the women's movement has created the space for a politically oriented lesbian identity. The changes that have certainly transformed the opportunities for being openly gay in our culture have been uneven in their impact and have in a sense been superimposed upon, rather than transformed, older patterns (Weeks, 1977; Altman, 1980).

Despite these qualifications, which account for some of the difficulties of research, it is still a little surprising that so little is known about the problems faced by older homosexuals,

for these putative problems have loomed large both in the
conventional social attitudes towards homosexuality and in the
mythology of the gay world itself. There is, for instance, a
widespread feeling that the commercial and also the more
politically orientated gay scenes are very youth orientated, with
a high premium on youthful good looks, affluence, an easy
going hedonism and success measured through the rate of
casual sexual pickups. The transience of many sexual encounters
in turn feeds fear of loneliness in old age. Moreover, the
organization of the gay subcultures around such activities as
cruising and discos is likely to be unappealing for many older
people, who might want a less frenetic or competitive life.
(West, 1977, p.142). Indeed, the contrast often drawn between
the glittering ephemerality of the youthful scene and the
loneliness of old age can act as a mechanism for the social control of homosexuality. As Kimmel (1978) has put it,

Fears about ageing as a gay person have been used to dis-
suade young people from accepting their homosexuality,
further hindering self-acceptance. Likewise, older gay
persons may believe their future development is reflected in
such a pathetic figure as the one created by Thomas Mann
in his 'Death in Venice'.

Not surprisingly, many individuals find it gets more rather
than less difficult to accept their homosexuality as they grow
older.

But even within the gay world itself, amongst those who
have accepted a homosexual way of life, there are very real
discrepancies of confidence and 'marketability' between young
and old. In part this is an effect of the greater self confidence,
or at least social ease, of those brought up and coming out
today in a less oppressive social situation, and can generate
real areas of difficulty. It may, as it has been well put, 'dis-
qualify a shy, unattractive old man and simply render him a
double failure: a failure in the heterosexual world and a failure
in the homosexual world' (Plummer, 1975, p.150). The traditional organization of the male homosexual world around sexual
contacts can inhibit the development of friendships across the
age barriers. One respondent of mine in his seventies felt it
necessary to curtail a (non-sexual) friendship with a man in
his twenties precisely because he was being gently teased about
its supposed sexual nature. Another respondent noted that
many gay people

tend to assume automatically that an older man that even
speaks to them is automatically wanting to go to bed with
them ... which can be absurd sometimes. You can offer someone a lift because they happen to live in the same locality
as you. And they'll refuse.

In their awareness of such attitudes, fears of ageing can
begin to dominate even quite self confident homosexual people
as they reach the threshold of middle life (Cant, 1980), though
these feelings seem to be stronger among homosexual men than

lesbians (Saghir and Robins, 1973). Lesbians have, for a
variety of historical reasons, been less orientated towards subcultural involvements and sexual self-marketing than have men,
and are consequently less likely to be concerned about competing
with younger 'rivals'. On the other hand, given the historically
shaped identification of womanhood with maternity, many lesbians who have lived independent lives may be more likely than
homosexual men to feel the absence of children.

The women's movement is, of course, challenging many of the
traditional assumptions about motherhood and femininity, and
many lesbians are bringing up children outside conventional
family patterns. This is likely to have major transforming
effects in the future. All that can be said at the moment is that
such changes as have taken place have aroused major con-
troversy, precisely around the topic of lesbian mothers
(Hemmings, 1980).

Given the strength of the familial ideology in our society,
it is not surprising that many homosexuals are apprehensive
about an old age without the supportive network of relationships
that the family by its very nature is expected to supply. It
needs to be said, however, that most people in old age living
outside a family situation are almost certainly heterosexual: the
family provides no guarantee of security in old age. But this
isolation from the family can be exaggerated. Given the absence
of a viable homosexual identity and way of life until the latter
part of the nineteenth century, and its only gradual and uneven
transmission in this century (Weeks, 1977), it is likely that
those with homosexual feelings did on the whole live in family
situations. The real problem was a different one: that of having to negotiate what was either a life of emotional frustration,
or a double life. The constant need for discretion is likely to
have been a more potent weapon of control than the nature of
the homosexual subculture itself. Its effects can stay even
when circumstances change. A respondent observed:

> The only time that I have really referred to my homosexuality
> explicitly was ... at the beginning of last year, when J. and
> I split.... without using the word homosexuality, which of
> course was not necessary ... to some friends I would say ...
> J. and I have split up.... I think I am readier now, if an
> occasion should arise, to say yes I am gay, but I don't make
> an occasion.

This was said by a man of sixty-nine, who had worked in a
theatrical ambience where such matters as homosexuality are
traditionally often seen as acceptable. The basic problem, then,
I would suggest, is not so much the nature of homosexuality
or of the gay subculture, which are after all historically formed;
the difficulties of older gay people stem from the hostile climate
in which they are likely to have become aware of their sexuality.
Ageing, as a result, is likely to bring a new inflection in the
force of stigma rather than a fundamental change of circumstances.

Despite all the qualifications we must make there is plentiful evidence that many homosexuals have fully accepted their homosexuality and have found viable ways of life. In this context, moreover, there are clear signs that facing old age was far from being a major crisis point, or a devastating break. Sociologists (e.g. Plummer, 1975) have identified a series of possible crisis points in the life careers of homosexuals; an awareness of difference, the association of this difference with a stigmatized way of life, the acceptance of oneself as homosexual, the problems associated with attempting to express oneself to others, coming out to parents, friends and at work, the formation or breakup of relationships, the mid-age crisis and the crisis of ageing. Of all these, it is likely that the most difficult to negotiate are the processes of self acceptance and coming out. Identification and coming out as homosexual can occur at any time from adolescence to old age. This can involve very strong emotional conflicts as the individual has to struggle, often in conditions of acute anxiety and isolation, against the received negative images to achieve a validation of her or his feelings. Once these crisis points are passed, however, others may seem insignificant in comparison. They may indeed 'provide a perspective on major life crises and a sense of crisis competence that buffers a person against later crises' (Kimmel, 1978).

Weinberg and Williams (1974) found no age-related differences in self acceptance, anxiety, depression or loneliness between older and younger homosexuals. In some cases, indeed, the older sample had a greater sense of well being than the younger. They tended to worry less about self exposure, they had a stronger sense of self and they tended to adopt less obviously stereotyped 'feminine' mannerisms. This latter point is less trivial than it seems, because 'camp' behaviour is often seen as indicating a degree of self advertisement; its absence, therefore, is likely to suggest some degree of self adjustment. There is also a good deal of evidence that most homosexuals adapt themselves with ease to the changes that their own self perceptions and expectations encourage. For instance, the much touted desire of homosexual men to look younger than they are is not substantiated by the evidence, certainly not amongst my interviewees. As one put it, 'I've never worn jeans. And now ... I couldn't, and that's that ... I've a very strong feeling about what we used to call mutton dressed as lamb. I don't attempt not to look my age ... at least I don't think so.' There are three important areas to consider where problems might arise: in relation to social interaction, social conditions and sex. In all these areas there are greater continuities with younger age groups than is often thought, but specific social needs do arise which are often ignored both in the wider community and amongst other homosexuals.

First there are discernible differences in the patterns of social intercourse. The evidence suggests, for example, that fewer older homosexual men do go to bars, and this is often

perceived by younger people as an inevitable result of ageing
(Weinberg and Williams, 1974). This can, however, be more
readily explained by historical factors. It may, for example,
reflect the relative absence of the social institution of the bar
in earlier times, and the greater reliance therefore placed on
the more private and informal network of friends. Organization
through coteries is still very widespread in the gay community,
particularly perhaps amongst lesbians, and is a phenomenon
that has been little studied (see Kimmel, 1978; West, 1977). It
is apparent that in the past such informal but tightly knit
groupings played an enormously important part in creating a
sense of self confidence, particularly as more public subcultural
forms were frequently harassed by police and social morality
campaigners. There is also some evidence that informal female
networks were a common development from the conditons of
women's subordination, as mutual dependence and emotional
sustenance became essential bulwarks against oppressive conditions. In such situations the question of whether these close
relationships were sexualized becomes almost irrelevant (Smith-
Rosenberg, 1975; Cook, 1977; Weeks, 1977). Its relevance
here lies in the fact that such firmly rooted phenomena obviate
the need for a more public, potentially competitive (and expen-
sive) social activity.

Their existence, however, cannot be taken for granted, and
this raises the second area, the social conditions of older
homosexual people. There is certainly some evidence that there
are greater numbers of older homosexuals living on their own
(e.g. see Weinberg and Williams, 1974, p.312). Again,
historical factors can help to explain this. In part it must reflect
the greater difficulties encountered in the past in establishing
partnerships. But this need not have negative implications: a
pattern of life organized around living alone could be as secure
as the more collective arrangements common in parts of the gay
community today. But in this context we must also bear in mind
some of the more obvious results of ageing. Partners do die.
Amongst my interviewees were several who had outlived their
partners; the crucial factor in their ability to continue on their
own was the support they gained from the network of friends
in which they were embedded. For those in more isolated
situations, bereavement could be devastating:

> They just thought we were close friends.... And this was
> the terrible thing when it happened, because they knew we
> were close friends, but they didn't know that sort of thing.
> So one had to control one's emotions, and that was a very
> difficult situation really.

More practical problems might also result from dissolution of
partnerships at death. Our property laws make no provision
for the easy transmission of property, even of shared personal
possessions, at death. Physical disabilities might further
inhibit an easy or satisfactory life on one's own. Factors such
as these can make for major difficulties in all older people but

homosexuals, because of the stigma still attached to their
sexuality, often find such problems are compounded, and this
must be taken into account when assessing social need.

With regard to our third area of interest, the sexual needs
of older people, there is frequent evidence for a lower incidence
of sexual activity (Weinberg and Williams, 1974, p.122). A
certain caution often intervenes, as a respondent suggested:
'now of course I'm much less promiscuous, much less. Have to
be after all. And therefore much more careful.' Amongst some
there is even a nostalgia for the secrecy and excitement of a
less open world - and this is particularly true for those who
have had a fairly integrated gay life. As a man in his eighties
said to me, 'Strangely enough since the law which has made it
legal ... the easy sort of public meeting of homosexuals ...
seems to have disappeared except in certain queer clubs.'
Another man, in his seventies, made a slightly different point:
'it was a wonderful conspiracy ... it had all the elements of
belonging to a freemasonry or a mystery ... exciting because
it was forbidden.'

On the other hand, Kimmel's survey confirms that his
respondents still felt sex was important to their lives (as it is,
of course, in the case of heterosexuals), and half of his sample
felt it was actually more satisfying and technically proficient
than when they were young. A 63-year-old noted 'less accent
on the genitals, more on the total person now' (Kimmel, 1978).
My own interviews suggest a similar pattern. Thus Gregory in
his eighties: 'Gerontophiles turn up. And it's a very good thing
that that is so.' Jack in his sixties: 'You'd be surprised at the
number of people who are gerontophiles you know, thank God.
Thank God.' And Felix in his eighties: 'I haven't got a regular
boyfriend now. But I'm still hoping. Oh yes. And I still have
sex now and again.'

We live in a general culture which privileges youth and
glamourizes their achievement. At the same time we are only
slowly chipping away at the hostility which homosexuality has
engendered. These two factors have inevitably had their impact
on the ways homosexual people have lived their lives, and it
is not surprising that, as we have seen, problems do arise
which are specific to older homosexuals. But, as I have stressed,
these problems are historically conditioned and changes are
manifestly taking place. The most important stem from the
emergence of openly gay self-help groups over the past decade,
many of them committed to responding to the social needs of all
groups of gay people, including the aged. The Campaign for
Homosexual Equality has at various times delegated executive
members to take on a portfolio for elderly gays. Telephone
advice lines are becoming more adept at recognizing and responding to the social needs of older people.

So it is likely that many of the 'problems' described in this
paper are in fact transitional ones. The growth of a more open
and variegated gay community has transformed the possibilities

of being homosexual in our society and this is demonstrable among older people as well as the young. Dank (1971) has cited an example of the impact when an older man joined a gay religious organization: 'I feel comfortable and relieved of tensions and self consciousness.... I'm alive at 65.' My own interviews reveal the same story. Contact with a gay organization can often be quite accidental. A respondent in his late sixties described one such random encounter:

I was looking down the deaths on the back of 'The Times', as I always do every day because I mean they're of far more interest to me now than births and marriages, and caught the name homosexuality. And in fact it was an advertisement for CHE which I'd never heard of. And I wrote off straight away sending a subscription ... and have been a member of the organization ever since.

Such contacts can bring an end to feelings of isolation and despair. A gregarious but isolated man in his seventies noted that: 'the big change [came] once I got involved in CHE. I was – I should say still am – sexually active, but not knowing anyone, had been very lonely, very frustrated. Suddenly I met a lot of people.' And in such situations the gap between old and young, while it does not disappear, seems much less pressing: 'I know plenty of young people and they're very, very pleasant and kind. The word kind, it's a silly word really. But I am treated very well.' Now the problems can be perceived as socially derived rather than individual ones, and these can be resolved by the development of a fuller social life: 'I've enjoyed life much more ... they're always ringing me up and you're never alone, you know, the type of thing you are before.'

There is no reason to think that the ways homosexuality is lived now will be the ways it is always lived. Our forms of sexual life, identities and behaviour are historically shaped, and are already being historically transformed. Similarly, our concepts of, and ways of living, the ageing process, are not immutable. What has to be recognized is that the possibilities of living a full life do not abate as one gets older; they can in fact increase. So it is likely that the difficulties now experienced by elderly homosexuals are products of a particular phase in the development of positive homosexual identities. Once we recognize this then we can pinpoint the difficulties that are socially created and sustained; and work to remove them.

NOTE

1 The interviews were part of an investigation into the organization and development of the homosexual subculture in England from the 1880s to the 1940s. The project was financed by the Social Science Research Council; the researchers were Mary McIntosh and Jeffrey Weeks.

SELECTED GROUPS AND ORGANIZATIONS

The list includes those referred to in Part Three. For additional information see 'Gay News' (fortnightly), 1A Normand Gardens, Greyhound Road, London W14 9SB.

Action for Lesbian Parents, c/o Womens Centre, Moor Lane, Lancaster.
Alcoholics Anonymous Gay Groups, Information AA, Tel.01-834-8202.
Campaign for Homosexual Equality, 42a Formosa St, London W9 2JP. Tel.01-289-9335.
EIRE: National Gay Federation, Hirschfeld Centre, 10 Fownes St, Dublin 2. Tel.710939.
Gay Activists Alliance, c/o 5 Caledonian Road, London N1.
Gay Christian Movement, BM Box 6914, London WC1N 3XX. Tel.01-283-5165.
Gay Legal Advice, Tel.01-821-7672, 7-11 p.m. nightly.
Gay Sweatshop Theatre Co., 5 Leonard Street, London EC2A 4AQ Tel.01-250-1762.
Gay Switchboard, Tel.01-837-7324, 24-hour information.
Gay Therapists Seminar, c/o London Friend, 274 Upper Street, London N1.
Gay Youth Movement, c/o 18 Moon Street, Birmingham.
Ice Breakers, Tel.01-274-9590, 7.30-10.30 nightly; or BM/GAYLIB, London WC1N 3XX.
Joint Council for Gay Teenagers, c/o Link, 14 Colquitt Street, Liverpool L1 4DE.
Lesbian Line, BM Box 1514, London WC1N 3XX. Tel.01-837-8602, Monday and Friday 2-10 p.m., Tuesday-Thursday 7-10 p.m.
Married Gays, c/o London Friend, 274 Upper Street, London N1. Tel.01-359-7371.
National Friend, c/o Campaign for Homosexual Equality, BM CHE, London WC1N 3XX.
NIGRA (Northern Ireland Gay Rights Association), PO Box 44, Belfast BT1 1SH.
PARENTS ENQUIRY: Rose Robertson, 16 Honley Road, Catford, London SE6 2HZ.
SHRG (Scottish Homosexual Rights Group), 60 Broughton Street, Edinburgh EH1 3SA. Tel.031-556-4049.
Sigma (support group for straight people in mixed relationships), Penny Edwards, 33 Springcroft Avenue, East Finchley, London N2 9JH.

CONCLUSION

The emphasis in this book has been on the way people who are homosexual see themselves and are seen by others. We have seen homosexuality as being what you are rather than what you do. This is to correct the overemphasis that has existed in the literature, observing the homosexual person as a sexual creature. However, we would at the same time recognize the need for studies which concentrate on the physiological aspects of people's sexuality, whatever their orientation. Masters and Johnson (1979) have pointed to the overwhelming similarity in the sexual responsiveness of homosexuals and heterosexuals.

Our emphasis on the centrality of sexual orientation in personal identity within our culture implies that identification as heterosexual or homosexual, unlike bisexuality, is likely to be a relatively stable aspect of self identity. However, rather than assuming the stability of sexual identity to be the result of determining etiological factors, we see as crucial the need to account for the maintenance of a homosexual identity. In the presentation in the book of an alternative model of homosexuality we have recognized this, and have attempted to consider factors which may interact to maintain a particular sexual identity.

In looking at the development of a homosexual identity we have moved away from causal explanations which have stressed one or more than one discrete event as resulting in avoidance of, or antipathy towards, the opposite sex. We consider that there are an infinite number of factors which may be important, and that no one of these has a necessary association with, nor is sufficient in itself to account for, the development of a homosexual identity. Implicit in such a perspective is the view that a homosexual identity can be a positive preference for relationships with the same sex, for whatever reasons, rather than the result of an aversion to the opposite sex. In this sense we would see the development of a homosexual identity as being a relative choice for the individual.

In the past, explanations of homosexuality have tended to assume not only a common causality, but a common experience of being homosexual. Our conceptualizations point to the uniqueness of both the development and maintenance of a homosexual identity, and its particular significance and meaning for each individual.

Some continuities of experience may, of course, exist - one of the most important being related to sex differences - and we would emphasize here the continuities, rather than the

186

discontinuities, in the social role experiences of all women, or
alternatively all men, irrespective of sexual orientation.

The differences for men and women in the development and
maintenance of a homosexual identity and lifestyle have been
ignored at the level of theoretical analysis by many writers.
This is to a large extent a reflection of the lack of cognizance
taken of female sexuality in general, and, within the literature
on homosexuality, of lesbianism in particular.

We also recognize that in what we regard as a necessary
emphasizing of individual differences we have not always
brought out a social structural level of analysis. We would, in
an ideal sense, consider such a perspective essential. One area
where we have tried to consider both the social and political
effects and the impact on the individual is in discussing the
secrecy surrounding homosexual lifestyles and identities. We
recognize that it is only a small minority of homosexual men and
women who feel able to come out as openly homosexual in most
of their encounters with other people. Obviously the stigmatization of homosexuality in society is important here, as is the
experienced or perceived risks involved in such a process for
each person.

Such a perspective is needed to understand the strength of
personal and societal opposition people often face in coming out.
Homosexuals who are open and positive about being gay pose
a very real threat to the way in which homosexuality has been
seen in society, whilst at the same time facilitating the process
of coming out for others by providing group support and
alternative role models with which they can identify.

Whilst, for reasons which will be obvious from our theoretical
orientation, we have not aimed to provide 'a handbook of treatment techniques', we still recognize that for individual homosexuals problems can arise, although we would stress that these
should be assessed within a social and political context. Such
problems may then be treated by behavioural or other counselling techniques.

Our aim is also to provide the counsellor with something to
say after 'I accept you.' Indeed, we would see the book as
hopefully leading not only to some attitude change in practitioners, but also to an increased knowledge base.

As we have already indicated, we consider the process of
coming out and the development of gay self-help groups to be
an important contribution to the therapeutic resources available
in helping individuals who are isolated or distressed. We feel
it important, however, to regard both self and professional
help as interdependant and in need of establishing a dialogue.
Our theoretical orientation we offer as a way of achieving this.

We have attempted in the book to place homosexuality in a
social and political framework. We would therefore see possible
factors in the development and maintenance of a homosexual
identity, the presenting of problems of homosexual women and
men and the range of homosexual identities and lifestyles

available, as being responsive to changes in the social climate. In this respect legal and social changes, especially related to the age of consent, may affect some of what we have written. What we would be certain of, however, is that the major influences on the experiences of being a homosexual man or woman in our society will come from changes in the gender-role system. We would draw attention to two aspects of the social experiences of homosexual women and homosexual men, which are emerging on both sides of the Atlantic. These are related to a reflexiveness about gender roles, which has taken the form for gay women of a rejection of traditional assumptions about the sexes and 'appropriate' role behaviour. This contrasts with the preoccupations of homosexual men with traditional masculine images, as a revolt against previous 'camp' effeminate stereotypes. This has led to the fashionable image of the homosexual male as a 'macho man', which emphasizes a hypermasculinity in appearance, sexual per-formance and attitudes to relationships.

This is occurring at a time when traditional gender roles can be regarded as bad for both mental and physical health reasons. The mental health problems of women have received some attention in relation to the position of women in the social structure, but we should also note the possible stresses involved for homosexual men in their role playing, especially if this results in a negation of their emotional needs as being 'unmasculine'. Between homosexual males, therefore, there may be an undervaluing of relationships which are not primarily concerned with sexual gratification. For gay women the rejection of gender-role stereotyping may involve having to face directly communicating sexual rather than emotional needs, which have not traditionally been seen as a necessary concern for women in relationships.

At the end of this book, after much discussion about theories of homosexuality and the presentation of a non-pathological model, we are left with the question, 'What do our readers want to believe about the theory and practice of homosexuality?' Clearly personal biases will play an important part here, and our own are manifested throughout the book. Whilst acknowledging this, we still feel that it is very important to direct the reader's attention to the need to question the development and maintenance of any sexual identity. We are concerned that there is a resistance on the part of both homosexual and heterosexual people to considering the develop-ment of their own particular sexual orientation, resulting in responses such as, 'I just am,' or, 'I was born this way,' or, 'I identify as gay because of the impossibility of having non-sexist relationships with the opposite sex in a capitalist society.' In each of these cases, the personal, the 'scientific' or the political response obviously does not in itself provide an adequate analysis of the diversity and uniqueness of the individual's reasons for coming to a particular sexual identity.

We hope that this book goes some way towards achieving this necessary synthesis.

BIBLIOGRAPHY
FOR PART ONE

Apperson, L.B. and McAdoo Jr W.G. (1968), Parental factors in the childhood of homosexuals, 'Journal of Abnormal Psychology', vol.73, pp.201-6.
Archer, J. (1978), Biological explanations of sex-role stereotypes, in J. Chetwynd and O. Hartnett (eds), 'The Sex Role System', Routledge & Kegan Paul, London.
Bailey, D.S. (1955), 'Homosexuality and the Western Christian Tradition', Longmans, Green & Co., London.
Bancroft, J. (1974), 'Deviant Sexual Behaviour: Modification and Assessment', Clarendon Press, Oxford.
— (1979), Treatment of deviant sexual behaviour, in R. Gains and B. Hudson (eds), 'Current Themes in Psychiatry', vol.2, Macmillan, London.
Barlow, D.H., Abel, G.G., Blanchard, E.B. and Mavissakalian, M. (1974), Plasma Testosterone levels and male homosexuality: a failure to replicate, 'Archives of Sexual Behaviour', vol.3, no. 6, pp.571-5.
Bell, A.P. and Weinberg, M.S. (1978), 'Homosexualities: A Study of Diversity Among Men and Women', Mitchell Beazley, London.
Bene, E. (1965a), On the genesis of female homosexuality, 'British Journal of Psychiatry', vol.111, pp.815-21.
— (1965b), On the genesis of male homosexuality: an attempt at changing the role of the parent, 'British Journal of Psychiatry', vol.111, pp.803-13.
Bieber, I., Dain, H.J., Dince, P.R., Drellich, M.G., Grand, H.G., Gundlach, R.H., Kremar, M.W., Rifkin, A.H., Wilbur, C.B. and Bieber, T.B. (1962), 'Homosexuality: A Psychoanalytic Study', Basic Books, New York.
Bieber, I. (1965), Clinical aspects of male homosexuality, in J. Marmor (ed), 'Sexual Inversion: The Multiple Roots of Homosexuality', Basic Books, New York.
Bobys, R.S. and Laner, M.R. (1979), On the stability of stigmatization: the case of ex-homosexual males, 'Archives of Sexual Behaviour', vol.8, no. 3, pp.247-59.
Brodie, H.K.H., Gartrell, N., Doering, C. and Rhue, T. (1974), Plasma testosterone levels in heterosexual and homosexual men, 'American Journal of Psychiatry', vol.131, pp.82-3.
Brown, W. Paterson (1964), The homosexual male: Treatment in an out-patient clinic, in I. Rosen (ed), 'The Pathology and Treatment of Sexual Deviation: A Methodological Approach', Oxford University Press, London.
Cautela, J.R. and Wisocki, P.A. (1977), Covert sensitization for the treatment of sexual deviations, in J.F. Fischer and H.L. Gochros (eds), 'Handbook of Behaviour Therapy With Sexual Problems', vols 1 and 2, Pergamon Press, New York.
Clarke, A.M. and Clarke, A.D.B. (1976), 'Early Experience: Myth and Evidence', Open Books, London.
Cooper, A.J. (1974), The aetiology of homosexuality, in J.A. Loraine (ed.), 'Understanding homosexuality: Its Biological and Psychological Bases', Medical and Technical Publishing Co., Lancaster.
Darke, R.A. (1948), Heredity as an etiological factor in homosexuality, 'Journal of Nervous and Mental Disease', vol.107, pp.251-68.
Delph, E.W. (1978), 'The Silent Community: Public Homosexual Encounters', Sage Publications, Beverley Hills/London.

Deutsch, H. (1932), On female homosexuality, 'Psychoanalytical Quarterly',
  vol.1, pp.484-510.
— (1947), 'Psychology of Women', vol.1, Research Books, London.
Diamond, M. (1965), A critical evaluation of the ontogeny of human sexual
  behaviour, 'Quarterly Review of Biology', vol.40, pp.147-75.
Dieckmann, G. and Hassler, R. (1974), reported in the 'Journal of the
  American Medical Association', vol.229, no.13, p.1716.
Doerr, P., Kockott, G., Vogt, H.J., Pirke, K.M. and Dittmar, F. (1973),
  Plasma testosterone, estradiol, and semen analysis in male homosexuals,
  'Archives of General Psychiatry', vol.29, pp.829-33.
Doerr, P., Pirke, K.M., Kockott, G. and Dittmar, F. (1976), Further studies
  on sex hormones in male homosexuals, 'Archives of General Psychiatry',
  vol.33, pp.611-14.
Dörner, G. (1968), Hormonal induction and prevention of female homosexuality,
  'Journal of Endocrinology', vol.42, pp.163-4.
— (1976), 'Hormones and Brain Differentiation', Elsevier, Amsterdam.
Dörner, G. and Hinz, G. (1968), Induction and prevention of male
  homosexuality by androgen, 'Journal of Endocrinology', vol.40, pp.387-8.
Dörner, G., Rohde, W., Stahl, F., Krell, L. and Masius, W.G. (1975), A
  neuroendocrine predisposition for homosexuality in men, 'Archives of
  Sexual Behaviour', vol.4, pp.1-8.
Duehn, W.D. and Mayadas, N.S. (1977), The use of stimulus/modelling
  videotapes in assertive training for homosexuals, in J.F. Fischer and
  H.L. Gochros (eds), 'Handbook of Behaviour Therapy with Sexual
  Problems', vols 1 and 2, Pergamon Press, New York.
Ehrhardt, A.A. and Baker, S.W. (1976), Prenatal androgen exposure and
  adolescent behaviour, paper presented at the International Congress of
  Sexology, Montreal, Quebec, October.
Ehrhardt, A.A., Epstein, R. and Money, J. (1968), Foetal androgens and
  female gender identity in the early treated adrenogenital syndrome,
  'Johns Hopkins Medical Journal', vol.122, pp.160-7.
Ehrhardt, A.A., Evers, K. and Money, J. (1968), Influence of androgen and
  some aspects of sexually dimorphic behaviour in women with the late-
  treated adrenogenital syndrome, 'Johns Hopkins Medical Journal', vol.123,
  no.3, pp.115-22.
Ettorre, E.M. (1980), 'Lesbians, Women and Society', Routledge & Kegan Paul,
  London.
Evans, R.B. (1969), Childhood parental relationships of homosexual men,
  'Journal of Consulting and Clinical Psychology', vol.33, no.2, pp.129-35.
— (1972), Physical and biochemical characteristics of homosexual men,
  'Journal of Consulting and Clinical Psychology', vol.39, no.1, pp.140-7.
— (1973), Biological factors in male homosexuality, 'Medical Aspects of Human
  Sex', July, pp.12-27.
Feldman, M.P. and McCulloch, M.J. (1971), 'Homosexual Behaviour: Therapy
  and Assessment', Pergamon Press, Oxford.
Fenichel, O. (1946), 'The Psychoanalytic Theory of Neurosis', Routledge &
  Kegan Paul, London.
Fischer, J.F. and Gochros, H.L. (eds) (1977), 'Handbook of Behaviour
  Therapy with Sexual Problems', vols 1 and 2, Pergamon Press, New York.
Freud, S. (1905), Three essays on the theory of sexuality, 'The Complete
  Psychological Works of Sigmund Freud', Standard Edition, vol.7, Hogarth
  Press, London.
— (1920), The psychogenesis of a case of homosexuality in a woman, in 'The
  Complete Psychological Works of Sigmund Freud', Standard Edition, vol.18,
  Hogarth Press, London.
— (1931), Female sexuality, 'The Complete Psychological Works of Sigmund
  Freud', Standard Edition, vol.21, Hogarth Press, London.
— (1933), Psychology of women, 'New Introductory Lectures on
  Psychoanalysis', Hogarth Press, London.
Gagnon, J.H. and Simon, W. (1974), 'Sexual Conduct', Hutchinson, London.
Gartrell, N.K., Loriaux, D.L. and Chase, T.N. (1977), Plasma testosterone

in homosexual and heterosexual women, 'American Journal of Psychiatry',
vol.134, pp.1117-19.
Glass, S.J. and Johnson, R.H. (1944), Limitations and complications of
organotherapy in male homosexuality, 'Journal of Clinical Endocrinology',
vol.4, pp.540-4.
Glass, S.J., Denel, H.J. and Wright, C.A. (1940), Sex hormone studies in
male homosexuality, 'Endocrinology', vol.26, pp.590-4.
Goldschmidt, R. (1931), Analysis of intersexuality in the gypsy-moth,
'Quarterly Review of Biology', vol.6, p.125.
Goy, R.W. (1968), Organising effects of androgen on the behaviour of rhesus
monkeys, in R.P. Michael (ed), 'Endocrinology and Human Behaviour',
Oxford University Press.
Grady, K.L., Phoenix, C.H. and Young, W.C. (1965), Role of the developing
rat testis in differentiation of the neural tissues mediating mating
behaviour, 'Journal of Comparative and Physiological Psychology', vol.59,
pp.176-82.
Green, R. (1974a), 'Sexual Identity Conflict in Children and Adults',
Basic Books, New York.
— (1974b), The behaviourally feminine male child: Pretranssexual?
Pretransvestic? Prehomosexual? Preheterosexual?, in R.C. Friedman,
R.M. Richart and R.L. Vande Wiele (eds), 'Sex Differences in Behaviour',
Wiley, N.York.
— (1976), Atypical psychosexual development, in M. Rutter and L. Hersov
(eds), 'Child Psychiatry: Modern Approaches', Blackwell Scientific
Publications, London.
Green, R. and Fuller, M. (1973), Group therapy with feminine boys and
their parents, 'International Journal of Group Psychotherapy', vol.23,
pp.54-68.
Griffiths, P.D., Merry, J., Browning, M.C.K., Eisinger, A.J.,
Huntsman, R.G., Lord, E.J.A., Polari, P.E., Tanner, J.M. and
Whitehouse, R.H. (1974), Homosexual women: An endocrine and psycho-
logical study, 'Journal of Endocrinology', vol.63, pp.549-56.
Hampson, J.L. and Hampson, J.G. (1961), The autogenesis of sexual
behaviour in man, in W.C. Young (ed), 'Sex and Internal Secretions',
vol.2, Ballière, Tindall & Cox, London.
Harré, R. and Secord, P.F. (1972), 'The Explanation of Social Behaviour',
Blackwell, Oxford.
Hart, J. (1979), 'Social Work and Sexual Conduct', Routledge & Kegan Paul,
London.
Hart, J. and Richardson, D. (1980), The differences between homosexual men
and women,'Bulletin of the British Psychological Society', vol.33,
pp.451-4.
Heim, N. and Hursch, C.J. (1979), Castration of sex offenders: treatment
or punishment? A review and critique of recent European literature,
'Archives of Sexual Behaviour', vol.8, no.3, pp.281-303.
Heston, L.L. and Shields, J. (1968), Homosexuality in twins, 'Archives of
General Psychiatry', vol.8, pp.149-60.
Higginbotham, H.N. and Farkas, G.M. (1977), Basic and applied research in
human sexuality: current limitations and future directions in sex therapy,
in J.F. Fischer and H.L. Gochros (eds), 'Handbook of Behaviour Therapy
With Sexual Problems', vols 1 and 2, Pergamon Press, New York.
Hocquenghem, G. (1978), 'Homosexual Desire', Allison & Busby, London.
Hooker, E. (1965), Male homosexuals and their 'worlds', in J. Marmor (ed),
'Sexual Inversion: The Multiple Roots of Homosexuality', Basic Books,
New York.
— (1969), Parental relations and male homosexuality in patient and non-
patient samples, 'Journal of Consulting and Clinical Psychology', vol.33,
pp.140-2.
Horney, K. (1939), 'New Ways in Psycho-analysis', Norton, New York.
Humphreys, L. (1970), 'Tearoom Trade: Impersonal Sex in Public Places',
Aldine Publishing Co., Chicago.

Hutt, C. (1972), 'Males and Females', Penguin, Harmondsworth.
Jay, K. and Young, A. (1979), 'The Gay Report', Summit Books, New York.
Johnson, A.M. and Robinson, D.B. (1957), The sexual deviant (sexual
    psychopath): causes, treatment and prevention, 'Journal of the American
    Medical Association', vol.164, no.14, pp.1559-65.
Kagan, J. (1964), Acquisition and significance of sex-typing and sex-role
    identity, in M. Hoffman and L. Hoffman, 'Review of Child Development
    Research', vol.1, Russell Sage Foundation, New York.
Kallman, F.J. (1952a), Twin and sibship study of overt male homosexuality,
    'American Journal of Human Genetics', vol.4, pp.136-46.
— (1952b), Comparative twin study on the genetic aspects of male
    homosexuality, 'Journal of Nervous and Mental Disease', vol.115, pp.283-98.
— (1953), 'Heredity in Health and Mental Disorder', Norton, New York.
— (1960), Discussion of Rainer et al.'s article, 'Psychosomatic Medicine',
    vol.22, no.4, pp.258-9.
Khan, M. Masud R. (1964), The role of infantile sexuality and early object
    relations in female homosexuality, in I. Rosen (ed.), 'The Pathology and
    Treatment of Sexual Deviation: A Methodological Approach', Oxford
    University Press, London.
Kinsey, A.C. (1941), Criteria for a hormonal explanation of the homosexual,
    'Journal of Clinical Endocrinology', vol.1, no.5, pp.424-8.
Kinsey, A.C., Pomeroy, W.B. and Martin, C.E. (1948), 'Sexual behaviour
    in the Human Male', W.B. Saunders & Co., Philadelphia and London.
Klaf, F.S. (1961), Female homosexuality and paranoid schizophrenia, 'Archives
    of General Psychiatry', vol.4, pp.110/84-112/86.
Klein, M. (1932), 'The Psychoanalysis of Children', Hogarth Press, London.
Klintworth, G.K. (1962), A pair of male monozygotic twins discordant for
    homosexuality, 'Journal of Nervous and Mental Disease', vol.135, pp.113-25.
Kohlberg, L. (1966), A cognitive-developmental analysis of children's sex-
    role concepts and attitudes, in E.E. Maccoby (ed.), 'The Development of
    Sex Differences', Stanford University Press.
Kolb, L.C., Reinder, J.D., Meznikoff, A. and Carr, A. (1961), Divergent
    sexual development in identical twins, 'Proceedings of the Third World
    Congress of Psychiatry', vol.1, McGill University Press, Montreal.
Kolodny, R.C., Masters, W.H., Hendryx, J. and Toro, G. (1971), Plasma
    testosterone and semen analysis in male homosexuals, 'New England Journal
    of Medicine', vol.285, pp.1170-4.
Kolodny, R.C., Jacobs, L.S., Masters, W.H., Toro, G. and Daughaday, W.H.
    (1972), Plasma gonadotrophins and prolactin in male homosexuals, 'Lancet',
    vol.2, no.7766, pp.18-20.
Lang, T. (1940), Studies on the genetic determination of homosexuality,
    'Journal of Nervous and Mental Disease', vol.92, pp.55-64.
Lange, J. (1931), 'Crime as Destiny: A Study of Criminal Twins', George
    Allen & Unwin, London.
Leschner, A.I. (1978), 'An Introduction to Behavioural Endocrinology',
    Oxford University Press.
Levitt, E.E. and Klassen Jr, A.D. (1974), Public attitudes toward
    homosexuality: part of the 1970 National Survey by the Institute for Sex
    Research, 'Journal of Homosexuality', vol.1, no.1, pp.29-43.
Limentani, A. (1979), Clinical types of homosexuality, in I.Rosen (ed.),
    'Sexual Deviation' 2nd edition, Oxford University Press.
Loraine, J.A., Ismail, A.A.A., Adamopoulos, D.A. and Dove, G.A. (1970),
    Endocrine function in male and female homosexuals, 'British Medical
    Journal', vol.4, pp.406-8.
Loraine, J.A., Adamopoulos, D.A., Kirkham, K.E., Ismail, A.A.A. and
    Dove, G.A. (1971), Patterns of hormone excretion in male and female
    homosexuals, 'Nature', vol.234, pp.552-5.
MacDonald Jr, A.P. (1976), Homophobia: its roots and meanings, 'Homosexual
    Counselling Journal', vol.3, no.1, pp.22-33.
McDougall, J. (1979), The homosexual dilemma: a clinical and theoretical
    study of female homosexuals', in I. Rosen (ed.), 'Sexual Deviation',

2nd edition, Oxford University Press.
McGuire, R.J., Carlisle, J.M. and Young, B.G. (1965), Sexual deviations as conditioned behaviour: a hypothesis, 'Behaviour Research and Therapy', vol.3, pp.185-90.
Manosevitz, M. (1970), Early sexual behaviour in adult homosexual and heterosexual males, 'Journal of Abnormal Psychology', vol.76, pp.396-402.
Margolese, M.S. (1970), Homosexuality: a new endocrine correlate, 'Hormones and Behaviour', vol.1, pp.151-5.
Margolese, M.S. and Janiger, O. (1973), Androsterone/Etiocholanolone ratios in male homosexuals, 'British Medical Journal', vol.3, pp.207-10.
Masters, W.M. and Johnson, V.E. (1979), 'Homosexuality in Perspective', Little, Brown & Co., Boston.
Mayerson, P. and Lief, H.I. (1965), Psychotherapy of homosexuals: a follow-up study of nineteen cases, in J. Marmor (ed.), 'Sexual Inversion', Basic Books, New York.
Meyer-Bahlburg, H.F.L. (1977), Sex hormones and male homosexuality in comparative perspective, 'Archives of Sexual Behaviour', vol.6, no.4, pp.297-325.
— (1979), Sex hormones and female homosexuality: a critical examination, 'Archives of Sexual Behaviour', vol.8, no.2, pp.101-19.
Mischel, W. (1967), A social learning view of sex differences in behaviour, in E.E. Maccoby (ed.), 'The Development of Sex Differences', Tavistock, London.
Money, J. (1961), Sex hormones and other variables in human eroticism, in W.C. Young (ed.), 'Sex and Internal Secretions', vol.2, Ballière, Tindall & Cox, London.
Money, J. and Ehrhardt, A.A. (1972), 'Man and Woman, Boy and Girl', Johns Hopkins University Press, Baltimore.
Money, J. and Ogunro, C. (1974), Behavioural sexology: ten cases of genetic male intersexuality with impaired prenatal and pubertal androgenization, 'Archives of Sexual Behaviour', vol.3, pp.181-205.
Money, J. and Schwartz, M. (1977), Dating, romantic and non-romantic friendships and sexuality in 17 early-treated adrenogenital females aged 16-25, in A.A. Lee, L.P. Plotnick, A.A. Kowarski and C.J. Migeon (eds), 'Congenital Adrenal Hyperplasia', University Park Press, Baltimore.
Morrow, J.E., Cupp, M.E. and Sachs, L.B. (1965), A possible explanation of the excessive brother-to-sister ratios reported in siblings of male homosexuals, 'Journal of Nervous and Mental Disease', vol.140, no.4, pp.305-6.
Munro, A. and McCulloch, W. (1969), 'Psychiatry for Social Workers', Pergamon Press, London.
Nash, J. and Hayes, F. (1965), The parental relationships of male homosexuals: some theoretical issues and a pilot study, 'Australian Journal of Psychology', vol.17, no.1, pp.35-43.
Neumann, F. (1966), Permanent changes in gonadal function and sexual behaviour as a result of early feminization of male rats by treatment with an anti-androgenic steroid, 'Endokrinologie', vol.50, pp.209-25.
Neustatter, W.L. (1954), Homosexuality: the medical aspect, 'Practitioner', vol.172, pp.364-73.
O'Connor, P.J. (1964), Aetiological factors in homosexuality as seen in Royal Air Force psychiatric practice, 'British Journal of Psychiatry', vol.2, pp.11-23.
Pare, C.M.B. (1956), Homosexuality and chromosomal sex, 'Journal of Psychosomatic Research', vol.1, pp.247-51.
Parker, N. (1964), Homosexuality in twins: a report on three discordant pairs, 'British Journal of Psychiatry', vol.110, pp.489-95.
Pearce, F. (1973), How to be immoral and ill, pathetic and dangerous, all at the same time: mass media and the homosexual, in S. Cohen and J. Young (eds), 'The Manufacture of News, Deviance, Social Problems and the Mass Media', Constable, London.
Perloff, W.H. (1963), The role of hormones in homosexuality,

'Journal Feinstein Medical Center', vol.11, pp.165-78.
Peters, J.J. and Roether, H.A. (1971), Group psychotherapy for probationed sex offenders, 'International Psychiatric Clinics', vol.8, pp.69-80.
Pillard, R.C., Rose, R.M. and Sherwood, M. (1974), Plasma testosterone levels in homosexual men, 'Archives of Sexual Behaviour', vol.3, pp.453-8.
Plummer, K. (1975), 'Sexual Stigma: An Interactionist Account', Routledge & Kegan Paul, London.
— (1981), The paedophile's progress: a view from below, in B. Taylor (ed.), 'Perspectives on Paedophilia', Batsford, London.
Policy Advisory Committee on Sexual Offences (1979), 'Working Paper on the Age of Consent in Relation to Sexual Offences', HMSO, London.
Pritchard, M. (1962), Homosexuality and genetic sex, 'Journal of Mental Science', vol.108, pp.616-23.
Raboch, J. and Nedoma, K. (1958), Sex chromatin and sexual behaviour, 'Psychosomatic Medicine', vol.20, no.1, pp.55-9.
Rainer, J., Mesnikoff, A., Kolb, L.C. and Carr, A. (1960), Homosexuality and heterosexuality in identical twins, 'Psychosomatic Medicine', vol.22, no.4, pp.251-8.
Rekers, G.A. (1977), Assessment and treatment of childhood gender problems, in B.B. Lahey and A.E. Kazdin (eds), 'Advances in Clinical Child Psychology', Plenum Press, New York.
Richardson, D. and Hart J. (1980), Gays in therapy: getting it right, 'New Forum: The Journal of the Psychology and Psychotherapy Association', vol.6, no.3, pp.58-60.
Roeder, F., Orthner, H. and Müller, D. (1972), The stereotaxic treatment of pedophilic homosexuality and other sexual deviations, in E. Hitchcock, L. Laitinen and T.K. Vaerne (eds), 'Psychosurgery', Charles C. Thomas Publishers, Springfield, Illinois.
Rogers, L. (1976), Male hormones and behaviour, in B. Lloyd and J. Archer (eds), 'Exploring Sex Differences', Academic Press, London.
Romm, M.E. (1965), Sexuality and homosexuality in women, in J. Marmor (ed.), 'Sexual Inversion: the Multiple Roots of Homosexuality', Basic Books, New York.
Saghir, M. and Robins, E. (1973), 'Male and female Homosexuality', Williams & Wilkins, Baltimore.
Schofield, M. (1965), 'Sociological Aspects of Homosexuality', Longmans, London.
Scott, P.D. (1964), Definition, classification, prognosis and treatment, in I. Rosen (ed.), 'The Pathology and Treatment of Sexual Deviation: A Methodological Approach', Oxford University Press, London.
Serber, M. and Keith, C.G. (1974), The Atascadero Project: model of a sexual retraining program for incarcerated homosexual pedophiles, 'Journal of Homosexuality', vol.1, no.1, pp.87-97.
Seyler Jr, L.E., Canalis, E., Spare, S. and Reichlin, S. (1978), Abnormal gonadotropin secretory responses to LRH in transsexual women after diethlystilbestrol priming, 'Journal of Clinical Endocrinological Metabolism', vol.47, pp.176-83.
Shaw, R. (1978), The persistent sexual offender: control and rehabilitation, 'Probation', vol.25, no.1, pp.9-13.
Siegelman, M. (1974), Parental background of male homosexuals and heterosexuals, 'Archives of Sexual Behaviour', vol.3, no.1, pp.3-18.
Simon, W. (1967), The lesbians: a preliminary overview, in J.H. Gagnon and W. Simon (eds), 'Sexual Deviance', Harper & Row, New York.
Slater, E. (1962), Birth order and maternal age of homosexuals, 'Lancet', vol.1, pp.69-71.
Socarides, C.W. (1963), The historical development of theoretical and clinical concepts of overt female homosexuality, 'Journal of American Psycho-analytical Association', vol.11, pp.386-414.
— (1979), The psychoanalytic theory of homosexuality, with special reference to therapy, in I. Rosen (ed.), 'Sexual Deviation', 2nd edition, Oxford University Press.

Spada, J. (1979), 'The Spada Report', Signet Books, New American Library, New York.
Stafford-Clarke, D. and Smith, A.C. (1979), 'Psychiatry for Students', 5th edition, George Allen & Unwin, London.
Starká, L., Šipová, I. and Hynie, J. (1975), Plasma testosterone in male transsexuals and homosexuals, 'Journal of Sex Research', vol.11, pp.134-8.
Storr, A. (1964), 'Sexual Deviation', Penguin, Harmondsworth.
Thomas, S.A. (1977), Theory and practice in feminist therapy, 'Social Work (USA)', vol.22, no.6, pp.447-54.
Thompson, N., Schwartz, D., McCandless, B. and Edwards, D. (1973), Parent-child relationships and sexual identity in male and female homosexuals and heterosexuals, 'Journal of Consulting and Clinical Psychology', vol.41, pp.120-7.
Tourney, G. and Hatfield, L.M. (1973), Androgen metabolism in schizophrenics, homosexuals, and normal controls, 'Biological Psychiatry', vol.6, pp.23-36.
Truax, C.B. and Carkhuff, R.R. (1967), 'Toward Effective Counselling and Psychotherapy: Training and Practice', Aldine Publishing Co., Chicago.
Ward, D.A. and Kassebaum, G.G. (1965), 'Women's Prison: Sex and Social Structure', Aldine Publishing Co., Chicago.
Warren, C.A.B. (1976), Women among men: females in the male homosexual community, 'Archives of Sexual Behaviour', vol.5, pp.156-75.
Wasserman, S. (1968), Casework treatment of a homosexually acting-out adolescent in a treatment center, in F.J. Turner (ed.), 'Differential Diagnosis and Treatment in Social Work', Free Press, New York; Collier-Macmillan, London.
Weeks, J. (1977), 'Coming Out', Quartet Books, London.
Weinberg, M.S. and Williams, C.J. (1974), 'Male Homosexuals: Their Problems and Adaptations', Oxford University Press, New York.
West, D.J. (1959), Parental figures in the genesis of male homosexuality. 'International Journal of Social Psychiatry', vol.5, pp.85-97.
— (1960), 'Homosexuality', Penguin, Harmondsworth.
Whitam, F.L. (1977), Childhood indicators of male homosexuality, 'Archives of Sexual Behaviour', vol.6, no.2, pp.89-96.
Wilbur, C.B. (1965), Clinical aspects of female homosexuality, in J. Marmor (ed.), 'Sexual Inversion: The Multiple Roots of Homosexuality', Basic Books, New York.
Working Paper on the age of consent in relation to sexual offences (1979), HMSO Policy Advisory Committee on Sexual Offences.
Young, W.C. (1961), The hormones and mating behaviour, in W.C. Young (ed.), 'Sex and Internal Secretions', vol.2, Ballière, Tindall & Cox, London.
Young, W.C., Goy, R.W. and Phoenix, C.H. (1964), Hormones and sexual behaviour, 'Science', vol.143, pp.212-21.
Zuger, B. (1966), Effeminate behaviour present in boys from early childhood: 1, The clinical syndrome and follow-up studies, 'Journal of Paediatrics', vol.69, pp.1098-107.

BIBLIOGRAPHY
FOR PART TWO

Bell, A. and Weinberg, M.S. (1978), 'Homosexualities: A Study of Diversity among Men and Women', Mitchell Beazley, London.

Berzon, B. (1979), Telling the family you're gay, in B.Berzon and R. Leighton (eds), 'Positively Gay', Celestial Arts, California.

Berzon, B. and Leighton, R. (eds), (1979), 'Positively Gay', Celestial Arts, California.

Campaign for Homosexual Equality (1979), 'Queers Need Not Apply', CHE, Manchester.

Crites, T.R. (1976), Coming out gay, in J.P. Wiseman (ed.), 'The Social Psychology of Sex', Harper, New York.

Dank, B. (1971), Coming out in the gay world, 'Psychiatry', May, no.34, pp.180-97.

de Beauvoir, S. (1953), 'The Second Sex', Jonathan Cape, London.

de Monteflores, C. and Schultz, S.J. (1978), Coming out: similarities and differences for lesbians and gay men, 'Journal of Social Issues', vol.34, no.3, pp.59-72.

Erikson, E. (1968), 'Identity: Youth and Crisis', Faber & Faber, London.

Erikson, E. (1977) 'Childhood and Society', Paladin, St Albans.

Ettorre, E.M. (1980), 'Lesbians, Women and Society', Routledge & Kegan Paul, London.

Fairchild, B. (1979), 'Parents of Gays', Lamda Rising Publications, Washington.

Foucault, M. (1979), 'The History of Sexuality', vol.1, Allen Lane, London.

Gagnon, J. (1977), 'Human Sexualities', Scott, Foresman & Co., Glenview, Illinois.

Gagnon, J.H. and Simon, W. (eds), (1967), 'Sexual Deviance', Harper & Row, New York.

Gay Christian Movement (1980), 'Explaining Lifestyles: An Introduction to Services of Blessing for Gay Couples', GCM, BM Box 6914, London WC1N 3XX.

Harry, J. and DeVall, W.B. (1978), 'The Social Organisation of Gay Males', Praeger, London.

Hooker, E. (1967), The homosexual community, in J.H. Gagnon and W. Simon (eds), 'Sexual Deviance', Harper & Row, New York.

Humphreys, L. (1979a), Exodus and identity: the emerging gay culture, in M. Levine (ed.), 'Gay Men: The Sociology of Male Homosexuality', Harper & Row, New York.

— (1979b), Being odd against all odds, in R.C. Frederico, (ed.), 'Sociology', Addison, Wesley, New York.

Jay, K. and Young, A. (1979), 'The Gay Report', Summit Books, New York.

Katz, J. (1976), 'American Gay History', Thomas & Cromwell, New York.

Kessler, W. and McKenna, E. (1978), 'Gender: An Ethnomethodological Approach', Wiley, Chichester.

Kimmel, D.C. (1978), Adult development and ageing: a gay perspective, 'Journal of Social Issues', vol.34, no.3, pp.113-30.

— (1979), Adjustments to ageing among gay men, in B. Berzon and R.Leighton (eds), 'Positively Gay', Celestial Arts, California.

— (1980), 'Adulthood and Ageing', 2nd edition, Wiley, Chichester.

Kinsey, A.C., Pomeroy, W.B. and Martin, C.E. (1948), 'Sexual behaviour in the Human Male', W.B. Saunders & Co., Philadelphia and London.

Lee, J.A. (1978), 'Getting Sex', Musson Books, Ontario.
Levine, M. (1979), Gay ghetto, in M. Levine (ed.), 'Gay Men: The Sociology of Male Homosexuality', Harper & Row, New York.
Levinson, D.J. (1978), 'The Seasons of a Man's Life', Knopf, New York.
Masters, W.H. and Johnson, V.E. (1966), 'Human Sexual Response', Little Brown & Co., Boston.
Miller, B. (1979), Unpromised paternity: lifestyles of gay fathers, in M. Levine (ed.), 'Gay Men: The Sociology of Male Homosexuality', Harper & Row, New York.
Millett, K. (1970), 'Sexual Politics', Hart Davis, London.
Money, J. and Tucker, P. (1977), 'Sexual Signatures', Abacus, London.
Morin, J.F. (1977), Heterosexual bias in psychological research on lesbianism and male homosexuality, 'American Psychologist', vol.32, pp.629-37.
Munro, A. and McCulloch, W. (1969), 'Psychiatry for Social Workers', Pergamon Press, Oxford.
Musgrove, F. (1977), 'Margins of the Mind', Methuen & Co., London.
Nicholson, J. (1980), 'Seven Ages', Fontana, London.
Plummer, K. (1975), 'Sexual Stigma: An Interactionist Account', Routledge & Kegan Paul, London.
— (1978), Men in love: observation of the male couple, in M. Corbin (ed.), 'The Couple', Penguin, Harmondsworth.
Plummer, K. (ed.), (1981), 'The Making of the Modern Homosexual', Hutchinson, London.
Ponse, B. (1978), 'Identities in the Lesbian World: The Social Construction of Self', Greenwood Press, London.
Rainwater, L. (1970), 'Behind Ghetto Walls', Aldine Publishing Co., Chicago.
Riddle, D.I. (1978), Relating to children: gays as role models, 'Journal of Social Issues', vol.34, no.3, pp.38-58.
Roazen, P. (1978), 'Erik H. Erikson', Free Press, New York; Collier-Macmillan, London.
Romm, M.E. (1965), Sexuality and homosexuality in women, in J. Marmor (ed.), 'Sexual Inversion: The Multiple Roots of Homosexuality', Basic Books, New York.
Ross, H.L. (1971), Modes of adjustment of married homosexuals, 'Social Problems', vol.18, pp.385-93.
Sagarin, E. (1975), 'Deviants and Deviance', Praeger, London.
— (1976), The high personal cost of wearing a label, 'Psychology Today', March, pp.25 et seq.
Saghir, M. and Robbins, E. (1973), 'Male and Female Homosexuality', Williams & Wilkins, Baltimore.
Sheehy, G. (1976), 'Passages: Predictable Crises of Adult Life', Dutton, New York.
Silverstein, C. (1977), 'A Family Matter: A Parents' Guide to Homosexuality', McGraw-Hill, New York.
Soares, J.V. (1979), Black and gay, in M. Levine (ed.), 'Gay Men: The Sociology of Male Homosexuality', Harper & Row, New York.
Socarides, C.W. (1963), The historical development of theoretical and clinical concepts of overt female homosexuality, 'Journal of the American Psychoanalytical Association', vol.11, pp.386-414.
Sonenschein, D. (1968), An ethnography of male homosexual relationships, 'Journal of Sex Research', vol.4, pp.69-83.
Spada, J. (1979), 'The Spada Report', Signet Books, New York.
Storr, A. (1964), 'Sexual Deviation', Penguin, Harmondsworth.
Tripp, C.A. (1976), 'The Homosexual Matrix', Signet, New York.
Tuller, R. (1978), Couples: the hidden segment of the gay world, 'Journal of Homosexuality', vol.3, no.4, pp.331-44.
Vaillant, G.E. (1977), 'Adaptation of Life', Little, Brown & Co., Boston.
Warren, C. and Ponse, B. (1977), The existential self in the gay world, in J. Douglas (ed.), 'Existential Sociology', Cambridge University Press.
Weeks, J. (1977), 'Coming Out', Quartet Books, London.

Weinberg, G. (1973), 'Society and the Healthy Homosexual', Colin Smith, Gerrards Cross.
Weinberg, M.S. and Williams, C.J. (1974), 'Male Homosexuals: Their Problems and Adaptations', Oxford University Press, New York.
Weinberg, T. (1978), On 'doing' and 'being' gay, 'Journal of Homosexuality', vol.4, no.2, pp.143-56.
Wilbur, C.B. (1965), Clinical aspects of female homosexuality, in J. Marmor (ed.), 'Sexual Inversion: The Multiple Roots of Homosexuality', Basic Books, New York.
Whitam, F.L. (1977a), Childhood indicators of male homosexuality, 'Archives of Sexual Behaviour', vol.6, no.2, pp.89-96.
— (1977b), The homosexual role: a reconsideration, 'Journal of Sex Research', vol.13, no.1, pp.1-11.
— (1980), The prehomosexual male child in three societies, 'Archives of Sexual Behaviour', vol.9, no.2, pp.87-100.

BIBLIOGRAPHY
FOR PART THREE

Ackerley, J.R. (1968), 'My father and Myself', Bodley Head, London.
Altman, D. (1980), What changed in the seventies, in Gay Left (ed.),
    'Homosexuality: Power and Politics', Allison & Busby, London.
Bell, A.P. and Weinberg, M.S. (1978), 'Homosexualities: A Study of Diversity
    among Men and Women', Mitchell Beazley, London.
Brophy, J. (1979), Motherhood, lesbianism and child custody, unpublished
    manuscript, University of Essex.
Burton, R.V. and Whiting, W.M. (1961), The Absent father and cross-sex
    identity, 'Merrill Palmer Quarterly', vol.7, pp.85-95.
Campaign for Homosexual Equality (1978), 'Homosexuality: A Fact of Life',
    CHE, Manchester.
-- (1979), 'Queers Need Not Apply', CHE, Manchester.
Cant, B. (1980), 35 into the 80s, 'Gay Left', no.10, p.30.
Cohen, S., Green, S., Merryfinch, L., Jones, G., Slade, J. and Walker, M.
    (1978), 'The Law and Sexuality', Grass Roots Books, Manchester.
Cook, B.W. (1977), Female support networks and political activism,
    'Chrysalis', autumn, no.3, pp.43-61.
Dank, B.M. (1971), Coming out in the gay world, 'Psychiatry', May, no.34,
    pp.180-97.
Donnison, D. (1978), Feminism's second wave and supplementary benefits,
    'Political Quarterly', vol.49, no.3, pp.271-84.
Driberg, T. (1977), 'Ruling Passions', Jonathan Cape, London.
Ettorre, E.M. (1980), 'Lesbians, Women and Society', Routledge & Kegan
    Paul, London.
Faraday, A. (1981), Liberating lesbian research, in K. Plummer (ed.),
    'The Making of the Modern Homosexual', Hutchinson, London.
Gagnon, J.H. and Simon, W. (1973), 'Sexual Conduct: The Social Sources of
    Human Sexuality', Hutchinson, London.
Gartner, A. and Riessman, F. (1977), 'Self Help in the Human Services',
    Jossey-Bass, San Francisco.
Gay Left (ed.), (1980), 'Homosexuality: Power and Politics', Allison & Busby,
    London.
Goodman, B. (1973), The lesbian mother, 'American Journal of
    Orthopsychiatry', vol.43, pp.283-4.
Green, R. (1978), Sexual identity of 37 children raised by homosexual or
    trans-sexual parents, 'American Journal of Psychiatry', vol.135, no.6,
    pp.692-7.
Harris, B. and Sisley, E. (1977), 'The Joy of Lesbian Sex', Simon &
    Schuster, New York.
Hart, J. (1979), 'Social Work and Sexual Conduct', Routledge & Kegan Paul,
    London.
Hart, J. and Richardson, D. (1980), The differences between homosexual
    women and men, 'Bulletin of the British Journal of Psychology', vol.33,
    pp.451-4.
Heiman, J., LoPiccolo, L. and LoPiccolo, J. (1976), 'Becoming Orgasmic:
    A Sexual Growth Program for Women', Prentice-Hall, Englewood Cliffs,
    New Jersey.
Hemmings, S. (1980), Horrific practices: how lesbians were presented in
    the newspapers of 1978, in Gay Left (ed.), 'Homosexuality: Power

and Politics', Allison & Busby, London.
Henry, S. (1978), The dangers of self-help groups, 'New Society', vol.44, no.820, pp.654-6.
Hooker, E. (1965), Male homosexuals and their 'worlds', in J. Marmor (ed.), 'Sexual Inversion: The Multiple Roots of Homosexuality', Basic Books, New York.
Kagan, J. (1964), Acquisition and significance of sex-typing and sex-role identity, in M. Hoffman and L. Hoffman (eds.), 'Review of Child Development Research', vol.1, Russell Sage Foundation, New York.
Kaplan, H.S. (1974), 'The New Sex Therapy', Ballière Tindall, London.
Kimmel, D.C. (1978), Adult development and ageing: a gay perspective, 'Journal of Social Issues', vol.34, no.3, pp.113-30.
Kirkpatrick, M., Roy, R. and Smith K., (1976), A new look at lesbian mothers, 'Human Behaviour', August, pp.60-1.
Leiblum, S.R. and Pervin, L.A. (eds.), (1980), 'Principles and Practice of Sex Therapy', Tavistock, London.
Lynch, A.C.E. (1979), Counselling and assisting homosexuals, 'Criminal Law Review', pp.630-44.
McWhirter, D.P. and Mattison, A.M. (1980), Treatment of sexual dysfunction in homosexual male couples, in S.R. Leiblum, and L.A. Pervin (eds.), 'Principles and Practice of Sex Therapy', Tavistock, London.
Masters, W.H. and Johnson, W.H. (1979), 'Homosexuality in Perspective', Little, Brown & Co., Boston.
Money, J. (1970), Sexual dimorphism and homosexual gender identity, 'Psychological Bulletin', vol.74, no.6, pp.425-40.
Morin, S.F. and Schultz, S.J. (1978), The gay movement and the rights of children, 'Journal of Social Issues', vol.34, no.2, pp.137-48.
National Council for Civil Liberties (1977), 'Homosexuality and the Social Services', National Council for Civil Liberties, London.
Osman, S. (1972), My stepfather is a she, 'Family Process', vol.2, pp.209-18.
Plummer, K. (1975), 'Sexual Stigma: An Interactionist Account', Routledge & Kegan Paul, London.
Plummer, K. (ed.) (1981), 'The Making of the Modern Homosexual', Hutchinson, London.
Policy Advisory Committee on Sexual Offences (1979), 'Working Paper on the Age of Consent in Relation to Sexual Offences', HMSO, London.
Powell, T.J. (1975), The use of self-help groups as supportive reference communities, 'American Journal of Orthopsychiatry', vol.45, no.5, pp.756-64.
Richardson, D. (1978), Do lesbians make good parents?, 'Community Care', no.224, pp.16-17.
Richardson, D. and Hart, J. (1980), Gays in therapy: getting it right, 'New Forum: Journal of the Psychology and Psychotherapy Association', vol.6, no.3, pp.58-60.
Riddle, D.I. (1978), Relating to children: gays as role models, 'Journal of Social Issues', vol.34, no.3, pp.38-58.
Saghir, M.T. and Robins, E. (1973), 'Male and Female Homosexuality: A Comprehensive Investigation', Williams & Wilkins, Baltimore.
Santroch, J.W. and Wohlford, P.L. (1970), Effects of father-absence: influences of, reasons for, and onset of absence, 'Proceedings of the 78th Annual Convention of the American Psychological Association', vol.5, pp.265-6.
Sarason, S.B. and Lorentz, E. (1979), 'The Challenge of the Resource Exchange Network: From Concept to Action', Jossey-Bass, San Francisco.
Silverstein, G. (1977), 'The Joy of Gay Sex', Simon & Schuster, New York.
Smith-Rosenberg, C. (1975), The female world of love and ritual: relations between women in nineteenth century America, 'Signs: Journal of Women in Culture and Society', vol.1, no.1.
Walker, M. (1977), 'Men Loving Men', Gay Sunshine Press, San Francisco.
Walmsley, R. (1978), Indecency between males and the Sexual Offences Act 1967, 'Criminal Law Review', pp.400-7.

Walmsley, R. and White, K. (1979), 'Sexual Offences, Consent and
  Sentencing', Home Office Research Study no.54, HMSO, London.
Weeks, J. (1977), 'Coming Out: Homosexual Politics in Britain From the
  Nineteenth Century to the Present', Quartet, London.
— (1981), Discourses, desire and sexual deviance, in K. Plummer (ed.),
  'The Making of the Modern Homosexual', Hutchinson, London.
Weeks, R.B., Derdeyn, A.P. and Langman, M. (1975), Two cases of children
  of homosexuals, 'Child Psychiatry and Human Development', vol.6, no.1,
  pp.26-32.
Weinberg, G. (1975), 'Society and the Healthy Homosexual', Colin Smyth,
  Gerrards Cross.
Weinberg, M.S. and Williams, C.J. (1974), 'Male Homosexuals: Their Problems
  and Adaptations', Oxford University Press, New York.
West, D.J. (1977), 'Homosexuality Revisited', Duckworth, London.
Wolfson (1971), 'Custody After Divorce', Centre for Socio-Legal Studies,
  Wolfson College, Oxford (SSRC 1971).

INDEX